W9-BTO-082

THE FATHERS
OF THE CHURCH

A NEW TRANSLATION

DIDYMUS THE BLIND

COMMENTARY ON GENESIS

Translated by

†ROBERT C. HILL

THE CATHOLIC UNIVERSITY OF AMERICA PRESS
Washington, D.C.

The paper used in this publication meets the minimum requirements of the
American National Standards for Information Science—Permanence
of Paper for Printed Library Materials, ANSI z39.48 - 1984.
∞
Library of Congress Cataloging-in-Publication Data
Names: Didymus, the Blind, approximately 313-approximately 398,
author. |
Hill, Robert C. (Robert Charles), 1931–2007, translator.
Title: Commentary on Genesis / Didymus the Blind ; translated by
Robert C. Hill.
Other titles: Eis tåen genesin. English
Description: Washington, D.C. : The Catholic University of America Press,
2016. | Series: The Fathers of the Church, a new translation ; volume 132
| Includes bibliographical references and index.
Identifiers: LCCN 2015035574 | ISBN 9780813228457 (cloth : alk. paper)
Subjects: LCSH: Bible. Genesis—Commentaries.
Classification: LCC BS1235 .D4913 2016 | DDC 222/.1107—dc23
LC record available at http://lccn.loc.gov/2015035574

TABLE OF CONTENTS

INDICES

1. Chapters 9–11 are missing from the manuscript, as are chapters 13 and 14.

NOTE TO THE READER

Robert C. Hill entered his repose in 2007. A mainstay of the Fathers of the Church series and a prodigious scholar until the end of his earthly life, he submitted the manuscript for this volume just a few months before his illness became critical. In view of his deteriorating medical condition at the time, it is not surprising that portions of his introduction and notes in this volume are adapted from, or are even reproduced verbatim from, one of his previous volumes, Fathers of the Church 111 (Didymus the Blind, *Commentary on Zechariah*).

Robert is sorely missed.

Carole Monica Burnett, editor
October 2015

ABBREVIATIONS AND SIGLA

Abbreviations

AB   Anchor Bible.

AnBib   Analecta Biblica. Pontificio Istituto Biblico, Rome.

CCG   Corpus Christianorum series Graeca. Turnhout:
        Brepols.

CCL   Corpus Christianorum series Latina. Turnhout:
        Brepols.

CSIC   Consejo Superior de Investigaciones Cientificas.

DS   *Enchiridion Symbolorum, Definitionum et Declarationum,*
        34th ed., ed. H. Denzinger and A. Schönmetzer.
        Freiburg: Herder, 1967.

FOTC   The Fathers of the Church. Washington, DC: The
        Catholic University of America Press.

ITQ   *Irish Theological Quarterly.*

KlT   Kleine Texte für Vorlesungen und Übungen. Bonn:
        A. Marcus und E. Webers Verlag, 1912.

LXX   Septuagint.

OCA   Orientalia Christiana Analecta. Rome: Pontifical
        Oriental Institute.

OTL   Old Testament Library.

PG   Patrologia Graeca, ed. J.-P. Migne. Paris, 1857–66.

PL   Patrologia Latina, ed. J.-P. Migne. Paris, 1878–90.

SC   Sources Chrétiennes. Paris: Du Cerf.

StudP   *Studia Patristica.*

TRE   *Theologische Realenzyclopädie.* Berlin: Walter
        de Gruyter, 1976–.

TQ	*Theologische Quartalschrift.*
VC	*Vigiliae Christianae.*
VTS	*Vetus Testamentum,* Supplement.

Sigla

Numerals in parentheses throughout the translated text indicate the page numbers in SC 233 or 244.

Words in square brackets have been supplied by the translator.

SELECT BIBLIOGRAPHY

Altaner, B. "Ein grosser, aufsehen erregender patrologischer Papyrusfund." *TQ* 127 (1947): 332–33.

Bienert, W. A. *"Allegoria" und "Anagoge" bei Didymos dem Blinden von Alexandria.* Patristische Texte und Untersuchungen 13. Berlin and New York: Walter de Gruyter, 1973.

Butler, C., ed. *The Lausiac History of Palladius* 2. Cambridge: Cambridge University Press, 1904.

Deconinck, J. *Essai sur la chaîne de l'Octateque.* Paris: Librairie Ancienne Honoré Champion, 1912.

Doutreleau, L., ed. *Didyme l'Aveugle. Sur Zacharie.* SC 83, 84, 85. Paris: Du Cerf, 1962.

Fernández Marcos, N. *The Septuagint in Context: Introduction to the Greek Versions of the Bible.* Translated by Wilfred G. E. Watson. Boston and Leiden: Brill, 2001.

Fernández Marcos, N., and A. Sáenz-Badillos. *Theodoreti Cyrensis Quaestiones in Octateuchum.* Textos y Estudios "Cardenal Cisneros." Madrid: CSIC, 1979.

Guinot, J.-N. "Théodoret a-t-il lu les homélies d'Origène sur l'Ancien Testament?" *Vetera Christianorum* 21 (1984): 285–312.

Hanson, P. D. *The Dawn of Apocalyptic.* Philadelphia: Fortress Press, 1975.

Hanson, R. P. C. *Allegory and Event. A Study of the Sources and Significance of Origen's Interpretation of Scripture.* London: SCM, 1959.

Hill, R. C. "Psalm 45: A *locus classicus* for Patristic Thinking on Biblical Inspiration." *StudP* 25 (1993): 95–100.

———. "A Pelagian Commentator on the Psalms?" *ITQ* 63 (Sept. 1998): 263–71.

Hill, Robert C., trans. *St. John Chrysostom. Homilies on Genesis.* FOTC 74, 82, 87. Washington, DC: The Catholic University of America Press: 1986, 1990, 1992.

———, trans. *Didymus the Blind. Commentary on Zechariah.* FOTC 111. Washington, DC: The Catholic University of America Press, 2006.

———, trans. *Cyril of Alexandria. Commentary on the Twelve Prophets.* FOTC 115, 116, 124. Washington, DC: The Catholic University of America Press, 2007, 2008, 2012.

Kahle, P. E. *The Cairo Genizah.* 2d ed. Oxford: Blackwell, 1959.

Kelly, J. N. D. *Early Christian Doctrines.* 5th ed. New York: Harper & Row, 1978.

Kerrigan, A. *St. Cyril of Alexandria, Interpreter of the Old Testament.* AnBib 2. Rome: Pontificio Istituto Biblico, 1952.

Kramer, B. "Didymus der Blinde." *TRE* 8 (1981): 741–46.

Lamirande, É. "Le masculin et le féminin dans la tradition alexandrine. Le commentaire de Didyme l'Aveugle sur la 'Genèse,'" *Science et Esprit* 41/2 (1989): 137–65.

Layton, Richard A. *Didymus the Blind and His Circle in Late-Antique Alexandria.* Champaign, IL: University of Illinois Press, 2004.

Lubac, H. de. *Histoire et Esprit: L'intelligence de l'Écriture d'après Origène.* Théologie 16. Paris: Aubier, 1950.

Nautin, P. With Louis Doutreleau. *Didyme l'Aveugle. Sur la Genèse.* SC 233, 244. Paris: Du Cerf, 1976, 1978.

———. "Didymus the Blind of Alexandria." In *Encyclopedia of the Early Church* 1:235–36. Edited by Angelo Di Berardino. Translated by Adrian Walford. With foreword and bibliographic amendments by W. H. C. Frend. 2 vols. New York: Oxford University Press, 1992.

Olivier, J.-M., ed. *Diodori Tarsensis commentarii in psalmos.* I. *Commentarii in psalmos I–L.* CCG 6. Turnhout: Brepols, 1980.

Quasten, Johannes. *Patrology.* Volume III. 4 vols. Westminster, MD: The Newman Press, 1960.

Rad, Gerhard von. *Genesis: A Commentary.* Rev. ed. OTL. Philadelphia: The Westminster Press, 1973.

Simonetti, M. "Lettera e allegoria nell'esegesi veterotestamentario di Didimo." *Vetera Christianorum* 20 (1983): 341–89.

———. "Didymiana." *Vetera Christianorum* 21 (1984): 129–55.

Sparks, H. F. D. *The Apocryphal Old Testament.* Oxford: Clarendon, 1984.

Speiser, E. A. *Genesis.* AB 1. Garden City, NY: Doubleday, 1964.

Tigcheler, J. H. *Didyme l'Aveugle et l'exégèse allégorique. Étude sémantique de quelques termes exégétiques importants de son Commentaire sur Zacharie.* Graecitas Christianorum primaeva 6. Nijmegen: Dekker & van de Vegt, 1977.

Zorell, F. *Lexicon hebraicum et aramaicum Veteris Testamenti.* Rome: Pontificum Institutum Biblicum, 1963.

INTRODUCTION

INTRODUCTION

The Genesis Commentary among the Works of Didymus

From its beginning in 313, Didymus's life spanned a period immediately following the persecution of Diocletian and including the ecumenical councils of Nicea and Constantinople I, whose terminology leaves an imprint on his work.[1] Despite the loss of his sight in early childhood, Didymus not only became a monk[2] but also attained such eminence as a scholar, adversary of heretics, and spiritual director as to win the admiration of a prelate like Athanasius and a hermit like Antony. It is therefore ironic that a teacher who attracted to his cell pupils like Rufinus of Aquileia and guests like the historian Palladius as well as Jerome and Paula, and who won the eulogies of church historians like Socrates and Theodoret,[3] should incur condemnation on charges of Origenism by church councils after his death in 398.[4]

1. For biographical details see P. Nautin, "Didymus the Blind of Alexandria," in *Encyclopedia of the Early Church* 1:235–36, ed. Angelo DiBerardino, trans. Adrian Walford, with foreword and bibliographic amendments by W. H. C. Frend, 2 vols. (New York: Oxford University Press, 1992); B. Kramer, "Didymus der Blinde," *TRE* 8 (1981): 741–46. Nautin does not repeat the biography in his critical edition of the Genesis commentary. In this work, unlike the Zechariah commentary, Didymus does not speak of the period of persecution; but in commenting on Gn 12.6 we shall find him using a key item of conciliar terminology, *homoousios.*

2. From the way in which Palladius (*The Lausiac History of Palladius* 2.20) mentions the admission of visitors to Didymus's "cell," Nautin concludes ("Didymus," 235) that "he led a monastic life and that his audience must have been mainly composed of monks."

3. In commending Didymus's rebuttal of heretical views (less a feature of this work than, e.g., of the Zechariah commentary), Socrates couples him with Gregory Nazianzen in his *Hist. eccl.* 4 (PG 67.528) as Theodoret couples him with Ephrem in his *Hist. eccl.* 4 (PG 82.1189).

4. J. Quasten, *Patrology* 3 (Westminster, MD: The Newman Press, 1960), 86,

3

The works of Didymus, dogmatic and exegetical, though in many cases destroyed as a result of this condemnation, are known to us by name from Rufinus and Jerome and in fragments in the catenae. Palladius tells us that he had "commented on the Old and the New Testament";[5] but it was feared that many of these commentaries were irretrievably lost. In 1941, however, a discovery was made at Tura outside Cairo of a partial commentary on Genesis along with those on Zechariah, Job, Ecclesiastes, and some Psalms.[6] If not complete, the Genesis commentary shares with the other Tura works the distinction of coming to us in Greek by direct manuscript tradition and of unquestioned authenticity, and has been critically edited.[7] Its appearance in English is overdue.

There arises the question of the place of the Genesis commentary among Didymus's other works.[8] In composing it he makes no reference to other works of his, not as in the Zechariah commentary, where (after admitting at the outset that it is not a full commentary on the twelve Minor Prophets that he is embarking on) he refers to earlier works on Leviticus, Psalms, Isaiah, the Final Vision of Isaiah, Hosea in part, Matthew, John, Romans, 2 Corinthians, and Revelation, as well as *On the Trinity, On the Holy Spirit* (extant in Latin), and a work on Ezekiel possibly only projected. Can this be taken to mean that with the Genesis work Didymus is at the beginning of his literary career? There are other clues pointing in the direction of such a conclusion. Differences in approach to the biblical text from the Zechariah commentary (highlighted in the text be-

---

attributes the loss of so many of Didymus's works to his condemnation along with other Origenists at the fifth ecumenical council in 553. See also DS, 519.

5. *The Lausiac History of Palladius* 2.19–20, ed. Cuthbert Butler (Cambridge: Cambridge University Press, 1904). Palladius speaks of Didymus as a συγγραφεύς.

6. See B. Altaner, "Ein grosser, aufsehen erregender patrologischer Papyrusfund," *TQ* 127 (1947): 332–33.

7. P. Nautin, *Didyme l'Aveugle. Sur la Genèse*, SC 233 and 244 (Paris: Du Cerf, 1976 and 1978). Nautin's collaborator was L. Doutreleau, editor of the SC edition of the Zechariah commentary.

8. Editor Nautin, SC 233.20, finds no internal evidence of the date of the commentary or its place among Didymus's works.

low), and rarity of reference to that prophet, would suggest the priority of the Genesis work. The commentator is consistently indebted throughout the work to his mentors Origen and Philo, often incorporating their commentary verbatim (as editor Nautin helpfully establishes); while the contributions of the former are anonymous (because of his suspect theology?),[9] the latter is invoked by name several times in comment on chapters 4, 5, and 16. If this degree of dependence suggests inexperience, so too does the relative reluctance to take issue with a rogues' gallery of heretics who appear frequently in that later and longer work; deviants mentioned in Scripture are cited, such as the Hymenaeus and Alexander of 1 Tm 1.20,[10] but even provocative texts like the opening declaration of the goodness of created things and the intriguing plural verb "Let us make" of Gn 1.26 draw no criticism of particular heretics' positions. Didymus's biblical canon here is conservative (apart from some willingness to cite Jubilees in support)[11] whereas the Zechariah work will enlist evidence also from *The Epistle of Barnabas* and *The Shepherd of Hermas*. And, finally, the length to which Didymus goes to deal with basic matters of interpretation, like the presence of metaphorical expressions in the Scriptures (for example, in Gn 6.5–7, on God's having second thoughts), could suggest that this commentary is an early work meant for readers whom he has not previously grounded in the elements.

It is not clear, likewise, who the intended readers of the Genesis commentary were; we have no reason to think that the work was commissioned by any patron or colleague, as the

9. Nautin, SC 233.23, is in no doubt that Didymus knew that Origen, having been the object of criticism before and after his death by bishops of Alexandria, was "très contesté." In the view of É. Lamirande, "Le masculin et le féminin dans la tradition alexandrine. Le commentaire de Didyme l'Aveugle sur la 'Genèse,'" *Science et Esprit* 41/2 (1989), 164, for Didymus Origen was known to be "suspect"; on the other hand, "grace à lui (Didyme), nous avons la preuve que les enseignements de Philon et d'Origène restaient bien vivants en Égypt" (154).

10. See commentary on Gn 3.15.

11. When citing Jubilees 4.23 to embroider the statement of Enoch's passing in Gn 5.24, he admits that the book is "not beyond dispute." See below, p. 139 in the present volume.

Zechariah commentary would later be written at Jerome's request.[12] Allegorical comment on the figures of Sarai and Hagar
and their offspring in chapter 16 develops into a lengthy lecture on the stages in spiritual growth towards perfection and
on the danger of proceeding no further than the introductory
stages. It begins thus:

> While Sarai is interpreted as virtue that is perfect and spiritual, then,
> the Egyptian handmaid Hagar is said by Philo to betoken the prelim-
> inary exercises, and by Paul the shadow. In other words, it is impossi-
> ble to grasp any of the spiritual or elevated ideas without the shadow
> in the letter or the introductory stages of initiation; it is necessary to
> produce offspring first from what is underlying.[13]

Continuance of the allegory throughout the whole chapter on
this same theme of growth from initial phases towards perfection leads one to conclude that Didymus has spiritual neophytes in mind, at least in this section of the work.

Text of the Commentary on Genesis; Didymus's Biblical Text

If we are grateful for the chance discovery in 1941 of this
authentic work of Didymus, we also regret that the text is not
complete or in a consistently good state of preservation (not
surprising, considering its likely completion by a copyist of the
late sixth or seventh century).[14] The opening pages on the first
five verses of chapter 1 are in a particularly fragmentary condition; subsequent lines and even pages are missing in places;
and commentary trails off in fragmentary fashion at the opening of chapter 17. We regret in particular the loss of Didymus's
comment on key passages dealing with life in the garden, the
two trees, the naming of the animals, and the making of wom-

---

12. In the preface to his own work on Zechariah (CCL 76A.747), Jerome
admits that Didymus "at my request dictated books of commentary [on
Zechariah], and along with three books on Hosea had them delivered to me."

13. SC 244.204. See below, p. 210 in the present volume.

14. So Nautin, SC 233.14, who also notes the lack of a title page, attributable
perhaps to the condemnation of Didymus at church councils before or about
that time.

an in chapter 2, the talking serpent in chapter 3, as well as all of chapters 9, 10, 11, 13, and 14. What comes to us by indirect tradition in the catenae and in extracts from Procopius of Gaza leads us to wonder if in fact Didymus, having treated of the Hexameron at length[15] and having taken Philo's lead to turn chapter 16 of Genesis into a lecture on stages of growth towards perfection, intended to proceed much further than the point he reached in chapter 17.

Without the ability to access the Hebrew text of Genesis, Didymus is working from a form of the Greek text available in Alexandria that (as we know from the Zechariah commentary) differed somewhat from that used by Cyril.[16] Though only in a few cases do we come across textual readings here (listed in the text below) that differ from the LXX generally, Natalio Fernández Marcos, who endeavors to identify an Alexandrian revision of the LXX among other forms,[17] remarks of the Tura findings that "the biblical text of Didymus the Blind may help to locate this possible recension in Alexandria and Egypt."[18] We would not expect of a blind commentator that he would busy himself with textual criticism; as is true of the Zechariah work also, Didymus rarely (and then with likely dependence on Origen)

---

15. Nautin, SC 233.22, observes that Origen's own commentary on Genesis reached only to 5.1, though Didymus might have had access also to his homilies.

16. See Introduction to Didymus the Blind, *Commentary on Zechariah,* trans. with intro. by Robert C. Hill, Fathers of the Church 111 (Washington, DC: The Catholic University of America Press, 2006), 6–8; and on the nature of Cyril's text in general, A. Kerrigan, *St. Cyril of Alexandria, Interpreter of the Old Testament,* AnBib 2 (Rome: Pontificio Istituto Biblico, 1952), 250–65.

17. Jerome, *Praef. in Paral.* (PL 28.1324–25), speaks of three forms of the LXX current in his time, viz., in Alexandria, in Constantinople-Antioch, and in "the provinces in-between." While P. Kahle, *The Cairo Genizah,* 2d ed. (Oxford: Blackwell, 1959), 236, would restrict the term "Septuagint" to the translation made in Alexandria in the third century BCE (the *Letter of Aristeas* speaking in legendary mode of such a translation of the Torah), others, such as N. Fernández Marcos, *The Septuagint in Context,* trans. Wilfred G. E. Watson (Boston and Leiden: Brill, 2001), 57, believe that "in the case of the LXX a process like that of the Aramaic Targums did not occur," though allowing that the LXX is "a collection of translations" (xi, 22).

18. *The Septuagint in Context,* 245. Fernández Marcos seems unfamiliar with Didymus's Genesis commentary and its critical edition.

cites alternative versions of the Hebrew associated with the names of Aquila, Symmachus, and Theodotion,[19] and nowhere any alternative forms of the LXX, *antigrapha*.

Didymus's Approach to Scripture and Style of Commentary

If both the extant text in its present condition and the indirect tradition of the work encourage a view that Didymus found not much more in Genesis beyond the Hexameron (and perhaps the flood story in chapter 6) that was grist to his mill (exegetically at least), we need to examine his approach to this seminal portion of Scripture. There is no doubt of his attachment to the inspired word of God, of his remarkable familiarity with it (considering his disability), and of his facility in moving from one scriptural text to another—a procedure not always conducive to systematic commentary. His endorsement of the charism of scriptural inspiration goes beyond the traditional formulations to speak rather of τὸ συγγραφικὸν πνεῦμα, where the accent falls less on the text than on its being inspired, as he says in comment on 6.9: "This, to be sure, is what the Spirit in Scripture teaches; when the passage comes to speak of the *generations of Noah* ..."[20] Inter-textuality is a feature of this work as well, though as noted it is not Zechariah and Hosea that loom large in the liberal scriptural documentation but, predictably, the staple works of the Psalter and Matthew's Gospel.

It could not be said of Didymus, then, in commenting on (a portion of) the work he refers to variously as κτίσις, κοσμογονία, and γένεσις, that he is primarily interested in it as a particular example of complex biblical composition in which a number of authors draw on strata of earlier compositions from various cultures that delve into the origins of the world and its peoples. The mentors whom he follows quite slavishly to interpret these primeval stories have snatched him immediately to an-

19. Of the three occasions where such reference is made, in the case of one text, Gn 4.23, it is (typically of Didymus) in reference to a subtext, Is 1.2, where the citation is made.

20. The phrase occurs also in comment on 1.26; 4.8; 6.2; 16.14.

other level. Attracted though he may instinctively have been to examine literal and even factual items in the text, as we shall see, he is not permitted to indulge that attraction at length; it is rare for him to supply background, such as identification of place names like Ai in 12.8, where he will usually settle for a popular (generally false) etymology that encourages an allegorical meaning. Consequently, we do not look to Didymus any more than to others of his contemporaries for an application of principles of literary criticism to this composite, multi-layered material. It is not the fault of the later chapter division of Genesis that leads him to ignore the sabbatical structure imposed by the Priestly author on the opening chapter, but the option of Pythagoras for six as a perfect number: "There is need to apply here what bears on the number six.... It would also be appropriate for a perfect number to be adopted in an anagogical sense; virtue is really something perfect, without fault and quite complete, being God's more perfect gift." The anthropomorphic style of the Yahwist is particularly obnoxious to him; he scornfully abjures a factual approach to 3.7–8 as inferior to one that focuses instead on "the divine element" in the text.

It would in fact be worthwhile for those adopting a factual approach to explain without absurdity how *they stitched together for themselves aprons from fig leaves,* how *they heard the sound of the Lord as he strolled* when they had committed deeds unworthy of it, why he was *strolling in the evening,* and finally how *they hid themselves* under the tree and what idea they had of God. In my view, in fact, it would not be possible for them to maintain a thread of factuality in all this worthy of an explanation deriving from the Holy Spirit. For ourselves, accordingly, as we did in what preceded, we shall focus on the divine element in these verses as well.[21]

He may advert to the differences in divine names employed, as he does in comment on 1.11; but we find the datum occurring already in Philo. The covenant of God with Abraham in 15.17–19, marked by fire and smoking pan, Didymus passes over quickly, seeing an anagogical significance in it, thus falling short of the requirements that the modern commentator Gerhard von Rad would set:

---

21. SC 233.196–98. See below, p. 84. For the number six, p. 77.

The narrative about God's making of the covenant is one of the old-
est narratives in the tradition about the patriarchs.... It has been
thought that this phenomenon [of the burning pan] could be understood as a mysterious preview of God's fiery mountain, and thus as a
reference to the conclusion of a covenant with Moses on Sinai. One
should beware, however, of treating as symbolic the intentional material aspect of the phenomenon. By subjecting it to a meaning that
appears reasonable, one loses the meaning of the whole.[22]

In short, the significance of primeval and patriarchal histories
in Genesis intended by a range of contributors is passed over in
favor of arbitrary spiritual meanings, which Didymus styles "the
divine element."

The reader of Didymus's commentary on any particular lemma appreciates the systematic shift of focus from the literal-
factual to the anagogical-allegorical level (if that is the appropriate terminology, as we must inquire below). The shift is
regularly signaled by words such as these: "So much for the literal; now we must move ..." after relatively brief attention to
letter and sometimes fact—what he sees "Paul" (Heb 10.1) calling "shadow." What is less helpful is the commentator's habit
(found also in the Zechariah work) of straying from the lemma
to a subtext, or string of subtexts, thought relevant, which can
become the text at the center of attention. The beginning of
the deluge in 7.6 prompts Didymus to return to the theme of
repentance developed earlier in connection with the building
of the ark, which leads him to find this theme in the song about
the unresponsive vineyard in Is 5.1–7, and then on to Sir 17.17,
1 Pt 2.9, Ex 19.6, Eccl 10.4, and Is 45.8, by which time the lemma has dropped from sight. Again it is a matter of priorities.

The priorities, of course, are those of his mentors, who have
less interest in real arks and real floods and more in what (*pace*
von Rad) they can be thought to symbolize. If Origen is prudently not cited by name, Didymus's indebtedness to him is
nevertheless unremitting and at times verbatim. In comment
on 1.21 he says, "The *huge sea monsters* by the norms of allegory
were the wicked powers, the devil and his angels, who are called

22. Gerhard von Rad, *Genesis: A Commentary*, rev. ed., OTL (Philadelphia:
The Westminster Press, 1973), 189, 188.

'dragons' by Scripture, a name clearly much more applicable to the devil," and he proceeds to cite even the Psalm and Job texts found in his *beau idéal*. We have seen him likewise relying heavily (out of inexperience?) on Philo, in this case occasionally by name. As we shall see, it is a reliance that can devalue the biblical text, as in the case of a proper understanding of "image" in that basic verse Gn 1.26, where Didymus introduces from his Jewish predecessor this critical nuance, with its hermeneutical and theological implications: "Now, it has been shown that it is not as a composite that [the human being] is an image: one element is a bodiless and spiritual essence, the other has a body with external form."[23] These two mentors also affect the stance Didymus takes to philosophical opinions, such as those of the Stoics; in chapter 7 on preparations for the deluge he cites Stoic views, rejecting some and accepting others accordingly as Origen dictates, and it may also be from Origen that Didymus takes single references to Plato and to Aristotle.

Didymus as Interpreter of Genesis

It was therefore inevitable that Didymus, so much under the influence of his respected predecessors, would in general adopt their hermeneutical stance towards the text of Genesis. And it is from them that in this work and elsewhere he can at times (as we have seen above) evince an intolerance of commentators wanting to respect the surface meaning of a text. Where 3.21 presents the Lord God in the wake of the Fall making garments of skin for the man and his wife—a point at which Chrysostom in his Homily 18[24] restricts himself to warning his listeners briefly against misinterpreting anthropomorphisms—Didymus

---

23. See below, p. 64. Cf. von Rad, *Genesis*, 58: "The interpretations are to be rejected which proceed from an anthropology strange to the Old Testament and one-sidedly limit God's image to man's spiritual nature, relating it to man's 'dignity,' his 'personality' or 'ability for moral decision,' etc.... Therefore, one will do well to split the physical from the spiritual as little as possible; the whole man is created in God's image."

24. PG 53.150.

takes a cue (from Origen, it seems)[25] to deny with some heat attempts of φιλίστορες to uphold a factual interpretation.

> It was fitting that *garments of skin,* in which there is reference to nothing else than their bodies, be made for the woman who was destined to be mother of all and for her husband, a partner in that destiny. In fact, if those bent on factual interpretation think that God made garments out of skin, why does the further phrase occur, *and clothed them in them,* when they were capable of doing so themselves?[26]

And yet, as we observed, there are many occasions in the commentary where we gain the clear impression that, instinctively, Didymus wrestles with details of the text before moving to another level, even addressing hypothetical or real ἄπορα that troubled readers and that were addressed in the *Quaestiones* of Antiochenes like Diodore and Theodoret.[27] When Didymus comes to the slaying of Abel by Cain in 4.8, for instance, he senses some such literalist objection and deals with it at the level of the questioner: "Some commentators also want to raise this question: What weapon did he use to do away with Abel? There is no problem in that; even if there was no iron, he could still have used stone or wood, as the Book of the Testament also suggests."[28]

On a score of occasions throughout the text, therefore, there is evidence of this instinctive response at a literal and/or factu-

25. M. Simonetti, "Didymiana," *Vetera Christianorum* 21 (1984), 130, sees (Plato via) Origen behind this interpretation found in Alexandrian commentators generally: "Didimo non solo, come ogni alessandrino, distingue platonicamente fra l'uomo creato ad immagine di Dio di Gen. 1,26 (= uomo interiore, anima) e l'uomo plasmato dal fango della terra di Gen. 2,7, ma condivide anche l'interpretazione, variamente attestata a partire dal II secolo, che ravvisava nelle tuniche de pelle, con cui Dio aveve coperto la nudità di Adamo ed Eva in conseguenza del peccato, il corpo materiale di cui è fornito l'uomo."

26. SC 233.250. See below, p. 104.

27. See J. Deconinck, *Essai sur la chaine de l'Octateuque* (Paris: Librairie Ancienne Honoré Champion, 1912), for what is extant of Diodore's work; N. Fernández Marcos and A. Sáenz-Badillos, *Theodoreti Cyrensis Quaestiones in Octateuchum,* Textos y Estudios "Cardenal Cisneros" (Madrid: CSIC, 1979).

28. Jubilees (which Didymus refers to as the Book of the Testament) 4.2, in fact, is no more explicit than the Genesis text. Nautin, SC 233.29, traces the reference to another apocryphal work preserved in Ethiopian.

al level before the commentator faithfully moves in the direction taken by his revered mentors.[29] Didymus finds significance in the difference in the order of wording of the text about the occupants of the ark in chapters 7 and 8:

In other words, when the destruction of humankind was imminent, it behoved righteous men to show fellow-feeling and thus to refrain from marital intercourse. He therefore separated wives from husbands in the words, *You are to board, you, your sons, your wife, and your sons' wives with you,* whereas when it was clear that procreation was once more assured, he returned his wife to Noah, as we explained, in the words, "Leave the ark, you and your wife, your sons and your sons' wives."[30]

On the other hand, his comment on the factual details of the ark's construction (despite modern commentators' observations that it amounts to a veritable supertanker)[31] in 6.14–17 is epitomized by his remark that "the literal meaning makes a lot of sense."[32] In such cases Didymus is in no hurry to move to a level of interpretation he would later more readily refer to (in the Zechariah commentary) as μυστικός.[33]

There is no doubt, however, that under his predecessors' influence, if not instinctively, Didymus devotes the bulk of his attention to that elevated level of meaning, or what he called

29. J. H. Tigcheler, *Didyme l'Aveugle et l'exégèse allégorique,* Graecitas Christianorum primaeva 6 (Nijmegen: Dekker & van de Vegt, 1977), goes to great lengths to show Didymus distinguishing between literal and factual senses of a text. The Genesis work would provide more evidence for his thesis than the Zechariah work; but Tigcheler was working before Nautin had completed his edition of the Genesis commentary, choosing to focus on the Zechariah commentary. What he is contesting is a statement of Didymus's hermeneutic such as that of A. Kerrigan, *St. Cyril of Alexandria,* 32, "Didymus, Origen's disciple, seems to recognize but two senses of Scripture, the literal and the spiritual."

30. See Didymus's comment on Gn 6.18 (SC 244.78) below, p. 162.

31. E. A. Speiser, *Genesis,* AB 1 (Garden City, NY: Doubleday, 1964), 52, estimates an ark of this size to be equivalent to 43,000 tons.

32. See below, p. 160.

33. The term occurs only thrice in the Genesis commentary. Simonetti, "Lettera e allegoria," *Vetera Christianorum* 20 (1983), 341, likewise observes of such differences of emphasis, "Com'è possibile che uno stesso esegeta sia stato tanto allegorista nel commentare *Zaccaria* e invece tanto poco nel commentare *Giobbe?*"

"the divine element in the verses," when expressing displeasure with the Yahwist's anthropomorphisms in the Fall account. He enunciates the principle in using the relationship of Sarai and Hagar as the basis for a treatment of stages of perfection: "No one, you see, who remains at the level of the letter or the introductory stage can lay claim to Wisdom herself" (on 16.7–8). In keeping with this principle, Didymus prefers to adopt what he generally calls an anagogical interpretation, as for example at the critical transition from primeval history to patriarchal history with the promise of universal fatherhood made to Abraham in the opening verses of chapter 12.

All this was not of a human kind, as we saw from the anagogical approach to the text, which we adopted from the outset. Every sinner has the devil for father, according to the statement, "Everyone who commits sin is of the devil"; just as the one doing God's will becomes his offspring—Scripture says, remember, "Everyone who does right has been born of God"—so "everyone who commits sin is of the devil," its father [1 Jn 3.8; 2.29], and has kinship with those born of this father.[34]

Such an allegorical treatment of a key stage in sacred history, in the view of modern commentators, succeeds only in trivializing its significance.[35]

Is Didymus deliberately using ἀναγωγή here where he proceeds to treat the fatherhood of all nations allegorically? Or does he simply employ the terms interchangeably, as L. Doutreleau,[36] W. Bienert,[37] and M. Simonetti[38] maintain? It is the thesis of Johannes Tigcheler's study (written before the release of

34. SC 244.138. See below, pp. 183–84.

35. See G. von Rad, *Genesis*, 154: "The transition from primeval history to sacred history occurs abruptly and surprisingly in vv.1–3. All at once and precipitously the universal field of vision narrows; world and humanity, the entire ecumenical fullness, are submerged, and all interest is concentrated on a single man.... What is promised to Abraham reaches far beyond Israel; indeed, it has universal meaning for all generations on earth."

36. *Didyme l'Aveugle. Sur Zacharie*, SC 83.51 and 68.

37. *"Allegoria" und "Anagoge" bei Didymos dem Blinden von Alexandria*, Patristische Texte und Untersuchungen 13 (Berlin and New York: Walter de Gruyter, 1973), 108.

38. "Lettera e allegoria," 346: "I due termini praticamente coincidono per il senso."

Nautin's critical text of the Genesis commentary) that, unlike Origen,[39] Didymus did preserve a clear difference, for example, ἀλληγορία for "langage figuré," ἀναγωγή for "extension de sens, signification profonde."[40] This thesis, vulnerable even on the evidence of the Zechariah work, would find no clear support in the Genesis commentary. While it is the latter term that is generally employed, the interpretation given is allegorical, as in comment on the respective gifts of Abel and Cain in 4.3–5 and the divine response to them:

> While the literal account provides this information, then, the ana-gogical sense would be as follows. People who pretend to be virtuous and make a display of it, not from a sincere intention but for some other reason, are procrastinators of a kind and dishonest, not offering first-fruits to God. The first-fruits of virtue, by contrast, come from free will, from where movement towards virtue arises.[41]

There is, however, little difference from the hermeneutical procedures adopted in the Zechariah commentary in other respects of the Genesis work. We are still justified in finding some of the spiritual meanings arrived at to be arbitrary, gratuitous, and (as other commentators, ancient and modern, would say of this style of interpretation) "self-opinionated."[42] It is possible to gain the impression that the commentator feels free to detect any "divine element" in the text he chooses, even if responding to cues from a predecessor. On Cain's slaying his brother in 4.8, for instance, we are told,

> So much for the factual sense (ἱστορία); but since we claim that Cain represents hypocritical behavior in the anagogical sense, this would be the case here as well. The *brother* of the exterior, visible man is the

---

39. See Tigcheler, *Didyme l'Aveugle,* 176–77: "Selon de Lubac, chez Origène, ἀλληγορία, τροπολογία et ἀναγωγή sont synonymes et signifient tous trois 'sens spirituelle.' Chez Didyme, croyons-nous, ce n'est pas le cas."

40. Ibid., 177.

41. SC 233.284–86. See below, p. 118.

42. Diodore's judgment in J.-M. Olivier, *Diodore Tarsensis commentarii in Psalmos* I, *Commentarii in Psalmos I–L,* CCG 6, 7. Cf. R. P. C. Hanson, *Allegory and Event. A Study of the Sources and Significance of Origen's Interpretation of Scripture* (London: SCM, 1959), 236, who says of Origen's system of interpretation, "The result, though it may be methodologically impressive, is to remove the reader one stage further from the original meaning of Scripture."

man hidden in thought; the zealous person should attend to both, using reason properly and wearing clothing suited to his behavior, as the Psalmist also teaches in the first Psalm, "Blessed the man who does not walk in the counsel of the impious" [Ps 1.1].[43]

The reader can find equally undisciplined the procedure of interpretation-by-association, where the commentator seems simply to flip through his mental concordance and light upon a series of texts containing similar terms to assemble a conglomerate meaning.

Noah opened the window of the ark, and so on [8.6]. Here, too, there is no obscurity in the text. If, on the other hand, you were to consider the anagogical sense, you would focus on mention of the *opening,* noting that a knowledge of times befits the righteous and is for their benefit and that of others: sometimes it is appropriate to close, sometimes to open. Thus, it was when the Savior had opened that it was said by those in the company of Cleopas, "Were not our hearts burning when he opened to us the Scriptures?" [Lk 24.32] You will also consider if the verse, "Open to me gates of righteousness" [Ps 118.19], bears on the passage, and you will consider in the same context the order given in Isaiah, "Open, you rulers" [Is 13.2 LXX], and likewise the closure in the statement, "Do not throw holy things to dogs" [Mt 7.6]. In other words, when one closes or opens properly, one is then an imitator of Noah.[44]

In the course of interpretation, both the Genesis and the Zechariah commentaries capitalize on etymology and on number symbolism, though it seems that in the early stages of the Genesis work the commentator is reserved in invoking them; lack of comment on chapters 10 and 11 may also be due to their genealogical character, where names and numbers proliferate. He forgoes the opportunity of following Philo into etymological comment on the successors to Cain's son Enoch in Gn 4.18: "If, on the other hand, you wanted to take this anagogically, you could begin the anagogy with a translation of the names and conduct it without undue detachment. Philo also treated of these matters, from which the students could on inspection draw due benefit."[45] What leads him into developing

43. SC 233.296. See below, p. 122.
44. SC 244.126–28. See below, pp. 179–80.
45. SC 233.320. See p. 131 below.

the significance of numbers is, for one thing, the numbers of animals admitted to the ark, where predictably he is unaware of the two traditions represented in chapters 6 and 7, one (the Priestly) staying with two, the other (the Yahwist, in 7.2) varying between seven and two in the cases of clean and unclean respectively. So he involves himself in a bewildering exposition of number symbolism, concluding, "What has been said about numbers is not without point, the truth being that no detail in the divine writings is superfluous" (on 7.2–3).[46]

Theological Accents of the Commentary on Genesis

A further contrast with the Zechariah commentary, and an index perhaps of relative priority, is that Christological interpretation here is rare and fleeting. The mention of the creation of human beings in God's image in Gn 1.26 elicits a passing mention of Jesus (though the accompanying denial of the relevance of the body to this image would allow only for the highest of Christologies); similar references do not exceed half-a-dozen, though of course there is constant inter-textual citation of the evangelical sayings of "the Savior." The term "God the Word," which Doutreleau found "surprenante" in Didymus's Zechariah work,[47] appears here in comment on Gn 12.6. Perhaps one consequence of this rarity, as was mentioned, and also an index of early composition, is the absence of theological polemic in the work by comparison with the frequency of (at least conventional) listing of heresiarchs in the later work. Didymus maintains briefly against "the Manicheans" that Gn 6.11, "The earth was corrupt in God's eyes," refers only to moral depravity. By involved reasoning the Ebionites of the early Church are brought into focus in a parallel between Hagar of chapter 16 and the recidivist Galatians.

Didymus does not moralize on the Fall; in fact, he can credit the guilty parties in chapter 3 with a role in bringing the Sav-

---

46. Simonetti, "Lettera e allegoria," 348, refers to Didymus's "simpatia tutta particolare per le simbologie numeriche, a volte complicatissime."
47. SC 85.808–9.

ior and in the foundation of the Church—if, as he says in this case, the scene is taken "allegorically" (he is ambivalent as to whether the man and the woman in this spiritual garden are historical or not).

On the other hand, interpreting the woman as the Church and Adam as Christ, an intelligent person would take the passage allegorically and consider whether the human race, from which the Church developed, by becoming guilty of transgression proved responsible for the descent of the Savior and his implementing the divine plan by which he became "curse" [Gal 3.13] and "sin" [2 Cor 5.21]—not that he was these, but took them on for our sake.[48]

He repeats the claim of a *felix culpa:* "In fact, if the human race had not become a transgressor, it would not have needed a healer, either, for there would have been no wound, and it was this that required his coming among human beings."[49]

It is perhaps in keeping with that underlying interest in literal and factual elements in the text, rather than with the encouragement he finds in his predecessors to spiritualize it, that Didymus can give evidence of a morality where free will and human effort are in balance with and even prior to the movement of divine grace—something we would expect rather of the Antiochenes.[50] The Noah of 6.8 is the paradigm.

Noah, on the contrary, found favor in the sight of the Lord God. It is a wonderful and heavenly thing to *find favor in the sight of God.* It is achieved on the basis of being pleasing to him, whereas the one who is pleasing to men is not guaranteed to be pleasing to God. ... Now, God gives this gift only when we provide the basis for receiving it; it is said in Proverbs, "Grace and peace bring deliverance, so preserve them for yourself and thus suffer no reproach" [Prv 25.10 LXX], for it is in the power of free will to preserve and practice them.

It was thus of his own doing that Noah *found favor in the sight of the Lord God;* he won grace for himself through the works of virtue, and for this he received grace from God. With those, in fact, who of themselves perform and achieve good works the God of all cooperates, and in addition he gives increase and leads to a great amount of good. Aware of this very fact, the Savior's disciples, who already

48. SC 233.220. See below, pp. 92–93.
49. SC 233.247–48. See below, p. 103.
50. In reference to Chrysostom see R. C. Hill, "A Pelagian Commentator on the Psalms?" *ITQ* 63 (Sept. 1998): 263–71.

of themselves had achieved the first step of faith in him, said to him in the knowledge that faith is also given by God, "Increase our faith" [Lk 17.5]. In other words, as "the utterance of wisdom is given through the Spirit" and "the utterance of knowledge according to the Spirit," so also "faith by the same Spirit" [1 Cor 12.8–9]. It is impossible, in fact, to receive the faith given by God as a grace without our having the faith which depends on us, as is exactly the suggestion of "Increase our faith." … This is the way we shall interpret as well the phrase "grace for grace" [Jn 1.16], understanding that which is from God to be coming in addition to what depends on us.[51]

Abram, too, illustrates this moral principle; when he comes in 12.6 to the oak of Moreh ("lofty" in the LXX), as to the oaks of Mamre of 18.1, Didymus comments, "[I]t is necessary to adopt such an interpretation also of the oak to which Abram came, under which he sat and was accorded a vision when he also received the promise about Isaac. It is therefore due to work and effort that he advances upwards, and shares in fragrance and insight into lofty and divine thoughts."[52]

There is clearly a dissonance here with theological positions that place the accent less on "work and effort," at least of a bodily kind. We observed Didymus insisting that it is not as a composite that the human being fulfills the divine design of "image," the body not being included under that rubric. The cursing of the ground in 3.17 evokes a similar principle: "Is there anything that is a consequence of the body and not a source of pain, since it is from it that pleasures and cares stem?"[53] If this principle is derived from Origen, so too are brief statements of his mentor's (condemned) views on the pre-existence of the angels (already fallen before material creation, in Origen's view) and of souls (also Origen's heterodox teaching) in the short extant fragment of commentary on chapter 2 and on 3.5. The clause in 1.27, "Male and female he made them," prompts a spiritual development of the relationship of the two that is repeated throughout: "And while in the case of material things a change of nature is out of the question, in the case of spiritual things the person now in receipt of teaching and hence in the position of a

51. SC 244.46–50. See below, pp. 150–51.
52. SC 244.154. See below, p. 189.
53. SC 233.242. See below, p. 101.

female could at some stage progress to being a *male* as a teacher of others, as in reverse you could through negligence forfeit being a teacher so as scarcely to be able to receive from someone else what you yourself taught others before."[54] The attitude to women that Didymus displays arises also from the "Pauline" analysis of the Fall in 1 Tm 2.14 (oft-repeated), to which he alludes in comment on the clause, "He drove out Adam" (LXX), in 3.24: "If you were to ask how it is that, though the serpent was responsible for the transgression, and the woman was the first to be deceived, reference is made not to their being expelled but to Adam, who, we are told by the wise Paul, was not deceived, our reply is that if the less guilty was expelled from the garden, much more those whose faults were greater."[55] At least Didymus avoids railing against the woman in the manner of a Chrysostom.[56]

Significance of Didymus's Commentary on Genesis

It is important for students of patristic biblical commentary ("exegesis" not a term applicable in this case)[57] that we have available to us from his cell in late fourth-century Egypt a work on a significant part of the book of Genesis by Didymus the Blind in his own Greek text. While the discovery at Tura provided us also with sapiential and literary works (on Job, Ecclesiastes, some Psalms), the lengthy prophetic/apocalyptic work that is the Zechariah commentary and here an Octateuchal[58]

---

54. SC 233.160. See below, pp. 69–70. Cf. Lamirande, "Le masculin et le féminin," 144–46.

55. SC 233.262. See below, p. 109.

56. See, e.g., *Homily* 17 on Genesis (PG 53.140). Also St. John Chrysostom, *Homilies on Genesis 1–17*, trans. Robert C. Hill, FOTC 74 (Washington, DC: The Catholic University of America Press, 1986), 238–42.

57. Cf. J. N. D. Kelly, *Golden Mouth. The Story of John Chrysostom, Ascetic, Preacher, Bishop* (Ithaca, NY: Cornell University Press, 1995), 94: "Neither John, nor any Christian teacher for centuries to come, was properly equipped to carry out exegesis as we have come to understand it."

58. The term "Pentateuch" was less familiar to authors in the early Church, according to O. Eissfeldt, *The Old Testament: An Introduction*, trans. Peter R. Ackroyd (New York: Harper and Row, 1965), 156.

commentary open up to us the thinking of a typically Alexandrian scholar of that period on the major categories of the
Hebrew Bible in its (or in a particular) LXX form. The loss of
the commentary on the opening five chapters of Genesis by
Origen, "la source principale" of Didymus in the view of editor Nautin,[59] who has painstakingly traced the latter's degree of
dependence throughout, makes this work even more valuable
as an exemplar of this style of commentary, and especially its
hermeneutic. Not only is the prophetic material of the Zechariah work quite different, especially parts that have been classed
as "full-blown apocalyptic,"[60] but we have identified features of
the Genesis commentary that themselves distinguish it and also
suggest an early date in the commentator's career.

Textually the Genesis commentary is not distinctive (at least
within the corpus of Didymus's works); the reader also notes
that once the Hexameron and narratives of Fall and Deluge
have been covered, the commentator (like his principal mentor) progressively loses interest, apparently not greatly moved
by patriarchal stories. Abraham's significance in sacred history is not highlighted, and matriarchs Sarai and Hagar are reduced to representing stages on the way to perfection. Clearly
the commentator is not focused on the literary techniques and
theological preoccupations of a diverse group of contributors
identified by his modern counterparts; an anthropomorphic
Yahwist is seized upon only as an irksome impediment to a
wholesale spiritualizing of life in the Garden by a commentator
under the dominant influence of Origen and Philo.

And yet in this apparently early work Didymus seems slow
to suppress an innate interest in literary and factual items in
the text (a distinction well vindicated by this work) in a manner that would have won the approval of an Antiochene like
Diodore. Time and again the commentator in this work (unlike
the Zechariah commentary) draws attention to such items before proceeding to develop a spiritual meaning, which he generally refers to as anagogical but which is frequently allegori-

59. SC 233.22.
60. P. D. Hanson, *The Dawn of Apocalyptic* (Philadelphia: Fortress Press,
1975), 369.

cal—an imprecision that has given rise to critical debate by his commentators. As is arguably true also of his mentors, movement to a range of spiritual meanings can be arbitrary and gratuitous; recourse to etymologies and number symbolism, which he notes is a feature of their work as well, does not predominate here. Perhaps because Christological interpretation is not often one of the levels of meaning he develops in this work, it does not display a polemical character. His treatment of the Fall is positive, free of moralizing; an accent on free will and human effort is a further unusual aspect of the work's moral teaching offered to readers, who would appear to be spiritual neophytes.

Incomplete though the *Commentary on Genesis* is, then, inexperienced though its author, and imperfect though its state of preservation, we can be grateful that we have a work in Greek from an author who is demonstrably faithful to the principles of his Alexandrian mentor Origen (if not always to the intentions of the biblical authors) in explicating this biblical material, which has attracted a variety of approaches throughout patristic literature.

COMMENTARY ON
GENESIS

CHAPTER ONE

N THE *beginning God made heaven and earth* (v.1).[1] The fact that God's creation involves visible and invisible things—namely, bodily things being the visible, and incorporeal and spiritual things the invisible—Scripture conveys, especially in the first book ...[2] when it says that they were made ... Egyptians worshiped the parts of the world and the world itself, and from them the Hebrews learned ... during all the four hundred and thirty years they were[3] ... Consequently, when the Law ... beginning ...

It was therefore necessary to convey that ... from what did not exist to ... because also from Creation[4] ... God can be spiritually perceived and made manifest ... It has rightly been said that *In the beginning God made heaven and earth;* visible creation[5] is encompassed by them, the earth encompassing animals and plants and waters, and heaven the vast number of the stars. So the earth is a presupposition for animals and plants and waters, since no existence would be possible for them without its underlying them, as also heaven in the case of stars and moon ... for without it which of them could exist?

Now, if you were to think that the *beginning* is a particular time ... on examination you would find it presupposes time;

1. Though, like Didymus's work on Zechariah, this work is entitled simply *On Genesis,* it is a formal verse-by-verse commentary, at least to the point it reaches in chapter 17. Here pages 25–34 reflect the many lacunae.

2. The manuscript is defective for the first five verses. Note from the FOTC editor: Words supplied by the SC editor appear in brackets in the SC edition, but here they have been assimilated into the translation.

3. The length of the captivity given by Ex 12.40–41.

4. The term used is κοσμογονία.

5. The term used is κτίσις.

the word *beginning* has not one meaning but many. In fact (without prolonging my treatment), sometimes it means the cause, as in this case: heaven and earth exist in the cause, (34)[6] wisdom being the cause of their existence and condition as well. The world, you see, did not come into existence independently, without being generated;[7] everything was made by the Word, remember, and in Christ Jesus "there were created things on earth and things in heaven, things visible and invisible"; in the Son and for him "all things hold together," for "he is before all things."[8] Without the Word of God, in fact, who is neither interior (ἐνδιάθετος) nor uttered (προσφορικός),[9] but an actual word, the substantial Word of God, nothing could exist. In other words, just as an architect ... designs a city for building ... (36) encompassing in itself. At other times the word *beginning* means kingly rule, so that here too he has made everything as king and possessing authority; ... he did not have material available to him for the substance of the universe ...

If, on the other hand, the substance underlying them ... being the basis and foundation of everything ... the Word of God, who is with the Father ... and is of one being with him, he is a simple substance ... to the created[10] things he has the relationship ... all things according to its[11] will ... but wisdom is substantial in itself ... as a partner.

The land was invisible and unfinished, and darkness was over the deep, and a spirit of God moved over the water (v.2). A study of the text suggests that the earth was lying under the water ... it was seen when God said, *Let the water under* (38) *heaven be gathered*

6. For ease of reference the page numbers of the SC edition are included in the text.

7. Editor Nautin sees dependence here by Didymus on Origen's commentary on the opening chapters of Genesis, itself inspired by the work of Theophilus of Antioch against Hermogenes, who spoke of pre-existent matter.

8. Col 1.16-17.

9. Nautin explains these two terms as Stoic vocabulary eliminated from Christian vocabulary. Didymus wants to deny the Word's being only a linguistic reality.

10. Participle of the verb δημιουργέω. Didymus has thus employed the whole available range of terms for creation, creating.

11. I.e., wisdom's.

together into one mass, and let the dry land appear (v.6): the earth
did not ... continue to hold so much water ... would be useful
also for the animals ... what it held could not continue ...[12] *was*
does not refer to what was not generated ... *God made heaven
and earth,* and so the earth was not ungenerated; nor does *was*
always mean what is eternal, but frequently ... is connected
with ... as in the verse, "That man was of noble birth."[13] ...

... *invisible* not ... on account of ... *unfinished,* since what was
capable ... reached that point. Whereas this ... of the text suggests a meaning ... the *invisible and unfinished* ... whereas by
definition it is lacking quality and form ... says in the book of
Wisdom, "Your all-powerful hand, which created the world out
of formless matter, did not lack the means ..."[14]

*And darkness was over the deep, and a spirit of God moved over
the water.* If you were to take this *darkness* as the visible kind,
you could ... because light had not yet been made. *Darkness*
was not a substance ... (40) when light was absent; it was *over
the deep.* The *deep* is water whose depth cannot be measured, by
comparison, that is, with length and breadth. The text says the
spirit moves on the water; that would be in the simpler sense[15] ...
part lying on the immeasurable mass of water and especially

12. At this point Nautin supplements the Tura text with a citation from
Procopius of Gaza (who, along with the catenae, is an indirect witness to
the text) to read, "The enemy of God Mani said that," implying it was Mani
and not Hermogenes who held the idea. Chrysostom in his Homily Two (PG
53.29) similarly said, "Even if Mani accosts you saying that matter pre-existed,
or Marcion, or Valentinus, or pagans ..."

13. Jb 1.1.

14. Wis 11.17. The puzzling phrase seems to arise from a copyist's reading
ἀόρατος, "invisible," for ἀόριστος, "shapeless." Even a limited commentator
like Severian will consult Origen's *Hexapla* to find in the alternative versions
(associated with the names of Aquila, Symmachus, and Theodotion) a
translation, "The earth was an empty void," closer to the meaning of the
Hebrew.

15. The term, Nautin points out, is Origen's in reference to the literal
sense, whereby water is water and *spirit* is breath. Likewise following Origen,
Didymus then moves to an allegorical level, whereby darkness is ignorance
(and the deep the devil and demons), the spirit is the Holy Spirit, and the
waters on which he is carried angelic powers, as is confirmed by Col 1.16; Ps
77.16 (modern numbering, as are all Psalm references in this volume, unless
otherwise marked).

... Now, since the Spirit in physical descriptions ... often also spiritual things, as he does also here ... So there is a distinction ... The *deep* would be ... ignorance to *darkness* and ... Holy Spirit *moves over* ... Spirit "rulers, powers, thrones, dominions" ... "The waters saw you, O God, they saw you and were afraid,"[16] obviously not in reference to material waters ... because they have neither fear nor sight, lifeless as they are; it is God who sees[17] ... but with understanding that is proof against confusion and defilement ... by nature but from knowledge ...

And God said, Let there be light, and there was light (v.3). (42) A light with the lights as in the verse, "Praise him, sun and moon, praise him, all the stars and the light,"[18] since they thought on this basis that there was another light than the sun and the other stars. But it is possibly not out of the question ... believing that before the sun ... they think that there was another light ... they say that not yet ... the one that in our view divides, but ... a certain beam leaps up from ... a beam from beyond that differs from the sun ... visible forms of the material ...

... beams of light as also of heaven ... Now, just as on earth ... plants themselves later ... a light as a pre-existing substrate ... providing the source ... many things for the allegory ... door, shepherd, way ... with benevolence and lovingkindness ... so too it is said by the Father to him, "I have given you as a light of the nations to provide salvation to the end of the earth."[19] Now, this verse teaches, not that God generated the Son from nothing, (44) but that the one who is light in essence was appointed by him as light for those ... It was, in fact, not when he was appointed light of the spiritual world that he came to be, being light eternal: "He was the true light, which enlightens everyone coming into the world."[20] Likewise, though being wisdom from eternity, the Son becomes wisdom for all

16. Ps 77.17.

17. Note from the FOTC editor: Nautin suggests ὁρᾶ[ται], "is seen"; SC 233.40, line B 11.

18. Ps 148.3. A problem offered by the Genesis account is the creation of light (in v.3) before the great lights (in v.14). Theophilus had suggested the Word as source of this light.

19. Is 49.6; Acts 13.47.

20. Jn 1.9.

by their being made wise, as one becomes a teacher for those desirous of learning. Far from commencing to be wisdom from that time, he has been such from eternity, whereas it is we who have become wise. In fact, wisdom says of herself, "When he established the heavens, I was with him"—the Father, that is— and became for us "wisdom, righteousness, sanctification, and redemption"[21] ... in every sense ...

... God by nature ... creation still ... likewise God is gener- ated ... allegorically ... in consequence ... the light ... to what was absent ... together with the origin ... (46) their substance, which was illuminated by God ... and preserve an uninterrupt- ed light ... of God; the text says, in fact, *And God saw that the light was good* (v.4), that is to say, the beings that are made to receive illumination ...

And God saw that the light was good. God's seeing the light must be taken in a manner befitting God ... in reference to God from the point of view of human experience or human reasoning ... "He spoke, and they came to be"[22] ... he spoke on the basis of providence so that we might get the impression ... in the sense of our receiving ... he wishes ...[23]

... we mention God's speaking ... (48) and in magnitude adding to the light that was made ... God would see the en- tire proportion and cause ... and the harmony of each with the others ... and we say that the painter sees things differently ... skill, despite his aesthetic application ... the artist, you see, on seeing the proportion of this part to that, and one part to another, grasps its beauty, whereas an unskilled person does not achieve that vision, which is the result of artistic perception and understanding ... the Savior is said to be in an allegorical sense Day, as in the verse, "The night is gone, the day is near," that is, he is Day and Light, Light in his essence ... darkness but ... enlightens the mind ... "For those who revere my name the

21. Prv 8.27; 1 Cor 1.30.

22. Ps 33.9. It follows that if Didymus, familiar with Origen's treatment, is ready to move from literal to allegorical meanings in the creation account, he wants to discourage anthropomorphic thinking in his readers.

23. There follow a dozen lines in the ms, still on anthropomorphisms (Nautin believes; SC 233.47), that contain scarcely anything legible. Didymus proceeds.

sun of righteousness will rise," a reference not to physical light
... "makes his own sun to rise[24] ...

And God called the light day, and the darkness he called night (v.5).
This must be taken in every sense: while some ..., there is also
need to consider that ... is made, which is *night*... creator; so by
the norm of allegory *day* ... enlightening and illumination and
... whereas *darkness* is ignorance: the verb *he called* ... that is, he
showed it must be taken ... (50) this constantly being the meaning in the ... the Scriptures: sometimes the verb "he made"
means "he showed"; the Jews said to the Savior, "You, though
only a man, are making yourself God," by "making" meaning
"showing" ... no one; and again it said, "This is the reason they
sought to kill Jesus, not only because he was breaking the sabbath, but also because he was calling God his own father, thereby making himself equal with God," which means equal to the
God who was not generated. John also writes about him in the
epistle, "If we say that we have not sinned, we make him"—God,
that is—"a liar," here "make" meaning "show." And in reference
to the priest who detects in ... "The priest defiles him,"[25] where
"defile" means showing him to be defiled, not him ... (52)

... from the outset God instilled reasoning, by which it is
possible to distinguish good and evil, found in those who have
not gone astray ... whereas others who have gone astray and
use things in opposition ... that good is to be chosen ... being
evil, as in most cases ... those who adopt these wayward ideas
... the Lord curses in the words, "Woe to those who call evil
good and good evil, who put darkness for light and light for
darkness."[26] While they do not do it in actual fact, since they do
not consider darkness to be light, yet in regard to behavior ...
he applies the curse to them ... love for the good and knowledge ... idle affair ...

And there was evening and there was morning, the first day.[27] (54)
... in what was said before this ... of visible creation ... often in

24. Rom 13.12; Mal 4.2; Mt 5.45.
25. Jn 10.33; 5.18; 1 Jn 1.10; Lv 13.3, 11, 44.
26. Is 5.20.
27. Nautin despairs of finding sense in the fragments of commentary on
this text. Note from the FOTC editor: This verse of Genesis does not appear
in Nautin's Greek text, but his French translation supplies it; SC 233.52–53.

the account ... surpassing ... thought is twofold ... the lights made ... which is different ... before every day and ... made second ... day made ...

... heaven where ... "Lo, heaven and the heaven of heavens belong to the Lord your God"[28] ... the heaven is different ... they claim seven heavens ... skilled in mounting ... are six heavens without ... of the heavens ... for while Paul ... citing three heavens[29] ... another of these ... by the three ... "heavens of heavens" ... he said; two ... "heavens of heavens"[30] ... for Scripture is in the habit ... (55)

... it is not beyond dispute ... Now, this has been put this way ... heavens are ... different from the earth ... which is properly said ... heaven was named ... heaven named in the beginning ... pondered in advance ... heaven is from ... it was one and the same ... of the Savior this ... "of this world" ... "By faith we understand that (56) the worlds were prepared by the word of God, so that what is seen was made from things that are invisible"[31] in imitation ... and marvelous, nor ... Moses erects under guidance ... was erected: "See that you make everything according to the pattern shown you on the mountain."[32] ... and Paul in his great wisdom in the epistle to the Hebrews in the more perfect and holy[33] ... with the result that it ... greater spirit ... (57)

... for as a building built on good foundations ... reveals a craftsman's, and a chariot ... and a ship the steersman's, so ... he is saying that from the magnitude and beauty of created things ... their Creator[34] is detected, for from the ... the surpassing quality of what is made ... will be astounded, for the greatly ... completion; not only in sensory perception but also ... these heavens the glory ... (58)

---

28. Dt 10.14.

29. 2 Cor 12.2. In commentary on 1.26, the creation of the human being in God's image, Didymus will cite Zec 4.10 about the Lord having seven eyes, and refer back to a development of the significance of the number seven—possibly this passage on seven heavens; see p. 63 below. Cf. his comment on 4.15, p. 127 below.

30. Ps 148.4.   31. Jn 8.23; Heb 11.3.

32. Ex 25.40; Heb 8.5.   33. Heb 9.11.

34. The term used is γενεσιουργός.

... to be understood in what was said before; for he speaks in proclamatory language. In fact, he proceeds from the use of proclamatory language to employ also interior language,[35] and it is an effect of composition ... the interior word ... (60)

And God said, Let a firmament be made in the middle of the water, and let it keep one body of water from the other (v.6).[36] ... otherwise the truth of the words ... the divine Scriptures concerning ... as in the Gospel, "Whoever believes in me," as Scripture said, "out of his heart rivers of living water will flow,"[37] which in a material manner ... of which it is said, "Much water will not be able to quench love" ... at the same time the opposite power of which ... the holy one cries aloud, "Rescue me from many waters," which ... he goes on, "from the hand of aliens," by "water" meaning the aliens. And again, "If you pass through fire, the flames will not scorch you; if through water, the rivers will not drown (62) you,"[38] which is the recompense given to the righteous. If you were to apply this verse to material rivers, it would not be difficult to be drowned by material rivers, since many other people, even rogues, have in the past met this fate. It is a considerable achievement, on the other hand, not to be overwhelmed by the flood of hostile powers and their immeasurable evil—a fitting reward and an appropriate end for the righteous.

With the rational animals represented by the water, therefore, the implication is that some were made in vice and some in virtue on their own impulse and volition. While all were made with the intention of their possessing virtue, in fact, some of their own accord did not preserve what was given. Since God had also made human beings upright, and yet they departed from uprightness ... different ... water not substantial ... Likewise, in fact ... the saving divine plan ..., yet it was not made in vain: there was a correction for the ... it is surely of their

35. For Didymus's use of these two Stoic terms, see note 9 above.

36. Note from the FOTC editor: This verse does not appear in Nautin's Greek text, but his French translation supplies it; SC 233.60–61.

37. Jn 7.38; Is 44.3; 55.1.

38. Song 8.7; Ps 144.7; Is 43.2. At this point the condition of the manuscript improves markedly. It is interesting that, at least in the text as we have it, Moses as author has not rated a mention.

own volition that some of the rational beings living together are good, and some evil.

The *firmament* made *in the middle of the water,* therefore, is reason, which is responsible for the difference obvious in the mindset;[39] coming from God, it is situated in the faculty of governance and distinguishes base behavior from good in choices we make. Now, distinction of this kind you would not interpret in a bodily sense when contemplating the response given by Abraham to the rich man asking that Lazarus be sent to him: "A vast chasm has been fixed between us";[40] that is to say, virtue is separated from vice not by place but in a difference of diversity and opposition; since (64) righteousness has no truck with iniquity, the righteous and the iniquitous cannot be together (speaking not of place but of attitude and disposition).

Just as in that context there is reference to virtue and vice in a "chasm" that separates evil from good, therefore, so too in this case God made *a firmament in the middle of the water,* that is, in the faculty of governance, so that there should be a discernment between good and evil. Of its nature the good draws one up, while the evil drags down the person who adopts it willingly; "the feet of folly bring her victims down to death and Hades," remember. What is bad is down, whereas the benefits of virtue are enjoyed by those above; "the Lord raises up the gentle," remember.[41] Thus the firmament, which is the basis of faith and virtue, is helpful in distinguishing malice from zeal, so that neither ... nor ... the firmament towards nature ... is possession of stability, but also in this way ... and also outstrips every bodily being. So *God said, Let a firmament be made in the middle of the water;* by the norm of allegory the water is understood to be one, since the rational being is one in substance,

---

39. For "mindset" or free will Didymus speaks of γνώμη. Nautin comments: "After having related the waters above and below to good things and bad, Didymus interprets the firmament which separates them as referring to reason, which distinguishes between good and evil"; SC 233.63, note 20, 1. One thinks, on the other hand, of the efforts made by Severian to explain the creation of the firmament: "In the middle of the waters there was set a crystal-like fixture, raising half the water on high, and leaving half below" (PG 56:442).

40. Lk 16.26.

41. Prv 5.5; Ps 147.6.

and the difference in the mindset is responsible for the separation.

And so it was: the will of the God of all had to be effected; the implementation quickly became obvious, following on both word and will. Now, the Son is his will, and through him all things have been established; as the wisdom of the one who generated him, he says, "When he established the heavens, I was with (66) him."[42] Hence, when we hear, *God said and so it was,* we take it to be the Son hearing and carrying out his will ... and do not take it in a human sense ... Instead, it is for us in our profession of the unity of Father and Son to believe from these expressions Father and Son as Creator of everything, instead of the Father being responsible for some things and the Son others. It is said in fact by the Son himself, "Whatever he does, the Son does likewise."[43]

God made the firmament, and God divided the water which was below the firmament from the water which was above the firmament (v.7). ... of the water, as was said before ... under the firmament ... what preceded.

God called the firmament heaven, and God saw that it was good (v.8). ... *God saw that it was good,* but such a degree of praise should be given that ... immediately the word *saw* gives a glimpse of beauty ... has the restoration ... and of the proportion he gives praise on seeing that ... to estimate the usefulness and the cause and the ... and some parts from matter, for being built is lacking in honor. It is possible to see other parts as lacking honor, such as hair and the like, and no one with the ability to judge the overall pattern of a city would blame the builder for building in the city a prison and other things along with what is honorable and beautiful. (68) After all, an individual item by itself is not so admirable as when you estimate the usefulness of everything together, as in the case of a city's appearance. Likewise in the case of creation, something even more admirable: it is impossible to mention this detail or that, since everything has been created for their use.

Evening came and morning came, a second day. Understand

42. Prv 8.27.
43. Jn 5.19.

that some people beyond the pale of religion have asked in an attempt to test us, "Why on earth in your view were the days mentioned when the sun was not yet in existence?"[44] For one thing, you could say to them that all this is to be interpreted in an anagogical sense; teaching through symbols is not out of the question for us. On the other hand, since it is normal for someone dealing with them to uphold even the literal sense, come now, let us take up a few details in regard to this. *Day* has two senses, temporal duration and light of the air about us; when it is said, "And on the third day,"[45] there is reference to the number of the day, not the day's brightness or gloom, whereas if you were to say that today is a gloomy day, you would not be speaking with reference to its number. So if the divine word says that a first and second and third (70) day existed before the creation of the sun and the other lights, we should consider the extent of temporal duration. To the person having difficulties with the divine Scripture the reply should be given that seventy-two hours, as it were, elapsed between the creation of the firmament and that of the lights, which is not surprising. Far from making the day, in fact, the sun indicates it, no more than anyone would say that instruments mechanically constructed make the hours: they only indicate them. So the sun and the moon indicate the times; they do not make them.[46] It is one thing to indicate, another to make, the result being that there is nothing illogical in such a lengthy period intervening between the creation of the sun and the other lights which, had

44. Origen had met and answered this question from Celsus, and in replying had upheld the value of allegorical commentary, as Didymus does; see SC 233.68–69, note 23,1, where Nautin refers to *Contra Celsum* 6.60.5-7 and 6.50.15-17.

45. Jn 2.1. It is interesting that Didymus, who believes that here he is staying with the text (τὸ ῥητόν) and not moving away from it to take refuge in allegory, does not consider the possibility of "days" in the figurative sense of stages in creation (not simply the "seventy-two hours" that Didymus cites). It is one thing to eschew literalistic interpretation, another to fail to explore the full sense of the literal. He will investigate the symbolism of the number six, and the sense of "day," when he reaches vv.14–19.

46. The point is Origen's, expressed here verbatim; SC 233.71, note 24,1. Didymus often makes it.

there been something to indicate it, would have been a period of three days.

God said, Let the water under heaven be gathered together into one mass, and let dry land appear (v.9). We take God's *saying* as anticipatory, as before when it was said, *God said, Let there be light,* and *Let a firmament be made.* The literal explanation of the present verse would be as follows: not all the water but only what is *under heaven* God orders to be *gathered together into one mass;* it had been said that the firmament was made *in the middle of the waters,* so that some water remained above, some below. He reveals the usefulness of the order in saying, *and let dry land appear;* it had been hidden with water on top of it, and in that condition was unsuited for producing plants and animals. (72)

He then says, *The water was gathered together into their masses* (v.9b LXX). Giving the order is one thing, so to say, carrying it out is another: *into one mass* describes collection of all the water, and the corresponding clause says that *the water was gathered together into their masses* and thus *the dry land appeared.* Now, the apparent discrepancy will be resolved by anyone familiar with the facts as follows.[47] The Ocean is a single sea surrounding the whole world; geographers say that what is for us an island by comparison with the whole sea, surrounded as it is and encompassed on all sides, the whole land and the whole world are by comparison with the Ocean. But there are, as it were, some inlets from the Ocean intruding into remote places, and these constitute the other seas. So if the text says *into one mass,* it means the mass across the world, which is normally called Ocean; what was gathered into one was gathered also into others, so to say, the individual masses.

Thus *the dry land appeared* (v.9b LXX). Note that he did not say, "All the dry land"; there was also land under the water, since it is impossible for there to be water without land or a solid body underlying it. Observe whether there is a difference in the words "dry" and "land" in the saying in the prophet, "Once again I shall shake the heaven and the land, the sea and the dry."[48] Now,

47. The problem arises from the inclusion in the LXX generally of v.9b, not found in most forms of the Heb. and in our modern English versions.
48. Hg 2.6.

somebody else will say that the same meaning is conveyed; but "dry" and "land" are used in different senses, "land" in reference to what is under heaven, and "dry" in reference to a moist substance. There is a statement, remember, "The sea itself (74) is God's and he made it, and the dry land his hands formed," and in reference to Jonah swallowed in the belly of the sea monster, "He ordered the sea monster, and he discharged Jonah on to the dry land" after being in a moist substance.[49]

So much for the literal sense. In regard to the spiritual sense that is in keeping with the preceding verses, our claim is that the waters abiding above the firmament are not material nor parts of these material waters; after all, there are no plants or animals there that are subject to this need of water. What has been said before this is sufficient proof that the water there is not material. Our claim, then, is that it is the rational beings abiding in a worse situation on account of their own vices that are the waters held under the firmament in many and varied *masses;* it is impossible for vicious people ever to share the same thinking, since it is a source of confusion and an enemy to unity. It is virtue, in fact, that is productive of unity, containing a mutual attraction as it does;[50] the temperate person is courageous, prudent, and just, and in possessing one virtue possessing the others, as is the case with the Beatitudes in the Gospel: those possessing what is productive of one Beatitude also possess what produces the others. It often happens, however, that there is a certain inclination for the same virtue, the result being that one person is described as merciful from an eminence in that area, another just, another temperate, and so on with the other virtues. The person possessing one in a perfect manner possesses also the others; I say "in a perfect manner" because often one is at the initial stage or is progressing. (76)

Now, that the virtues possess a mutual attraction is clear

49. Ps 95.5; Jon 2.10. Didymus, for all his interest in a higher level of meaning of texts, can be precise about textual matters, even where an otiose distinction may be involved. Under the skin he may not have been different from Severian—but nurture affected nature.

50. The notion occurring here, as often elsewhere in Didymus (Nautin notes; SC 233.75, note 26,2), is Stoic. He proceeds to develop the notion at length (what would be known to Christian moralists as the four cardinal virtues).

from what follows. The rational being who proposes to live in accordance with virtue exercises prudence so as to judge what is to be done and not to be done, what is to be chosen and avoided, what involves blame and commendation; we definitely need the knowledge to distinguish between good and evil so as to choose one and shun the other. The person with prudence like this, who distinguishes evil from good and has a clear knowledge that good is to be chosen and done, chooses it, while shunning the opposite in the knowledge that it is to be shunned, is harmful, ... and damaging. Such a person also has need of justice so as to accord to each one what is their due: to the good, choice; and to the bad, avoidance. With the knowledge of what is to be blamed and what is to be commended, therefore, such a person has need of fortitude so as to despise deceit and not fall foul of those who opt for it. Hence such a person is also temperate, temperance being something appropriate to the rational being. You observe that the person possessing one possesses all, and that like the Beatitudes they have the one end, though being different from each other; just as in a city there are different entrances, and the person entering through one is still in the city, so too with the virtues. Virtue is therefore something unifying, as Paul also says to those living in that fashion, "May you be united in the same mind and the same will."[51] Vice, by contrast, is not like that: excess cannot be consistent with defect, since the person with audacity does not also have dread. Likewise, piety holds the middle ground between impiety and superstition: piety accepts and reverences what it should, whereas superstition has reverence for everything, even what should not be reverenced, and impiety has reverence for nothing (78) and holds nothing reverend, which is true of atheists. So superstition and impiety are inconsistent.

Since what was under the firmament, then, were rational beings in the grip of vice and a tendency to evil, and since vice is disordered and confused, it is impossible for them to be in the one "will" and choice. After all, just as when people in casting their vote are in the right, they proclaim their being in the right by a unanimous vote, while those in the wrong achieve a

51. 1 Cor 1.10.

lesser vote or an excessive one in different degrees, so too in the case of vice the person falling short of truth is caught up in various forms of vice. This is the case also with travelers: false trails are very numerous, while there is one straight path.

There was a dispersion, therefore, of the waters, which we assumed to be the rational beings in the grip of different mindsets and morals. So God wants them to be one, since he deigned to bring them benefits, being their Creator. It was mentioned before, remember, that he is the author of their being, whereas each of them is responsible for the diversity of their mindset. It is God himself, then, who orders them to be *gathered together into one mass* so that they may become water like that which is above the heavens—*one,* not in number, but in accord. Actually, the "one heart and soul"[52] of all the believers is a matter not of number; instead, it is realized as one in accord and in pursuit of the same purpose and the one goal.

The God of all therefore orders the things that were divided to be brought into harmony; this is the intention of the beneficent God. Since they were confused and at odds in their mindset, they were first gathered together in *masses.* (80) There was no inconsistency between the order given and the statement that they *were gathered together into their masses* although God had said, *Let the water be gathered together into one mass;* befitting those not yet arrived at the goal of the highest virtue is the gathering that is progressing toward it.[53] Just as if you want to teach your child perfect lessons, you entrust him to a teacher, and if he first drills him in the letters, then the syllables, it would not be in opposition to the one who entrusted him, so too from this stage he would arrive at perfection. Likewise, if a king ordered his subjects to build a city, and if he then gave instructions about the way the construction would be done, it would not be at variance with his orders; the building would be completed on that basis and through those means. In this way, too, the rational beings subject to vice would not succeed in ar-

52. Acts 4.32.

53. As observed in n. 47, this rationalization would have been unnecessary if Didymus had been in a position to check the Heb. text, where (at least in most mss, as in Eng. versions) v.9b does not occur.

riving at the ultimate goal unless different stages occurred, like the heaps of waters; he bids completion in *one mass* be arrived at after progress is made. So what happened was not inconsistent with the order; instead, just as the order contributes to the completion of the order, there is an overall plan predisposing the rational beings, insofar as they are able, to reach the goal in this way.

And so it was; and the water was gathered together into their masses (v.9). On the one hand, God's purpose was for what was dispersed to be assembled into one—what he says, in fact—(82) and in their case, on the other hand, after falling short for a while of their goal they were *gathered together into their masses,* which were the stages of development.

God called the dry land earth, and he called the masses of the waters seas (v.10). We said that the earth that was made in the beginning with heaven had this same name, and heaven this same name, whereas what was made after heaven and earth in the beginning is more properly *firmament,* though given the added name *heaven.* So too the land along with the heaven made in the beginning was given this same name, whereas the land referred to here is named *dry* and given the added name *earth: God called the dry land earth,* as it was said, *He called the firmament heaven.*[54] In terms of allegory, when God calls the dry land *earth,* he does not grant it a new name; instead, since he had ordered that the waters that were covering it and were related to the deep should withdraw, he calls it *dry land*—the text saying, *And let the dry land appear*—so that the soul, though remaining in its own substance, is functionally called *earth* while the waters remain, and when liberated by God for reception of the divine seed it produces ripened fruit "a hundredfold, sixtyfold, thirtyfold."[55] In other words, in the same way as with cultivated soil, one soil yields a crop more promptly, and another produces more slowly depending on the attention of the farmer

54. With his eye for detail, Didymus has detected some inconsistencies in the text, viz., how the words "earth" and "heaven" are used twice as though new names each time.

55. Mt 13.23. Didymus can move to a subtext and develop it to the point where it becomes the text.

or the type of ground, so too with souls: some receive the seed but stifle it with cares and worries, whereas others receive intense farming and engage in education to such a point as to draw benefit themselves and reveal to others the goal of the benefit. (84) The difference in the plants, in fact, is manifold and various, the worst being variable, being such only from its treatment, which shows that dry land is better than bad soil; the seed amounts to nothing as long as it is in poor terrain.

And God saw that it was good. God saw that it was good for the land to be cleared of what covered it in order that it might become earth; so the literal sense is clear here, too. When hidden by the waters, therefore, the earth was not dry and could neither nourish living beings nor produce crops; so after the setting-up[56] of the world it was *good* that there were animals which would have offspring, and in addition it was *good* that there were plants and trees and edible crops of which the animals partook. Since, then, as was said before, on seeing the interrelationship God approved and commended it, it is therefore said, *God saw that it was good,* the verb *saw* being taken in the previous way,[57] that he did not ... As craftsmen their crafts, and to a far greater extent, ... God sees pre-eminently, but not by sense.

And God said, Let the earth put forth a crop of vegetation (v.11). Once separated, the earth that had been submerged under the wet substance was given the name *dry land* and the added name *earth,* and had the ability to produce crops. (86) Now, it should be noted that throughout the entire process of creation there occur the formulae *God said* and *God made,* obviously in reference to his creative work. In this name, in fact, there is particular reference to his creative work, whereas the name *Lord* conveys the sense of ruler and king. So the statement occurs, *In the beginning God made,* not the King or the Lord—not that God is other than the King and the Lord, but that the name God places greater emphasis on his creative work. So when the commandment is given to Adam, the phrasing is, *The Lord God*

56. The term used is κατάστασις, another term for "creation."

57. As in comment on Gn 1.4, where readers were warned not to misinterpret anthropomorphisms. See p. 29 above.

commanded Adam,[58] and rightly so: giving laws and commandments belongs to a lord and king.

*And God said, Let the earth put forth a crop of vegetation, plants
yielding seed, each according to its kind and likeness.* In other words,
of the things that grow from the earth some are trees, some
vegetables. When Moses in Deuteronomy wanted to name the
trees, he called those that bear fruit simply trees "of wood,"[59]
by the phrase "of wood" referring to vine, fig tree, olive tree,
whereas there is obviously need to mention as well all the
plants not known to most human beings ... to people involved
in healing bodies ... as Solomon also, in bringing out their value, said he had received knowledge of them from God: "For it
is he who gave me unerring knowledge of what exists, to know
the structure of the world and the activity of the elements,"
and a little later "varieties of plants and powers of roots" and so
on,[60] no longer referring to them as "of wood." ... In our text,
on the other hand, by *crop of vegetation* he refers to everything
(88) vegetable, also referred to in the Gospel as "vegetation of
the field."[61]

... plants in general, while by *each according to its likeness* he indicates the species. Now, the fact that Scripture also knows what
is meant by "species" he conveys by saying, "Abstain from every
species of evil," using the word "species" in its precise sense,
though often it also uses it in the sense of "form": "And we saw
him, and he had no form or beauty," and, "We walk by faith,
not by form,"[62] implying that the person whose knowledge is not
based on visible shape walks by faith, whereas ... by form.

After having referred to the ground-hugging plants as *plants
yielding seed, each according to its kind,* therefore, he proceeds to
refer to the trees as *fruit trees bearing fruit.* Every plant, you see,
has in it a nature which comes from its seed, such that some of
them are edible, others ... useful for different needs that are
known in some cases also to men, in others only to God.

---

58. Gn 2.16. While we find this precision in distinguishing the divine
names typical of Didymus, Nautin informs us that it had occurred already in
Philo, with whom Didymus was very familiar; SC 233.86–87, note 31,4.

59. Dt 28.42.   60. Wis 7.17, 20.
61. Mt 6.30.   62. 1 Thes 5.22; Is 53.2; 2 Cor 5.7.

So much for the literal sense; the allegorical sense in my view is somewhat as follows. Having created the human being upright in the sense of bearing fruits of virtue and setting store by knowledge of the truth, God instilled in him good thoughts. The earth, understood in a spiritual sense, on the other hand, had been drawn away from its own mindset ... when the human being was sown with thorns as a result of the Fall. All those, for example, who were the beneficiaries of divine teaching but did not respond to the sowing of the word are told, "You have sown wheat and have reaped thorns";[63] in other words, their purpose in sowing would not have been to reap thorns ... because they did not cultivate properly or ... judged worthy of the blessing Jacob gave (90) his son: "Lo, the smell of my son is like the smell of a prosperous field which the Lord has blessed." On the other hand, the one who has cultivated it properly will be told, as was the bride, "A locked garden is my sister, my bride."[64]

The phrase *And so it was* occurs by way of response.

And God saw that it was good (v.12). It should be noted that, although two commands were given and implemented, reference is made to one, *God saw that it was good;* consideration was given to the goal and purpose in saying, *God saw that it was good,* the vegetation and the rest proliferating for the sake of the human beings. Now, if he said that what displayed proportion in material things was *good,* much more so what is to be found in virtues, harmony of a soul that lives a good life, is rational, chooses what is virtuous, and is zealous for a virtuous goal.[65]

God said, Let lights be made in the firmament of heaven for lighting up the earth to separate day from night. Let them act as signs and indicate times and days and years. Let them provide light in the firmament of heaven to shine upon the earth. And so it was until there was *a fourth day* (vv.14–19). In beginning of the book we said that as an efficacious being God has only to wish for what he wishes to exist. In his case, you see, it is out of the question

63. Jer 12.13.

64. Gn 27.27; Song 4.12.

65. Here, where the goodness of created things is asserted, this would have been an occasion for firing salvos at a rogues' gallery of heretics; but since he moves quickly to a spiritual level, he does not take the opportunity.

that action should precede effect, as is the case with human en-
deavor, where only after action does the work come into being,
and after the building process the house; (92) the house does
not exist during the building process, nor the ship during the
shipbuilding, since the actions themselves require time. God,
on the other hand, acts outside of time in bringing into being
what he wishes; the outcome is definitely not a consequence.

It was therefore simultaneously that he wished the lights
to come into existence, and they were; and simultaneously he
wanted the water to be gathered together into a single mass,
and his command was executed; and in saying *Let a firmament
be made*, it came into existence. Hence, in consequence of this
thought ... we should think of the six *days* not as though cited
as part of a chronological presentation but as a rational basis
peculiar to God's creation and the force of the number.[66] Six,
in fact, is the first of the perfect numbers; they say that perfect
numbers are those composed of their own parts, and there are
only four between 1 and 1000. So the first is 6, half of which
is 3, a third 2, a sixth 1, and when added together they total 6.
The same is true of 28: its half is 14, its quarter 7, its seventh
4, its fourteenth 2, its twenty-eighth 1, and when likewise added together they make 28. Beyond them there are two others,
and if addition is made of others than the perfect ones, there
is some excess or defect. Look at 8, for example: its half is 4,
its quarter 2, its eighth 1, which when added together give a
lower number. On the other hand, 12 gives a higher number
when addition is made: its half is 6, its third 4, its quarter 3, its
sixth 2, its twelfth 1. So the experts in these matters call the
ones that fall short defective, and those that surpass excessive,
while those composed of their own factors are perfect. So God,
who is responsible for a creation that is perfect, brought it into
being in the first perfect number, definitely not for us to claim

66. We noted above (n. 45) that Didymus had not seen the use of a "day"
of creation as a figure. Here, while he warns against taking it as twenty-four
hours, and insists on "order" in creation, he does not see the Priestly author's
order moving towards a seventh day, the sabbath rest. Instead, under the influence of Philo he indulges in number symbolism regarding the six days of
creation, the Hexameron.

that six days passed as the sun followed its course six times, (94) the sun not having existed in the first three days, but because the number six was adopted for the sake of reasonableness and harmony.

Now, this is the reason Moses precisely gave in summarizing the main points about created things: "This is the book about the origin of heaven and earth when they were created on the day when God made heaven and earth"[67]—not that heaven and earth were made in a *day* but *in the beginning,* nor that all things came into existence in a single day. Instead, the meaning is that, with all things being made simultaneously, this number was adopted, as I said, for reasons of order and harmony, and in addition on account of our limitations and inability to understand in a way other than what suits us. Let the statement be clear from an example: our body has both color and size as it has substance; they did not come into being separated from one another by an interval of time; only in thought is one being before the other and one later. Likewise, the world, too, was made with an order that was due to a separation not of time but of harmony; it is impossible to think of a part of the world that is not coordinated with the others as far as existence is concerned.

The lights emerge as worthy of honor for being made on the fourth day, since it is on that basis that they are said to be made with a reason for them. A group of four, you see, having the force of ten, indicates honor; throughout Scripture ten is an object of praise. The fact that the indication of a number in the divine (96) writings conveys not principally multiplicity but significance it is possible to grasp from the statement by God, "I kept for myself seven thousand men who have not bent the knee to Baal"; if that had been the number, the prophet would not have said, "I am left alone,"[68] nor would they have had any association with one another, since they did not shun one another. The significance of seven, which is without mother or father, is to the effect that the saints have the same power, even if amounting only to one, because they constitute something

67. Gn 2.4.
68. 1 Kgs 19.18, 10.

divine, superior to human beings in contemplation and life.
When John says in the Apocalypse that there were a hundred
and forty-four thousand men following the Lamb, who is the
Savior, and they were virgins, not defiled by women,[69] he shows
that there is an element of honor attached to this number. Let
no one say that so large a crowd of virgins was gathered together from among the believers in John's lifetime, since the believers were probably not so numerous. Our claim, therefore,
is that the world was made in a six-day period for reasons given
above, and the lights were made on the fourth day as explained
before, namely, that a group of four, having the force of ten, is
worthy of honor; Moses gave ten commandments, offerings are
made in tenths, and you would find other instances of distinction accorded groups of ten.

Let lights be made in the firmament of heaven, therefore. This
teaches us that they are not gods, as the Egyptians thought in
their deception. Now, he did well (98) to say *in the firmament*
and not "above the firmament"; this is something visibly true.
Their role, it says, is *lighting up the earth* and *separating day from
night;* dawn brings on day, and sunset night. Another role of
theirs is to act as *signs;* the stars signal many things, as does
the sun itself—signal, not by causing them but by making them
obvious. The fortune-tellers, on the other hand, claim that they
are actively involved, the movement of one to another having
a certain effect. This is not what they are for, however; their
purpose is to signal hours, months, and years, signaling not being causative. *Let them act as signs and indicate times and days and
years,* the text says, which means signaling the seasons of the
year—spring, winter, and the rest—the sun having this effect if
it is in one or another region. If, on the other hand, the astrol-
ogers, who concur in the meaning of the *signs,* claim that this
too introduces the doctrine of fortune, this would not be plausible, either; human nature would not be able to grasp such
signs when, even according to them, the sky moves so quickly
that it would be impossible to take the horoscope of a newborn.

The phrase *And so it was* acts as a response, and brings out
that the Son effected what the Father (100) wanted to be estab-

69. Rv 14.1.

lished; without his saying how many lights would be made, the text proceeded, *And God made the two lights,* and thus the will and implementation of Father and Son are identical. The *rule* of the lights was determined, the sun presiding over the day, and the moon and other stars over the night. *He set* them,[70] the phrase *he set* not being synonymous with *he made* in such a way that they were not first made and then set; one stage was bringing into being, and the other was allotting to other parts of the world.

To make a remark further regarding what was said about the text properly mentioning six *days,* not hours or months or years: saying months or years would imply slowness, and hours would be incomprehensible, since the person unable to grasp *day* would not understand "hour," either. Having given a perfect number, therefore, it was only right and proper to adopt *days.* Likewise, the phrase *God saw,* in saying that God saw they were well made, is understood as in the case of what preceded.

While this is what we have to say in clarifying the literal sense, the anagogical sense would be as follows. It was said before that the phrase *Let there be light* should be applied to the Savior, not that he was brought into being from what did not exist, but by comparison with those to whom he gives light. In the case of those given light, some receive less light, others more, and in addition to them (102) there are some that are in the dark of night. Accordingly, today as well the thoughts of the Son prove to be lights, as the intent of the text in hand can logically be understood. He is adapted to the measure of each one, to the more elevated being the Sun of Justice,[71] while to the less developed he provides in appropriate measure the light of the Spirit in the manner of the moon. Those illuminated in the night, on the other hand, would be everyone who, though mature, is necessarily subject to the needs of the body; the person who is mature, even though being such, nevertheless has a body and so needs nourishment and is subject to the other

70. Gn 1.17, whereas the "making" of the lights occurs in v.16, and their "ruling" in v.18—precision again. Didymus will proceed to make spiritual capital out of the terms.

71. Mal 4.2.

needs of the body. These he meets in the manner of a mature person, and hence has light; but as such it is a light in the night, since tension of this kind from the needs of the body, even if not disappearing, is relaxed.

Just as the moon, as some people claim, receives beams from the sun, and becomes a secondary light derived from the greater one, so too the Church is a light to the world. For instance, the Lord said to his disciples, "You are the light of the world," not a light like the sun, since it is he who is the "Sun of Justice," but a lesser one and derived from him. And the Apostle, in saying, "You are among them like lights in the world," shows that they are a "light of the world" through sharing in "the true light"; in fact, he went on, "By holding fast to the word of life."[72] The moon would represent the presence in them of the light itself; the Lord did not say, "You are the lights," but the "light," since in having unity among themselves they all are one light, being Church as they are. (104) The *stars* among them could be taken allegorically as those elevated by the Word above the others whom they illuminate; such ones would be prophets, who before the rising of the sun dispatch the beam of prophecy.

It was he, at any rate, who in rising enlightened the whole world, and showed everything to be one light through the participants being shown to be a perfect light. Scripture says, remember, that the righteous will shine "like the sun in the kingdom of their Father"—not the sun, but "like the sun," as is also said in the Song of Songs about the one who shares in the light, "Who is this who peeps out, fair like the dawn, chosen like the moon, astonishing like the sun?"[73] Note that in this some stages of development are indicated: first there is the "dawn," then "chosen like the moon" in the sense of full and entire like a full moon—after all, even if it is the same moon when in the first and fourth quarter, its state is complete when it is full, and it is to this he likens the bride—and after this like the sun, "astonishing" in its final stage and unity. People who become like this are not light by nature, only through participation in "the

72. Mt 5.14; Mal 4.2; Phil 2.15–16; Jn 1.9.
73. Mt 13.43; Song 6.10.

true light."[74] They also separate *day from darkness,* discriminating between vice and virtue, and thus illuminating people on earth, who are not yet heavenly in their behavior. They signal *times and days* and months *and years* as applies, making known the stage achieved by each and the way for each to follow towards instruction, just as we say that a physician prescribes the times for nourishment in consideration of the well-being of the one to be nourished; sometimes, in fact, the patient is fed at night. (106)

The Sun of Justice, therefore, the moon mentioned with him, and the stars signal a time of this kind, such as a time of learning, a time of progress, a time of beginning, and even actual behavior; when someone is enlightened, their underlying behavior is pure. The Sun of Justice did not come into being when he gave the signal; he existed from eternity, signaling only when those who made their approach were in need of a guide. Hence they are also said to have been made *on the fourth day,* "being made" taken in an allegorical sense to mean their relation to rational creatures; as was said before, since we have the capacity for virtue, we need people to incite us to the practice of the virtues, the practice passing from a group of four to a group of ten. Four has the force of ten, remember, since the factors of four make up ten.

Now, the *firmament,* in which the lights occur, should be understood as faith and virtue in perfection, which the Psalmist possessed in saying, "The Lord was my support"; and of the Church it is said, "What is that which comes up, leaning upon her nephew?"[75] Without the Word, in fact, it would not be possible for the Church to exist; he is its support and foundation. These lights for their part act as *signs,* signaling in the literal sense a kingdom, or droughts, or heavy rain, or anything else of great consequence, and in a spiritual sense, as was mentioned, progress, and often the soul's desolation, something the lights suggest in an allegorical sense. (108) They also illuminate peo-

74. Jn 1.9.
75. Ps 18.18; Song 8.5. The firmament, of course, had been interpreted differently at its first appearance (as reason); see above, p. 33.

ple *on earth;* everyone unable to share in the pure, perfect light is illuminated by that of the saints. Moses conveyed as much in saying, "I stood between the Lord and you" to offer to God your supplications and minister to you the graces coming from him. Likewise, the Savior also in becoming man is "a mediator between God and man":[76] as God he connects us to the Father, and in becoming man he also somehow speaks to us in his lov- ingkindness what he heard from the Father. Among the lights inferior to the sun would also be the Law, of which the Psalmist said, "Your Law is a lamp for my feet," implying that the Law sheds light on the progress and advance of the soul. Likewise il- luminated, Paul also says, "Let us live honorably as in the day"; being in Christ, such people belong to him and say individual- ly, "It is no longer I who live, but it is Christ who lives in me," and "I know a person in Christ."[77] For thus they become light from light in such a way that they illuminate others through their instruction.

The phrase *He set* should be taken to mean "show" as in the reference to the Savior, that the Father "set him as heir of all things" in the sense of "showed":[78] far from making him heir at a later stage, he made manifest what he was.

God saw that it was good: it was good to be illuminated by the light of the senses, and much more by a spiritual one. (110)

And God said, Let the water produce reptiles with living souls, and on the earth winged creatures flying across the firmament of heaven. And so it was. God made the huge sea monsters and every single living reptile of various kinds produced by the waters and every winged, fly- ing creature of various kinds. And God saw that they were good. God blessed them, and so on to *the fifth day* (vv.20–23). Since among the things on earth the creation of the human beings, who are mortal beings, is pre-eminent, consequently the other animals and plants serving their needs are created; some are for food, others to tend them, while others are for bearing burdens and others for their needs, nothing existing without a purpose.

76. Dt 5.5; 1 Tm 2.5.

77. Ps 119.105 (where the Alexandrian text reads not "word" but "Law"); Rom 13.13; Gal 2.20; 2 Cor 12.2.

78. Heb 1.2. We have seen, and will see, Didymus often making this point.

God therefore says, *Let the water produce reptiles with living souls, and on the earth winged creatures flying;* they were required to exist to meet human needs.

After mentioning the reptiles' bodies, he calls them all *living souls;* even if they were without reason, he still equips their body with a life force that will perish with them, whereas that of the human being will survive the dissolution of the body. Some of the birds fly up high, whereas most have a lower flight and they most of all are assigned to be for human food; so is it of the majority that he says, *and on the earth winged creatures flying;* this is probably the reason they do not fly on high like the eagle and such like, to be accessible to human beings, for whom also they were made. (112) *Across the firmament of heaven,* it says, not that in flying they come near it, but that they are under it, even if not reaching it. For example, Scripture calls the clouds that bear rain "heavenly," and says the rain comes from heaven, although the clouds are composed of air, and it is from them that rain comes. Such clouds are said to be no more than a few miles above the earth, and often mountains are found to rise above the clouds, and the clouds to be lower than they are. So the answer is that the sky is often referred to as "heaven" and "firmament." *And so it was* is to be understood in a way similar to the previous cases.

Why does it say, *God made the huge sea monsters?* It should be noted that it does not say in reference to the sea monsters, "Let the waters produce sea monsters," but just the fact that he made them. They are so huge that the naturalists marvel, comparing them to islands, and claim that people often travel towards them in the belief that they are going to dry land, only to discover that they are sea monsters when they make it obvious by moving. Note also the further statement, *God made the huge sea monsters and every single living reptile:* the waters produce their bodies—I mean the bodies of those that get their existence from the waters—and God makes the monsters along with the other animals by providing them with the life force. Not that their bodies exist first and then are animated (the soul of brute beasts does not have life apart from their bodies); (114) rather, since it is by the will of God that they come into existence at the same time, Scripture says that their bodies emerged from the water and God made their souls, namely, their animation and movement, not from the waters but from God's willing it. The phrase *of various kinds* clearly means by *kinds* in this case "species."

And God saw that they were good. In the previous cases it was said, remember, *it was good,* on account either of what was made being one, or of its existing in one part of the world. Since in this case, on the other hand, they were allotted to different places, some traveling in the air, some being in the water, it was logically said, *God saw that they were good.*

And God blessed them. Why on earth, when in the other cases preceding this one there was no blessing offered, in this case is it said, *And God blessed them?* Take note, at any rate, as to whether it is not added on account of offspring being associated with these creatures. They are not blessed, note, in the way human beings are, of whom it is said, "Blessed be the God and Father of our Lord Jesus Christ, who has blessed us with every spiritual blessing in the heavenly places."[79] These are spiritual blessings given to the intellect and the interior person, which are not applicable to brute beasts, the term "spiritual" being added to highlight the fact that there are also bodily blessings, like bodily wellbeing and things that are indifferent. So the increase and the large numbers which he bade happen with the animals he called *blessing.* The phrase *in the seas* is said simply of the marshes and rivers, (116) with the intention of indicating waters of every type by mentioning the greater ones. Logically there is reference to the winged creatures in the phrase *on the earth* on account of their being close to the earth; they could not live in the sky because of its warmth.

Evening came, and morning came, a fifth day (v.23), and rightly so: it was quite appropriate for brute beasts gifted with senses to be made on the fifth day, since the number five is suggestive of sense. After all, even if human beings have a share in senses, their intellect and reason are greater than senses, whereas brute beasts have senses alone.

79. Eph 1.3.

So much for the literal sense, then. In an anagogical sense, "water" was said in what went before to refer to evil by the norm of allegory, especially when we cited the verse, "Much water will not be able to quench love."[80] This is not an effect of material water; rather, it is said to be the cause of a diminution of virtue, "the love of many growing cold on account of the increase of lawlessness."[81] Is not lawlessness, therefore, the water that tries to quench the impulse of love? By stirring up hatred, in fact, it constrains love, which consists of sharing and mildness, which are natural to human beings. So God's intention is that the *reptiles* and *winged creatures* be made from the waters understood in this sense, and they suggest differences (118) in behavior. Some descend to the depths of evil, and as a result are contemptuous—Scripture says, remember, "When the impious fall to the depths, they are contemptuous of troubles"—like reptiles coiled around earthly things and clinging to the mass of this water, of which it is said, "To be sure, our soul passed through the irresistible water,"[82] but the benefactor wishes to deliver us from such severe trouble. Others, having faulty ideas, are called *winged creatures,* head in the air and mind on things different from other people, yet the loving God wishes them to emerge from this condition so that they may bring their thinking, which they devoted to improper interests, to appropriate objects befitting their rational nature, so that in this way they may recover the ability of divine flight, which they forfeited.

The *huge sea monsters* by the norms of allegory were the wicked powers, the devil and his angels, who are called "dragons" by Scripture, a name clearly much more applicable to the devil. It is said in reference to the Savior, for instance, in the form of a hymn: "You crushed the heads of the dragon; you crushed the heads of the dragons in the water."[83] Now, it is clear that they were made by God, not as being evil but in regard to their underlying substance; God did not make devil or demons as

80. Song 8.7, cited in comment on 1.6. Didymus systematically moves to an anagogical or allegorical sense after dealing (as he sees it) with the literal— though in this case number symbolism is regarded as part of the literal.

81. Mt 24.12.   82. Prv 18.3; Ps 124.4.

83. Ps 74.14, 13.

such—they brought ruin on themselves, Scripture affirming that they are angels that did not preserve their rank. (120) The fact that the devil is called a sea monster is stated in the book of Job: "The one destined to curb the huge sea monster";[84] and by him the sea monsters under heaven were tamed. It is also possible that the clause *God made them* means "showed"; by *made,* Scripture often means "showed," as in the statement, "If we say that we have not sinned, we make him a liar," not that we become creators of God, but that we show him to be a liar as far as this is possible for us. The same meaning emerges also from the saying by the Jews, "Though you are a man, you are making yourself God," in the sense of showing. This is what God does also in showing the wicked powers and making them obvious as such lest they escape detection and cause immeasurable harm, and in order that those whose contest is with them may recognize them,[85] this being the way to be contemptuous of them.

Now, God wants these creatures to be out of the waters, his intention being that as initiates in virtue they should keep their distance from evil.[86] The person in the grip of vice to this degree, you see, does not all at once undergo a transformation to perfection; instead, gradually and by degrees these people move steadily to some degree of virtue. So his purpose is that in this way they may become *winged creatures* of heaven and part company with earth, like those who were told, "If you lie down among the lots, a dove's wings covered in silver, and its back in the pallor of gold,"[87] by "lots" meaning the crossing of the waters, as in the verse, "Isaac (122) desired what was good in resting between the lots."[88] These would be the Old and New Testaments, which

84. Jude 6; Jb 3.8.
85. 1 Jn 1.10; Jn 10.33; cf. Eph 6.12.
86. What follows is a classic example of Didymian interpretation-by-association. Wanting to take the production of creatures by the waters in the sense of neophytes "keeping their distance from evil," he speaks (against the evidence of the text) of their being "out of" the waters, which then leads to the citation of a notoriously obscure psalm verse (Ps 68.13), which as subtext—in the manner of Didymus—becomes the text, and itself gives rise to further subtexts that themselves lead the reader further from the Genesis text.
87. Ps 68.13, where Theodoret also saw reference in "lots" to OT and NT.
88. Gn 49.14, which in fact is referring rather to Issachar.

give wings to the one who rests between them and compares the prophecies with their outcome, as though having wings of a dove, like the Holy Spirit coming down on Jesus.[89] These wings are thoughts which have heavenly elevation and magnitude, and are hence called "doves," as the bride is called by her spouse, "My dove, my perfect one."[90] It is also said of the saints, "Who are these who fly like clouds and like doves with their young?"[91] where by "doves' young" is meant those under instruction by those who are advanced, as Paul is a dove with Timothy as his young, and Peter with the evangelist Mark.[92] Even in olden times some people were given the title "sons of prophets,"[93] and you would not be wrong to refer to them as "doves' young," that is, the prophets' young. Now, the same people are referred to as "young" and "clouds," but under different aspects: insofar as they bear a divine and spiritual rain, transmitting it to others for their benefit, they are "clouds," whereas insofar as they are stamped with a share in the Holy Spirit, they are "doves" in that they are "covered in silver," adorned with the divine word, instructed in the divine Scriptures. That "silver" means the word, in fact, emerges from the verse, "The tongue of the righteous is silver tested in fire";[94] it is not material silver, but since the tongue is an instrument of the word, it is also taken as its symbol. Now, it is "tested in fire" insofar as it deals not with ordinary things but with heavenly light which Jesus "came to cast on the earth" (124) wishing it to be "already kindled." To the apostles also "tongues like fire" appeared, resting on each of them,[95] signifying the divine word that teaches. Their "backs"—the doves', I mean—were adorned "in the pallor of gold," by "gold" indicating the intellect, and by "pallor" its being living and immortal. All who are adorned with wisdom, therefore, in virtue of which God wants the reptiles to be removed from the

89. Jn 1.32.   90. Song 5.2.

91. Is 60.8.

92. Didymus acknowledges Peter and his (traditional, if not scripturally confirmed) relationship with Mark, and their association with the see of Alexandria, in his other works as well.

93. 1 Kgs 20.35.   94. Prv 10.20.

95. Lk 12.49; Acts 2.3.

waters, are "doves" in having a different intelligence, elevated by the wings of truth and always in possession of the "life-giving Spirit."[96]

It is these creatures that God blesses so that they may receive the faculty of *increasing* and *multiplying*,[97] *increasing* in producing others to imitate them, and *multiplying* in always having in their own case a longing for progress towards the perfect good. The phrase *And fill the waters* would mean, "In your case, no longer be people of the depths, caught up in the bonds of sin; instead, be the ones in control of them, and live your life at a distance from them." Or perhaps, since the water has its own fullness and usefulness in providing clean drinking water, being caught up and held in check, his advice is to keep at a distance from what is opposed to your intention and purpose—I mean being caught up and held in check, shackled in the toils of sin—and move towards those benefits, being given clean water to drink that is not stifling, and being purified by freedom from every taint, discharging these functions of water, given undying water to drink, and purified without being held in check.

Evening came, and morning came, a fifth day (126) can be explained as follows: the day of material things came to an end for those moving to spiritual things; the end of the day that passes brings on the beginning of the succeeding one. So they leave what is material and move to what is perfect, as is indicated by the number six: there is progress in going from five to six. Now, attention need only be given to numbers on the basis contained in the numbers, five suggesting material things, six in the present case perfection.

And God said, Let the earth bring forth living souls in their various kinds, four-footed creatures, reptiles, and wild animals (v.24). The statement *God said* is to be taken as before. Now, he told the earth to *bring forth living souls*, which shows that the souls of brute beasts were incorporated at the same time as their bodies insofar as they perish along with them. This is not the case with human beings; after their dissolution the souls continue living.

---

96. Jn 6.63. After all that escalating digression, Didymus comes back to the reptiles of the Genesis text.

97. Gn 1.22.

The general run of people are agreed on this, even those outside the faith; they believe there is a Hades, of which they have
a vague idea ... yet they are inclined to believe that there is a
place where souls live after their departure from here.[98]

At any rate, the command regarding the brute beasts suggests that the *earth bring forth living souls according to their kind,
four-footed creatures, reptiles, and wild animals,* the order implying
that the earth has power over the brute beasts issuing from it
for the reason that the Logos Spermatikos[99] is in some way existing in it, (128) or rather in the seeds of the animals. The
only thing surer is that the souls of brute beasts are the source
of their bodies' force of imagination and impulse, being themselves bodily—or, rather, they are in the body itself and in its
composition. Scripture says, remember, "The soul of every animal is its blood."[100] What is common to them is being nourished, waking up, sleeping, getting tired. The commandment
does not refer to every soul, but only to the irrational; the soul
of the human being has been created in God's *image and likeness* (v.26), as will be grasped more precisely in what follows.

Then, since the animals brought forth from the earth are
not all of the same species, but in kinds that underlie the different species, he said *according to their kind,* whereas the term *in
likeness* suggests species. So the *kind* is common to them: all that
have souls are separated by essential differences, the essence
of a horse being different from that of an ox, and likewise the
others. The command applies to three categories: *four-footed
creatures, wild animals, and reptiles.* So by *four-footed* it would now
be referring to all tame animals serving human beings, by *wild*
to the four-footed animals that are untamed, and by *reptiles* to
all in the form of snakes—their differences not unknown to
naturalists.

And so it was (v.24). In other words, existence had to follow

98. Nautin appropriately cites the *Ad Autolycum* of Theophilus of Antioch
for the widespread belief in basic truths among peoples of all religions and
none; SC 233.126–27, note 48,3.
99. The term, denoting the activity of the Logos among all people and
things, is found in Justin's *Second Apology* 13 (PG 6:465).
100. Lv 17.11.

the command. You could wonder, however, why ... after the clause, *And so it was,* (130) there followed *and God made* (v.25). In fact, since, in generation of the animals, generation in this kind of origin involves emission of seed, whereas it is God who shapes and forms, it is expressed this way, the command coming first and then the production of the seed with God's involvement ... a time interval from the first creation ... Instead, consider that at once by God's power the emission of seed happens and the formation of the ... in the case of the human being God said to Jeremiah, "Before I formed you in the womb, I knew you."[101] There is considerable difference, however, in the creation of the animals: some in the beginning have their origin from earth and water, and their generation varies, some laying eggs, and from them come the eggs, while others produce living offspring. It is the will of God that produces the different forms of their existence.

Of these it is also said that *God saw that they were good* (v.25 LXX), not *it was good;* instead of a single work, there were different ones. To this statement one could make the objection that in the case of light, the firmament, the sun, and the like the phrase logically ensues, *it was good,* but how does the phrase *they were good* apply to *wild animals* and venomous *reptiles* when their appearance is repulsive? The reply to this is, firstly, that as a work of God they are *good* and commendable, even if the precise reason for their existence is hidden from us. You would next find, on studying the usefulness of their existence and examining the natural qualities of each animal, that in one case their mildness contributes to human beings by being an example to aggressive and irascible people, and in another case (132) attentiveness and concern stimulate the indifferent, as the divine book of Proverbs also encourages the slothful to adoption of virtue and adduces the example of brute beasts in saying, "Go to the ant, lazybones, and be wiser than it."[102] And such a person would find brute beasts contributing to temperance, respect for ancestors, and virtue in general, even the smallest one offering correction to the one made *in the image*

101. Jer 1.5.
102. Prv 6.6.

who has become negligent, if one were to read the works of naturalists.

So much for a literal rendering, then; the spiritual interpretation should be taken. The sinful soul, experiencing a flood of earthly passions, "bears the image of the man of dust," and becomes completely earthly in pondering earthly things. It is said of such base people, "They will go to the depths of the earth," not this earth of ours, but the earth in a figurative sense, of which it is said by some, "You have hidden in deep places," and "You stretched out your right hand, and the earth swallowed them,"[103] although they were not swallowed by the earth. People under the earth in the sense explained, therefore, the process of repentance coming from God's command draws out and withdraws from sin in order that they may throw off "the image of the man of dust" and take on that of "the man of heaven." Of people like this and of himself the blessed Paul says, "He raised us up with him and seated us with him in the heavenly places,"[104] in order that those who bear the image of the man of heaven from here-below may also be granted their way of life, just as those who adopt the opposite lifestyle in keeping with their earthly behavior may also experience a place befitting them. (134)

It brought forth, then, every *living soul in their various kinds*, where by *in their various kinds* we understand "in order": far from forsaking vice and at the same time reaching the goal, there is need of progress by individual stages towards complete reform leading from different vices to virtue. Thus some people in their behavior are horses, of whom it is said, "They were lusty stallions, each neighing for his neighbor's wife"; on ceasing to be like that, they became well-bred horses, judged worthy of carrying the word by a participation in virtue, so that in their case and because of them it was said, "Your riding is salvation."[105] Other people are oxen, of whom it is said, "Is it for oxen that God is concerned? Or does he not speak entirely for our sake, that whoever ploughs should plough in hope,

103. 1 Cor 15.49; Ps 63.9; Jer 30.25; Ex 15.12.
104. 1 Cor. 15.49; Eph 2.6.
105. Jer 5.8; Hab 3.8.

and whoever threshes should thresh in hope?"[106] So all who pass from being devoted to earthly things to attention to the divine would be oxen like this. Still others are lethargic and lazy like asses, bearing the burden of vice, and for this reason are lethargic, like those who say, "There is a lion on the road, murderers on the street!" They are freed by the Lord's command from this lethargy, their symbol being the ass "in the opposite town" let loose by the disciples sent by the Lord so that the Lord might ride it and free from the bonds of lethargy and lack of reason the cattle-like people signified by it.[107] Camels, too, in their behavior are people who have difficulty entering the kingdom of heaven, set free also in their case by being rid of the harmful burdens of vice with which they are laden (136) in the words of the prophet Isaiah, "To be found there ... and flying serpents, which were carrying their riches on asses and camels"[108]—clearly not that a serpent or lion possesses material riches; instead, the figurative reference is to evil powers that are symbolically called "serpents" and "lions" and possess riches that they load not on a rational animal or on oxen capable of carrying a respectable and useful burden, but on "asses and camels," which have a hump and are unclean. It is these people, then, who are brought forth from their desperate condition by a process of repentance, as the text says, when God commanded it; he wishes "not the death of the sinner"[109] as much as his repentance.

And God saw that they were good. What is *good* is the change from vice to virtue. Now, it should be remarked that God made these creatures by transforming them so that the wild beasts that once were venomous might be rid of their savagery and rendered tame. Just as if I say that the potter works the clay, I suggest that he is anxious not for the clay to remain as it is but that it become a pot by turning firm and no longer being fluid, so, allegorically speaking, God made the wild animals, not for them to remain wild but to change from the wildness of vice to the gentleness of virtue. And since people's ways are different, it was therefore put in the plural: *God saw that they*

---

106. 1 Cor 9.9–10.
108. Is 30.6.

107. Prv 22.13; Mt 21.2.
109. Ezek 33.11.

were good. The fact that people's ways are suggested by brute beasts is confirmed by the book of the Acts of the Apostles, where some men came to the chief of the apostles inviting him to come and preach the Gospel to them, (138) since they were foreigners. When Peter, the text says, "went up on the roof to pray," he had a vision of "something like a sheet with four corners coming down" from heaven to earth, "in which were all kinds of four-footed creatures, reptiles, and wild animals of the earth." A voice from heaven came to him and said, "Get up, Peter, kill and eat." He replied, "'By no means, Lord, for I have never eaten anything profane or unclean.' And a voice came to him again a second time, 'What God has called clean, you must not call profane.'" The vision of the animals in the sheet Peter himself interpreted when he came to those who invited him and said, "God has made it clear to me as well not to call any person profane or unclean,"[110] applying the four-footed beasts and wild animals in his vision to human beings who are purified by rejecting vice.

Now, it should also be said that God was not content with saying *Let them bring forth* as a command; instead, *He made.* In other words, God not only makes a recommendation to virtue but also gets involved in the process; with someone choosing the good, God cooperates to achieve the good, his purpose being that, having resolved to carry out his command, they may succeed in bringing their resolve to its conclusion. Even if you opt for virtue of your own volition, in fact, you have need of God to grant the outcome and the happy result. It is of this, to be sure, that the Savior gives evidence, regarding his miracles, in requiring the willingness of those being healed when he says, "What do you want me to do for you?"—something he hears from the leper ready to believe, "If you wish, you can heal me."[111]

God said, Let us make a human being in our image and likeness. Let them have control of the fish of the sea, the birds of heaven, (140) *the cattle, all the earth, and all the reptiles creeping on the earth. God made the human being; in God's image he made him; male and female*

110. Acts 10.9–15, 28.
111. Mt 20.32; 8.2.

he made them. God blessed them in the words, Increase and multiply; fill the earth and gain dominion over it; have control over the fish of the sea, the birds of heaven, and all the cattle, all the earth, and all the reptiles creeping on the earth (vv.26–28). The *human being* means both the living thing composed of soul and body, and also in particular the soul. Hence Peter, the chief of the apostles, speaks of the soul as "the human being hidden in the heart," and the blessed Paul, "I take pleasure in the law of God according to the inner human being,"[112] that is, according to the intelligence, according to the soul. On the other hand, when it is said, "There was a human being in the land of Uz," and, "When human beings began to multiply,"[113] there is reference to the composite. So if we take it in the literal sense, *God said, Let us make a human being*, it refers to the composite human being. The blessed Paul, however, refers not only to the composite but also extends the meaning of *human being* to what is visible and obvious to the senses, that is, the body: "Even if our outer person is wasting away, the inner person is being renewed day by day."[114]

While on first impression each of us is composed of soul and body, there are those who claim that the human being is composed of three things: soul, body, and spirit. They make this claim with support from the apostolic saying, "May the God of peace sanctify you entirely, (142) and may your spirit and soul and body be kept sound,"[115] their belief being that it is not logical for mention to be made of the "soundness" of the Holy Spirit when it is not his nature to be a victim of weakness. In confirmation of this, therefore, they adduce another text to this effect: "It is that very Spirit bearing witness with our spirit"; our spirit, they claim, is different from the Holy Spirit, receiving witness from the Holy Spirit when it is well-disposed. And the saying from Daniel, "Spirits and souls of the righteous, praise the Lord,"[116] suggests the same idea, in their view. On the other

---

112. 1 Pt 3.4; Rom 7.22.   113. Jb 1.1; Gn 6.1.

114. 2 Cor 4.16.

115. 1 Thes 5.23. Nautin sees Didymus here responding to Philo's distinguishing three elements in the human person; SC 233.141, note 55,1.

116. Rom 8.16; Dn 3.86.

hand, those who do not wish to take the spirit as different from the soul claim that by "the spirit" it means the mindset, or that by the term "spirit" it referred to the soul itself. Those opposed to this say that by employing the conjunction "and" in the verse "spirits and souls of the righteous" it indicates that the soul is different from the spirit. Now, to establish that the human being is composed of soul and body they adduce the clear statement in the Gospel, "Do not fear those who kill the body but cannot kill the soul; rather, fear the one who can destroy both soul and body in hell."[117] If people kill one but not the other, the body and the soul are two.

In speaking of *human being* only as the body, then, we did not mean the human being pure and simple, but external man with that qualification; nor by only the soul did we mean the human being pure and simple, but interior man. For the composite we spoke of *human being* pure and simple with no qualification. So the question here is to whom reference is made by the God of all, *Let us make a human being in our image and likeness.* Accordingly, it was not the human being as a composite that was made *in the image* of God, since God does not have human form. The divine teaching confirms this; it is said that God is "spirit" and "light," and light and (144) spirit do not have human form. Scripture also declares that God has seven eyes surveying all the earth,[118] whereas the human being has two; the human being will surely not be found to be in the image of God if we take this view. We do not claim, however, that the human being is an image of a God with seven material eyes; rather, we investigate the way he is an image of God. It was, in fact, to suggest his perfect power of sight that the text employed the number seven, as the virtues are seven in number, as was mentioned previously.[119] Likewise, God is said to have wings, as the holy one says: "In the shelter of your wings you will shelter me,"[120] whereas the human being is a being without wings, and what is

117. Mt 10.28.

118. Jn 4.24; 1 Jn 1.5; Zec 4.10.

119. Didymus is probably referring back to mention of seven heavens in commentary on 1.5 (cf. 4.15), a section now mutilated, on p. 54 of the SC text. Regrettably, the section on 2.2 in reference to the seventh day is also mutilated.

120. Ps 17.8.

without wings cannot bear God's image and likeness—not that we understand God's wings as material ones, but as thoughts elevating and lifting up those who desire it.

There is need to examine, therefore, how the human being was made *in the image and likeness* of God. Paul in his wisdom, remember, applied this term to the human being in saying, "A man should not cover his head, being God's image and glory." Now, it has been shown that it is not as a composite that he is an image: one element is a bodiless and spiritual essence, the other has a body with external form. There is assuredly need to understand in a different way his being made *in image and likeness.* Having made everything as governor and leader of all, then, since as creator he is governor and king, and having made the human being so that he should also govern the wild beasts, cattle, and birds made on his account, God shows that the human being is his image in respect of governance. (146) That this is the case we can learn from the apostolic statement, "But I want you to understand that Christ is the head of every man, and the husband is the head of his wife";[121] as the husband is under the command of Christ, so too the wife is under the command of her husband, with him as her head. The comparison, in fact, should be taken proportionally; it is not identical in both cases. It is like our saying that the physician is to healing what the architect is to house-building, each producing an effect.

If there is a resemblance, then, between God and the rational human being created to govern those subject to him, he can in this respect be *in the image and likeness* of God. It is, however, particularly in the sense outlined that the text can be taken; it was said above that the intelligence or the soul is the human being in a proper sense. Sharing in God, the soul becomes by virtue of this sharing his image, as we say that the person who participates in virtue is a replica of it; Paul understood this when, speaking in Christ, he says to those whom he urges to be a replica of Christ, "until Christ is formed in you,"[122] making it known that the understanding of Christ that dwells in the soul stamps it with his image. (148)

---

121. 1 Cor 11.7, 3.
122. Gal 4.19.

Let us make a human being in our image and likeness. God's image is his only-begotten Son; Paul teaches this in writing, "He is the image of the unseen God," though "image" is being alike in substance and proof against change. Scripture says, remember, "The one who has seen me has seen the Father." From God's saying, *Let us make a human being in our image and likeness,* we should not form the idea of different images: there is not one image of Father and another of Son; if the person who saw the Son saw also the Father, and, as Paul says, the Son is "the exact imprint of God's very being,"[123] we should not think in terms of a different image, there being nothing created that is image and imprint of God as far as being is concerned. Hence it is not said, "Let us make a human being as an image," but *in our image;* it is from that image that we become images and resemble it, since the human being has been made capable of receiving the image. There is, on the other hand, also need to consider that there are two things that God mentions happening, *Let us make a human being in our image and likeness.* My view, in fact, is that *likeness* betokens a surpassing resemblance that is proof against change, such that a likeness is an extraordinary kind of image, whereas an image is not so precise as to be a likeness that is proof against change. So an image would be the beginning and commencement of a likeness, as it were.[124]

There was, therefore, need for him to be made *in the image* first, and then *in the likeness*—first, not in the sense of time, (150) especially when it was the first creation of the human being, but in the sense of our imagining. That this is the case the co-author, the Spirit, confirms: *God made the human being, in the image of God he made him,*[125] no longer adding *in the likeness.* The mind that comes to acknowledgment of God, you see, is stamped with the *image* of God, and later gradually comes to perfection *in the likeness* of God, as blessed John declares, "Beloved, we are now children of God, and it has not yet been revealed what we shall be; we know that, when he is revealed,

123. Col 1.15; Jn 14.9; Heb 1.3.
124. Didymus is right to be tentative in explaining what seems to be a tautology.
125. Gn 1.27.

we shall be like him"[126]—in other words, being in his image, we hope to be in his likeness.

Now, the fact that this interpretation is reliable Paul also confirms in encouraging some people to make progress in virtue: "In order that you may be in the image of the Creator," although they were so on the basis of substance.[127] What he means is something like this: every person, as a creature of God and gifted with reason, is *in his image,* capable of receiving the image, as we said, and suited to a share in it; but if they acquire it in actual fact, like the human being created in the beginning, they already have the condition of image realized within them. Let us take an example to clarify what is being said: the human being is rational; disposition to it is natural for an infant, but not reason itself. So the infant has (152) this potency, and will give evidence of it when reason is fully developed if it is amenable to correction. So, too, the character of *image,* as long as it is not overwhelmed, evinces the dignity of the original creation; but if vice and malice choke it, a broom is required, as the Gospel says[128]—namely, the process of repentance—in order that by clearing away the mist we may reveal the outline of the image.

The verse, *Let them have control of the fish of the sea, the birds of heaven, the cattle, all the earth, and all the reptiles creeping on the earth,* would imply according to the former explanation the human being's governance over the animals subject to him. One would, in fact, wonder how with nets and snares he could hunt animals that exceeded his powers, were wild, and at the same time disposed to do him harm, and, moreover, huge; it would not have happened like that unless he had command over them from God. In fact, sometimes numerous herds of different animals are driven along by a child or otherwise by a weak person, which clearly shows the divine power instilled in the rational animal, by which they have been subjected to him. Now,

126. 1 Jn 3.2.

127. Cf. Col 3.10. Nautin explains that Didymus is not claiming for human beings consubstantiality with God—only that they enjoy the faculty of governance (e.g., of animals); SC 233.151, note 59,2. Didymus also offers a clarification almost immediately below.

128. Lk 15.8.

governance is nothing other than lawful oversight; none of the others, for instance, governs its fellows, unless on occasion the sheep called "ram" commands a herd by giving a lead, doing so not by reason, as with human shepherds, but by nature. A human being, on the other hand, was made *in the image and likeness* of God to govern the ones mentioned.

Now, since we claim in another sense that the human being, who by an order was made *in God's image and likeness,* is man's intelligence (154), we take it, correspondingly, to be in control of those wild beasts whom the holy one mentions in offering his prayer: "Do not deliver to the wild beasts the soul that confesses to you." They would be the hostile forces from which he prays the confessing soul to be delivered, or evil thoughts prompted by them. Again, it is said by Job, "See, the wild beasts among you eat grass like oxen,"[129] not that the wild beasts in the literal sense familiar to Job have changed their nature, but that the savagery of the hostile powers has been tamed so as to make no impact on the magnitude of the holy man's virtue. And you can find many animals interpreted spiritually[130] in Scripture, *fish* being used symbolically of some people whom the kingdom of heaven draws up when it has been cast into the sea; the preaching of the word brings those "of every kind,"[131] that is, people of every sort of custom and every nation—so it governs also these *fish. Birds* are also taken spiritually, some culpable, some commendable; "the young vultures fly high," Scripture says, and of the person who slanders father or mother it is said, "The ravens of the valleys will peck him, and eagles' young eat him."[132] This would not happen in actual fact, since a slanderer of parents would not be found in every place, nor ravens everywhere; instead, clearly the person guilty of this fault is in a fashion overcome and devoured by the powers of darkness, which keep to the ground and normally inhabit "valleys."

129. Ps 74.19; Jb 40.15. If the psalmist could arguably be taken as speaking allegorically, presumption that the same is true of Job is at variance with the author's clear intention.

130. The term used is μυστικῶς.

131. Mt 13.47.

132. Jb 5.7; Prv 30.17. As elsewhere, Didymus will strive to show that a literal sense of a passage is out of the question.

(156) And the literary person will find in the case of the other animals some taken in a commendable way, others culpably.

The human being, therefore, is appointed to *have control of* all these, being made *in the image* of God. The apostles arrived at this condition of being *in the image and likeness* of God, and *had control of the fish* of the spiritual sea, being made fishermen by Christ, who said to them, "Follow me, and I shall make you fishers of people," as also to Peter, "From now on you will be catching people,"[133] meaning those swimming in the sea understood in the sense described. And in proof of their being in control also of wild beasts, they received "authority to walk on snakes and scorpions and on all the power of the foe." In the Psalm as well it is indicated that authority over such things is given by God to the righteous, the Holy Spirit saying to the virtuous, "You will tread on the asp and the basilisk, and trample down the lion and the dragon."[134] He gave them also power over the *birds* that snatched the seed sown by the word, the purpose being that they might hunt them down and chase them off, and as well over bestial people, of whom it is said, "Do not be like horse and mule, lacking intelligence," and "You turned into lusty stallions."[135] The saints exercise control over all these people, bringing them from vile ways to better ones through the word. The human being also received authority over the *reptiles,* which you would not be wrong in taking as pleasures and passions, by maintaining a distance from fleshly desires through resistance to them and "putting to death whatever is in you that is earthly: fornication, impurity, passion, evil desire."[136]

Now, it did well to say in the correlative clause, *God made the human being; in the image of God* (158) *he made him* (v.27). While the command included his becoming *in the likeness* as well as *in the image,* the correlative clause says, *In the image he made him,* not adding *in the likeness.* Of this matter we gave an explanation a little above.

The clause *Male and female he made them* must be examined: how is it that after God had given the command about a single human being, the correlative clause says, *he made them?* At

133. Mt 4.19; Lk 5.10.
135. Ps 32.9; Jer 5.8.
134. Lk 10.19; Ps 91.13.
136. Col 3.5.

the literal level this would be proof that the woman is of one substance with the man, both occurring in the one species as implied by *Let us make a human being*, whereas the phrase *male and female* suggests the division that God was responsible for with a view to procreation. At the same time it brings out that the woman also is *in the image of God*, that both have the same capacity: of being a representation of God, of a share in the Holy Spirit, and of acquisition of virtue. And since we said that the term *human being* is employed in the sense of the intelligence and soul, we shall take an anagogical sense of *male and female* as follows. The intelligence capable of being a teacher, of introducing the seed of the word in souls capable of receiving it, would in that sense be a *male;* and the term *female* would be applied symbolically to those incapable of themselves of giving birth to anything, instead accepting teaching like seed from someone else. And while in the material order *male* and *female* are made by God, in the spiritual order it is up to you for yourself and of your own choice either to fill the place of a teacher—that is, *male* or sower of good things—or to be a disciple accepting seed from someone else, (160) which in that respect is being *female*.

While this is the meaning if you consider the superior beings by comparison with lesser ones in terms of rational capacity, by contrast if you wanted to apply it to the Word of God, it is the whole of rational nature that has the role of *female* in relation to him. He is the bridegroom of the rational being: "He who has the bride is the bridegroom."[137] And in the Song of Songs the wedding song is sung by the bride to the groom, the bride being understood as the Church or the perfect soul already capable of being attached to the Word. He is the inseminator of every rational being in its receipt of benefit from him in moral matters and doctrinal truths. And while in the case of material things a change of nature is out of the question, in the case of spiritual things the person now in receipt of teaching and hence in the position of a *female* could at some stage progress to being a *male* as a teacher of others, as in reverse you could through negligence forfeit being a teacher so as scarcely to be able to

137. Jn 3.29.

receive from someone else what you yourself taught others before. A text referring to those receiving seed from the Word would be the verse, "From fear of you we conceived in the womb, suffered birth pangs, and brought forth a breath of salvation on the earth." Now, it is fear that causes the holy conception where God is concerned; Scripture says, "The fear of the Lord is pure, abiding forever," and "Fear of the Lord surpasses everything."[138] Anyone in possession of it advances in it so as also to become husband of a spiritual wife and hence earn the blessing mentioned in the Psalm, "You are fortunate and will prosper, your wife like a flourishing vine around your house, your sons like olive shoots around your table. Lo, this is the blessing of the one who fears the Lord."[139] (162)

At the level of fact this is not beyond dispute, since many of those who had fear of God lived a childless life or waited till old age, as in the case of Abraham and Zechariah, father of John. So the meaning is something like this: the mindset and faith which the blessed man adopted is a *female* partner for him, capable of giving birth to godly works, words, and thoughts. Scripture says, remember, "For a man wisdom brings forth good sense," and the sage says of it, "I was enamored of her beauty"—wisdom's, that is—and "I brought her to live with me."[140] So those who fear the Lord have for their partner this wisdom, faith, virtue, and with it they do not give birth to any *female,* only *males;* they do not give birth to behavior that is reprehensible or thoughts that are decadent or censurable, but only things that are vigorous and strong. Scripture says, remember, "Your sons like olive shoots," and the oil from them promotes light and soothes pain; the spiritual person who is ever advancing evinces behavior like oil fueling his own light, which contributes to courage in contests against the opposing power.

We take *male* and *female,* then, in the sense mentioned, *male*

---

138. Is 26.18 LXX; Ps 19.9; Sir 25.11. The progress from the status of female to male is reminiscent of the final saying in the Gospel of Thomas, Saying 114: "Every female (element) that makes itself male will enter the kingdom of heaven."

139. Ps 128.2–4.

140. Prv 10.23 LXX; Wis 8.2, 9.

as the one who teaches, *female* as the one who receives offspring either from a teacher or from the Word, forms them, brings them to maturity, and gives birth to the divine virtues, thanks to which she is brought to be a "mature man."[141]

God blessed them in the words, Increase and multiply, fill the earth and exercise dominion over it, have control over the fish of the sea, the birds of heaven, and all the cattle, all the earth and all the reptiles creeping on the earth. And God said, Lo, I have given you every (164) *crop upon all the earth bearing seed fit for sowing, and every tree containing fruit with seed fit for sowing; they will be for your food, and for all the wild animals of the earth, all the birds of heaven, and every reptile creeping on the earth—whatever has a spirit of life in it—I have given every green crop for food. And so it was. God saw all the things he had made, and, behold, they were very good. Evening came and morning came, a sixth day* (vv.28-31). It is not surprising if, after mentioning man and woman, the clause *God blessed them* is phrased in the masculine; it was necessary that the combined reference be made from the more honorable. After all, in speaking of males and females, you would never choose to designate them by the females.

He blessed them in consummating their union and beginning their reproduction, proceeding to say as much in the words, *Increase and multiply*, suggesting that there was no veto or obstacle to having children and what was required for it, since in that way they would become parents of the offspring who would in accord with the divine command *fill the earth*. The text says, in fact, *And fill the earth*, which should be taken rather prudently; if not, it would conflict with the proverb, "The Lord made spaces and uninhabited regions";[142] there exist, in fact, uninhabited places and regions. The command *Fill the earth* should be taken to refer to inhabiting in the sense explained, of filling the earth suited to it.

And exercise dominion over it, which refers to the extent of authority; anyone with partial authority is not said to have *dominion*. Now, God has given this to the human being, (166) as we

141. Eph 4.13. Note from the FOTC editor: The word for "man" here is ἄνδρα (ἀνήρ), that is, an adult male.
142. Prv 8.26 LXX.

explained, so that the cultivated terrain and the land rich in metals of many and varied kinds should be under his control. The human being, in fact, gets copper, iron, silver, gold, and many other metals from the earth, and it is given to him also for food and clothing. A human being receives such considerable lordship over the earth as to develop it by his skill when he transforms it into glass, pottery, and similar things, as is also suggested by the human being's having control of *all the earth.*

He proceeded to say, *Let them have control over the fish of the sea, the birds of heaven, and all the cattle.* As already mentioned before, in fact, these creatures are ... by human beings in traps, machines of a kind, and hooks, so that even the more fearsome, such as the lion and the panther, which are naturally very savage, are often tamed by human beings. This is the way *control* is exercised over them, with God committing it to them. It should be recognized, however, that control takes different forms: there is a control which is lawful oversight both of ruler and ruled; the law gives authority and ... of control to ruler and subject in order that in virtue of the same law a ruler rules and the subject is submissive, the law providing guidance that this is the way it should be done. In a different fashion a teacher has control of students, and, again differently, a master of his slaves and a general his army. So the human being has control of the brute beasts in different ways, as was said, of the tame ones in one way, and of the savage ones in keeping with their nature; not all are edible, some contributing to his well-being (168) or to other needs, as the naturalist will find.

Following on from this comes the verse, *And God said, Lo, I have given you every crop upon all the earth bearing seed fit for sowing.* In other words, God gave authority and knowledge so that the human being should know which of the plants on the earth are fit for eating, which for well-being, and which for other needs. There is a difference in their nature: some are trees, some are vegetables, some herbs; in all cases, some are edible, while others are for a different use. One should not be ignorant of their use, according to the command before this, when God said, *Let the earth put forth a crop of vegetation, plants yielding seed, each according to its kind,* and added, *and fruit trees bearing fruit,* because trees differ from vegetation, and so he calls them *fruit trees*.[143] The human being had authority not only over the products of farming; but he had it already even over produce which he had neither sown nor farmed, and so he met different needs from it as well. God made them available, in fact, not far from inhabited places—obviously for people's needs—and germination took place for all of the plants, since he had made them all for their needs.

Now, the providence of the God of all is indicated particularly in the statement, *They will be for your food, and for all the wild animals of the earth and all the birds of heaven*. It was fitting, in fact, that the one who had care for human beings should show providence also for those animals made for their need and service and for other benefits for them. After all, if he did not exercise providence for the brute beasts on that primary basis, he still did so for the sake of the human being.[144] (170)

Once again God saw that everything was good, the text proceeding, *God saw all the things he had made, and, behold, they were very good*. Whereas before this, then, the text praised everything that was made in the words, *God saw that it was good* or *they were good*, here instead it says shrewdly *very good*, in view of the concord and harmony of everything. Let us take an example to clarify the statement. Someone wanting to form a choir chooses the best choristers one by one, the result being that none of them leaves anything to be desired in performing their part. If he also surveys them as a group in light of the task he had in mind for them, he would find the result of their harmonizing clearly surpasses what would have been possible from one person alone. You would find this also in the case of an army: the foot-soldier has to be at his best, as also archer, general, adviser, so that when the time comes, the coordinated effort of them all emerges in the extent of the commendation proposed for the joint purpose. To give evidence of the relationship of all these beings with one another, their harmony, concord, and interconnection, as well as the compatibility of opposites, the text proclaims that *they* all *were very good* when judged, as said

143. Gn 1.11.
144. The comment arises from one way of dividing vv.29–30.

before, not by sense but by reason. *Evening came and morning came, a sixth day.* It had to be, in fact, that a vast and wonderful world was made in this number of days, its significance having been mentioned in what went before, and yet to be detailed still further in what follows.[145]

So much for the literal sense, then; but since in what went before as well we also spoke on the anagogical sense in addition to the textual, (172) this should be done here as well. The human beings were *blessed* for *increasing and multiplying* by this form of association. Now, it has been said before that the male is the one who sows and teaches good things, whereas the female is the soul that receives lessons from the teacher, shapes them, and gives birth to them, resulting in an achievement of them both, of the teacher as introducing them to her, and of the disciple as providing a docile heart for the completion of the good action. And since the divine teaching involves introduction, progress, and completion, it is in that sense that *increase* should be understood; to indicate the notion of introduction, and aware that those at that stage are infants, blessed Paul says, "I fed you with milk, not solid food," whereas to the mature he says, "I promised you in marriage to one husband, to present you as a chaste virgin to Christ." The Church, you see, being mature, is attached like a bride to Christ, and has one husband, of whom it is said, "Lo, a husband, his name is Dawn."[146]

Blessing, therefore, is for all who move to maturity after being small, and learn greater insights after lesser ones, being in receipt of *increase* in virtue and *multiplication* of spiritual goods by being attached to God. This is also the way they *fill the earth* with their fruitfulness; the Savior in the Gospel in reference to the seed taught that the rich earth was a good heart, which received the divine seed and brought forth a numerous yield in keeping with the verse, "Sow for yourselves righteousness, reap the fruit of life."[147] It is also possible, on the other hand, to take

145. Didymus had expatiated on the significance of the number six in connection with 1.14–19, and will again at the close of the chapter.

146. 1 Cor 3.1–2; 2 Cor 11.1–2; Zec 6.12, where the LXX has read "Dawn" for "Shoot (of Babylon)" in reference to Zerubbabel, and where the sense "husband" (for ἀνήρ) is less appropriate than simply "man."

147. Hos 10.12.

as a reference to a teacher increasing and multiplying his disciples the blessing (174) that says, *Increase and multiply, fill the earth and exercise dominion over it;* he has *dominion* in reaping what he has sown, and so it is said of him and such people, "They will come home joyfully, carrying their sheaves,"[148] whether with divine insights and deeds or with disciples, since it is no small gain that comes to the teacher even from them.

The verse, *Let them have control over the fish of the sea, the birds of heaven, and all the cattle,* should be taken in the following way. There are different forms of behavior among people, such that some are told, "You brood of vipers," and it is said of others, "You turned into lusty stallions," and again, "Though enjoying a state of honor, a human being did not show intelligence, being comparable to brute beasts and likened to them," and, "Do not be like horses and mules, that have no understanding";[149] a student will find other such statements scattered throughout the divine Scriptures. You could say, then, that it is the one who surpasses the others who by education saves the aforementioned from being irrational. On the other hand, it is possible to take it this way: the different passions and movements of the soul are many and varied, and are guided by the soul as by a charioteer,[150] which, instead of allowing itself to be dragged in the wake of the billows of their impulses, keeps them in check and under control in keeping with the authority given it: *Let them have control over the fish of the sea,* and so on. Or is there not control of fish in the case of the one who by the word of divine instruction lifts from the depths those like Peter caught up in the billows of this life,[151] or draws downwards those carried away with conceit and imparts a saving sense of humility? (176) The Lord recommends this in the words, "Learn of me, that I am gentle and humble of heart," the purpose being that in this way they may be lifted up by it to the divine heights and borne aloft like eagles, taking wings like those of a dove and flying to

148. Ps 126.6.

149. Mt 3.7; Jer 5.8; Pss 49.20; 32.9.

150. Nautin notes Didymus's use here of Plato's celebrated image (*Phaedrus* 253 CD); SC 233.175, note 70,1.

151. A reference to Mt 14.31?

their appropriate resting place.[152] The person who tames those who have become savage gives evidence of the great power of control. On the other hand, the one who by reason struggles against his own impulses that resist and rebel against the intelligence proves that the power given by God has dominion over them. He has control *over all the earth,* that is, all bodily passions, by "putting to death whatever is earthly: fornication, impurity, passion, evil desire,"[153] which you would not be wrong to call *reptiles.*

He is said to have control of them as well by the one who gave *every crop bearing seed fit for sowing* and other nourishment, which could reasonably be taken to be the teachings of the divine Scripture, which are heavenly nourishment. Scripture says, remember, "A human being does not live by bread alone, but by every word that comes from the mouth of God."[154] Now, God gave also another form of nourishment *upon the earth*; in creating us in the beginning, he fixed in our reason sound thoughts, and if one preserves them in such a way as to keep this ever life-giving nourishment, one will enjoy permanence in virtue by not wasting the good things given us by God in our minds in the beginning. God gave *every fruit tree bearing* (178) *fruit,* from which again some nourishment is given; those who are more mature and minister to people's salvation would be *trees* according to the statement, "All the trees of the field will applaud with their branches," rejoicing in the salvation of the repentant. They resemble the person declared blessed in the first Psalm, the word likening him to "the tree planted near water courses,"[155] constantly given drink by its attention to divine matters and yielding its fruit in due season.

The verse, They are given *for your food, and for all the wild animals of the earth, all the birds of heaven, and every reptile creeping on the earth,* should be understood as follows. The Lord, who cares for the salvation of all, has given different remedies for a range of ailments so that those who did not enjoy any may be without excuse ... did not have opportunities for the word. Likewise, its ministers are suited to each one, as Paul says ..., "I have be-

---

152. Mt 11.29; Ps 55.6.
154. Mt 4.4; Dt 8.3.

153. Col 3.5.
155. Is 55.12; Ps 1.3.

come all things to all people so as by all means to save some,"
... and appropriately suited to each one, not "casting what is
holy to dogs, nor pearls before swine,"[156] but leading them
away from their own individual situation in which they found
themselves of their own volition, and through a word suited
to them bringing them to instruction. Lest anyone be a reptile and hence descend to the depth of evil, no one is deprived
of the knowledge of the good; this is the nourishment *on the
earth* that God gave to the soul from the beginning by instilling
fine thoughts, and the one who keeps them pure will enjoy life-
giving nourishment.

*God saw all the things he had made, and, behold, they were very
good.* Just as was said about material things that (180) the harmony of one thing with another shows the intensity of their
beauty, so too in regard to virtue the proportion of one to another and their relationship to their common end show that
what was described is *very* commendable.

Evening came, and morning came, a sixth day. There is need to
apply here what bears on the number six, and to a greater degree since what is now commended surpasses the material level. In the case of the latter, remember, it was said that it was appropriate for this world, which contains a passive and an active
element, to be made in this number, which is a perfect number
composed of its own factors.[157] This world, in fact, is both cause
and recipient of many things in itself, even if not at the same
time; the naturalists say that this is true symbolically also of
this number. It would also be appropriate for a perfect number
to be adopted in an anagogical sense; virtue is really something
perfect, without fault and quite complete, being God's more
perfect gift.

Now that we have addressed all that was created in the six
days that have been clarified, we shall round off our treatment
by praying the God of all and Creator of the perfect and complete world to grant also in what follows a perfect understanding of the text.

156. 1 Cor 9.22; Mt 7.6.
157. Nautin sees the influence here of a Neopythagorean source, perhaps
through the medium of Origen; SC 233.180–81, note 73,2.

CHAPTER TWO

EAVEN AND earth and all their array were completed. God completed on the sixth day the works he had done, and on the seventh day he rested from all the works (182) *he had done. God blessed the seventh day and sanctified it for the reason that on that day he rested from all the works God had begun to do* (vv.1–3). The term *completed* sometimes suggests destruction, sometimes existence. For example, when the disciples asked the Savior, "When will this be, and what will be the sign of your coming and the end of the world?"[1] the word "end" means "finish," which is normally taken to mean the destruction of the world. In this case, by contrast, *completed* occurs in the sense of "accomplished"; it was not their existence that was over and done with, but their creation, as we say also in the case of builders when they bring their work to an end, Lo, the ship or the house is completed. So, for its part, heaven was completed in receiving its particular harmony, being given its fulfillment with the firmament and the lights as well as the stars, and for its part the earth with the animals and the various plants. While the term *completed* was not appropriate when each of them was created, it was logical to proceed to say, now that everything had received concord and harmony, *Heaven and earth and all their array were completed.* The earth's *array* is also called its "fullness" in the verse, "The earth is the Lord's and its fullness." The fact that the variety of heaven is also called *array* Moses himself confirms in these terms: "When you look up to heaven and see the sun, the moon, and the stars, all the array of heaven, do not be led astray and bow down to them"; it is by the positioning given them by God that they display their beauty, some moving in

1. Mt 24.3.

one (184) orbit, others in another, some taking a direct path, others an oblique one.

There is reference, at any rate, to the army of heaven on account of their arrangement in the verse, "His hands created the whole army of heaven."[2] People without a good understanding of it have made the mistake of introducing it as predestined and presuming that everything is determined by fate; they present the stars as influencing people's lives and other events, although they are placed as a sign and not as a cause as … about them in explaining in connection with what was made on the fourth day the verse, "Let them act as signs and indicate times and months and years,"[3] when we showed that human life is not determined by the stars. In fact, those who perish in war and in universal disasters do not fall under the one constellation. Furthermore, fatalism is refuted by the laws; all Jews are circumcised on the eighth day after birth and experience the knife while still in swaddling clothes, but you would not claim that all alike are delivered at the one hour, since Jews are born almost everywhere on earth every day. They also say that some Ethiopians have the muscles of their knees removed as soon as they are born, and yet they do not have the same birthday. In short, the differences in customs and laws throughout the nations disprove fatalism.

If instead this does not occur through fate, much less do acts of free will; if fate is responsible for (186) what happens, whereas free will is for what is affected by it, fate does not affect the latter. It is in fact virtue and vice that bring their possessor what benefits him in one case and what harms him in the other, and everyone acting by them is either punished for bad behavior or commended for doing good. What happens of necessity, on the other hand, … no one is praised or blamed for acting under necessity; otherwise, if the laws were the result of fate and those disobeying them did so as a result of fate, it seems fate would disprove and refute itself. The stars, therefore, give signals, they do not cause; they signal conditions of prosperity and depression and anything else that God in his providence wishes.[4]

2. Ps 24.1; Dt 4.19; Hos 13.4 LXX.
3. Gn 1.14.
4. So Didymus would support astrology as far as premonition goes.

So much for this topic. Let us return to the text from the beginning: *God completed on the sixth day the works he had done,* which brings out the fact that the achievement refers only to what he had made. There are in fact also works which have not yet been accomplished, but foretold as happening in the future, like the resurrection of the dead and, in a word, what is due to happen by providence, since they are done by God in a particular sequence—hence the appropriate addition, *the works he had done.*

Now, there is need to observe that instead of doing anything on the seventh day, *God rested*—everything was completed, after all—*blessed* only *the seventh day and sanctified it,* and [the text] adds the reason for this in saying that *on that day he rested from all the works God had begun* (188) *to do.* The text says, *had begun to do:* a beginning to all the works did not occur on any of the six days; angels and archangels and the whole spiritual order did not receive its beginning. That this is the case God himself says in Job, "When the stars were made, all my angels praised me in a loud voice."[5] ...

5. Jb 38.7 LXX. Because four pages of the papyrus are missing at this point, we do not see whether Didymus discussed the possibility of pre-existence of the angels or of souls. We are left to regret also the loss of Didymus's treatment of life in the garden, the two trees, the naming of the animals, and the making of woman.

CHAPTER THREE

...NOW MADE.[1] Hence this prior warning: "If the ire of the ruler rises against you, do not leave your post."[2] This pretext, in fact, becomes the cause of many evils, as the devil proceeds to make further suggestions. He now engages in introducing the idea of God's jealousy, with the claim that God's veto was not to prevent their being harmed by refraining only from the tree of the knowledge of good and evil—rather, it was to prevent their becoming gods by having a knowledge of the future. From this distortion, of course, has sprung the whole heresy that is called Ophian,[3] which reveres the serpent and, it is thought, treats it as important; their claim is that God wants human beings to live in evildoing, and that not to know good and evil is evildoing, and so they maliciously make this claim: It was the serpent that made the human being good. They also come up with other fairy stories about the serpent, thus maligning the God they have fashioned for themselves.

Nevertheless, the serpent chooses the moment to conduct its deception, (190) persuading them only to develop a facility not for doing good—not as the Apostle said, "I want you to be wise in what is good, and guileless in what is evil."[4] The serpent instead wanted them to be wise in evil, and wished to open their eyes, which were averted from it. When virtue is being practiced, they are not open, remaining closed with a useful blind-

---

1. The extant commentary resumes at Gn 3.5. We have thus missed Didymus's interpretation of the talking serpent: the devil in person, or merely his instrument? From what follows, it would seem the former.

2. Eccl 10.4.

3. The name (from ὄφις, "serpent") was one of those given to gnostic groups.

4. Rom 16.18.

ness, which Jesus says in the Gospel is his role: "I came so that those who do not see may see, and those who do see may become blind."[5] Now, in actual fact, instead of making anyone blind, Jesus gave sight to the blind. So it is clear that he blinds those who see badly, and makes them see again with eyes that bring benefit, those of the interior man, which preserve purity of vision, not in a physical sense but spiritually; having enjoyed knowledge beforehand and applying reason to sensation, they hide it, as the saying goes, "Wise people will hide sensation."[6] To clarify the statement with an example: the sense of touch detects hot and cold, hard and soft, rough and smooth—things that are obvious even to the touch of an animal and a child; but when a physician touches a swelling, he "hides the sensation" by applying reason to the throbbing. Likewise with paintings: ordinary people look at them only with the senses, artists with their reason. Before the transgression, therefore, the human being had eyes to look at things as he should, that is, to apply understanding to things in knowledgeable fashion. (192) So as long as his eyes were looking at sights appropriate to him, he had no knowledge of evil; far from experiencing it, he did not admit it; but when they were blocked up and opened to turn towards evil, then they were also expelled. This was the devil's intention in tricking the woman; he leads her to think that God is jealous, and makes lavish promises with the intention of beguiling her in the words, *You will be like gods, knowing good and evil* (v.5), as well as making the suggestion of many gods. Since at that time there was no practice of idolatry involving statues, there is reference to the angels that accompanied him.

She saw that the tree was good for eating, pleasing for the eyes to behold, and attractive to contemplate. She took some of the fruit and ate it, and gave it to her husband, who was with her. They ate, and the eyes of both were opened, and they realized that they were naked (vv.6–7). The effect of the serpent's deception that had inveigled her produced in her a contrary judgment; instead of her judging by sight what was set before her for food, the prior de-

5. Jn 9.39; Is 6.10. Didymus seems to be nuancing the sense of the Gospel (and Isaian) text here to make his point.
6. Prv 10.14.

ception aroused a certain satisfaction and enjoyment, and then she urged the man, who was deceived, to get involved. After being enticed, at the word of the serpent she *took* with full consent and *ate* to bring the deed to completion; she also made her husband an accomplice, being guilty herself and making him assist in the deception, such being the sensation that we said was a block on the woman's reason.[7] (194)

With the opening of their eyes, *they realized that they were naked*. This often happens with people who have been deceived; after the act the shamefulness of their evil behavior becomes clear as they realize that they have been stripped of virtue. It, too, is a gift of the merciful God, to prevent the one guilty of evil from living completely insensible and remaining utterly divested of virtue. So this is the purpose of the devil's deception: that what is seen in the light of true reason by the pure eye of the soul he causes to be seen in opposite fashion, suggesting what is pleasant in place of what is good, and presenting what is good as a nuisance. Thus, for example, eyes that previously were beneficially closed became open; the soul, you see, has an eye which of itself has regard for spiritual things, and an ear which responds to instruction from someone else. By distorting them the serpent achieved deception, the result being damage to the senses and the mind; when the senses suffer distortion, then the mind's choices are also distorted. Scripture says of people who treat things in a perverted fashion, "Woe to those who call evil good and good evil."[8]

They fell victim to pleasure, then, which was the cause of their fall; it is on this basis that philosophers give the preference to what is pleasurable[9] ... The general run of people, in fact, prefer ease to virtue, finding the effort unacceptable, and

7. The responsibility of the woman for the man's fall, which roused Chrysostom to such a lengthy diatribe, passes without development by Didymus. He is more concerned with deception at a philosophical level (probably under influence from Philo and Origen). For Chrysostom on Eve in the fall, see his *Homily* 16.5–13 on Genesis, trans. Robert C. Hill, FOTC 74 (Washington, DC: The Catholic University of America Press, 1986), 210–26.

8. Is 5.20.

9. The Epicureans, specifically. In his philosophical treatment of the Fall, then, Didymus sees pleasure-seeking as the cause.

are (196) deprived of virtue. That which is pleasurable, then, is to be despised, being the basis of sin. There are some commentators who claim that Adam's eating *with her* suggests his considerateness, to prevent her perishing completely. They cite in support the statement by Paul, "Adam was not deceived; rather, the woman was deceived and became a transgressor";[10] so he was capable by himself of removing from evil her as well.

They stitched together fig leaves and made themselves aprons. They heard the sound of the Lord as he strolled in the garden of Paradise in the evening; both Adam and his wife hid from God's presence among the trees of the garden of Paradise (vv.7–8). We apply these verses in the light of the previous interpretation of the garden, of Adam and his wife.[11] Since *they realized that they were naked, they stitched together fig leaves and made themselves aprons. They heard the sound of the Lord as he strolled in the garden in the evening; they hid from the Lord's presence among the trees of the garden.* It would in fact be worthwhile for those adopting a factual approach to explain without absurdity how *they stitched together for themselves aprons from fig leaves,* how *they heard the sound of the Lord as he strolled* when they had committed deeds unworthy of it, why he was *strolling in the evening,* and finally how *they hid themselves* under the tree and what idea they had of God. In my view, in fact, it would not be possible for them to maintain a thread of factuality in all this worthy of an explanation deriving from the Holy Spirit. For ourselves, accordingly, as we did in what preceded, we shall focus (198) on the divine element in these verses as well.[12]

The word presents two forms of nakedness, one before the transgression and another after it, one involving no shame and another deliberate and a cause of shame. It was explained also in what was said before that when they had done nothing shameful and instead were free of every blemish, they had a

10. 1 Tm 2.14. The term for "considerateness" is συνκατάβασις. Nautin believes that the view quoted here is that of Origen; SC 233.196, note 83,6.

11. The interpretation would have been given in the missing pages of the ms on Gn 2.4–3.5.

12. For someone like Didymus, whom we have seen denying the possibility of a factual/historical interpretation for some passages in Scripture, the anthropomorphic style of the Yahwist might have been particularly obnoxious in these verses.

confident mindset before God, which is what virtue is like. But
when they became transgressors of God's commandment, they
were then divested of the beauty of virtue; they felt shame for remaining stripped of it, pondering all the good things they had
exchanged for bad, since sensation was still active, and from
then on they *hid* from the God of all as he *strolled*. The sinner, in
fact, not having yet lost a sense of it but still conscious of sin, is
censured by the normal thoughts imparted by God,[13] by which
the Creator ceaselessly cries aloud, but being in the grip of the
deception of his fall he often *stitches together* excuses for his sins.
Is this not evident in many people? The one who is guilty of anger, for instance, often adduces specious excuses by which he
will present the reasonableness of anger, sometimes quoting the
Scriptures in support of his willfulness. This is *stitching together*
incomplete cover from *leaves* and not from fruit, presenting only
an *apron;* you can hear of people (200) in anger, like a holy man
who gave vent to anger in destroying groups of fifty,[14] and of
others, without remembering that they did these things without
use of sword or any means of defense. Instead, they called on
God himself and by prayer won him over to help them; if they
had offered prayers in anger, God would not have heeded them,
since as befits him he urges the one who prays "to raise holy
hands free of wrath and disputation."[15]

Those who claim excuses on the basis of the saints' virtue,
therefore, and wish to *hide* their own falls by *stitching together*
leaves think they thereby mount a defense of themselves, as
happened also in the case of the first-formed. Those adopting
such a pretense the Lord through the symbol of the fig tree
admonished in the Gospels when he came to it and found only
leaves: "May no fruit ever come from you again." We claim that
the admonition was not directed at the fig tree itself; it was not
the fault of the material fig tree that it bore no fruit. Instead,

13. Nautin traces this idea to the Stoics, and Origen also voiced it; SC
233.198–99, note 85,1. Didymus is proceeding to make a case for taking at
least the stitching of leaves in allegorical fashion, as he will the garments of
skin God gives them in 3.21.

14. 2 Kgs 1.10.

15. 1 Tm 2.8.

the reference was to Israel's lapse into impiety: "There are no grapes on the vine, or figs on the fig trees."[16] *They stitched together fig leaves,* then, to mount a specious defense, as was mentioned before, and the text follows the outline of the story. Since mention was made of the garden of Paradise, of nakedness and recognition of it after the offense, the text says that a cover was made of leaves, using elements of the story, in the manner of the inspired Scripture. Often, in fact, the soul is referred to as a vine, as a sheep, as a bride, by way of divine instruction, (202) and the text continues in the same vein in each case. For instance, when it presents it as a vine in the words, "Israel is a luxuriant vine," it then refers to the teachers as vine dressers and to schemers as foxes: "Catch us the little foxes that ravage the vines"; and when it calls it a sheep, it calls the teachers shepherds, and those who led them astray wolves and lions: "Israel is a sheep led astray; lions drove it away";[17] and when it calls it a bride, it uses the term "bridegroom" of the one who leads it to the truth, and the term "adulterer" of the one who harms it. Now, all of these things, even if there are different terms, still receive, when applied to the soul, a particular sense appropriate to the divine Spirit, without its being a sheep or a bride or a vine. Consequently, then, with the mention of a garden, on account of the outline of the story he made mention of *leaves,* which those who have fallen away from virtue in the sense explained *stitched together.*

Now, it was they who *heard the Lord as he strolled in the garden in the evening.* Before the transgression he did not stroll as though apart from them: he was with them—something that is the privilege of the person who preserves virtue and is in it so as to be able to say, "I saw the Lord always in my presence, because he is at my right hand to prevent my being shaken," and "I am always with you."[18] When man is with God, God is also with him; Scripture says, "Draw near to God, and he will draw near to you." But when some people forsake him, they will be told, "They came to me treacherously, (204) and I will go to them

16. Mt 21.19; Jer 8.13.   17. Hos 10.1; Song 2.15; Jer 50.17.
18. Pss 16.8; 73.23.

in hostility and anger."[19] And just as the person who avoids the sun and closes his eyes does not cause any diminution in the sun, which continues to shine, so the one who avoids God does harm to himself, avoiding God not as though he were localized, but forsaking virtue, like those of whom it is said, "God will reject them because they did not hearken to him, and they will be wanderers among the nations"[20]—in other words, since they did not listen, he in turn rejected them.

Although they are alienated from him as a result of the transgression and he keeps his distance from them, yet out of his characteristic goodness he *strolls,* giving them an impression by way of the commonly-held ideas, as explained before,[21] so that they may be brought around. It happens *in the evening,* as is appropriate for transgressors; for the virtuous person the light of truth is at its zenith, never being in a condition of darkness—you can hear, for example, the holy one saying, "As night departs, my spirit rises to you, O God," and "O God, my God, I rise to you," and "In the morning I shall come before you and watch."[22] But *evening* comes and darkness ensues and the hour turns to nightfall when one departs from the light by being in ignorance and vice, so that God says to the sinful soul, "I made your mother like night"; some people become children of night and darkness,[23] the result being that the sinner is affected by the darkness of ignorance, impiety, and vice. Now, it shows that it was not all of a sudden that the light left them by saying that *in the evening* they heard God strolling; (206) after enjoying a fresh sensation and then being reduced to a condition without that freshness, they still did not descend to utter ignorance. Instead, by God's lovingkindness they were aroused by his crying to them in their depths in order that thereby they might reach repentance so as to learn that "weeping there will be in the evening, and joy in the morning," so that it could be said of such people what is said of someone sensing the extent of her

19. Jas 4.8; Lv 26.23–24.
20. Hos 9.17.
21. A reference to the Stoic notion acknowledged in note 13 above.
22. Is 26.9; Pss 63.1; 5.3.
23. Hos 4.5; 1 Thes 5.5.

troubles, "At a late stage she gave vent to lament." On repenting they will move from there to the light, and so say, "This is the day the Lord has made, let us be glad and rejoice in it."[24]

On hearing *the sound of the Lord as he strolled,* as Scripture says, *they hid from the face of the Lord God.* The expression *the face of the Lord God* should not give the impression of human form; Scripture says, remember, "God is spirit,"[25] and a spirit is not composed of parts, one of them being called "face" or another human member. We should not, in fact, take in a human fashion the statements about God, which are expressed that way to help us. It is not surprising if these references are made to God when it is the way we learn even about material things. In Proverbs, for instance, it is written, "Death and life are in the hand of the tongue," which we take not in the sense that the tongue has hands, but that it has an action that is called its "hand." Also it is said, "By your words you will be justified, and by your words you will be condemned,"[26] which is the meaning of "in the hand of the tongue"—in language, that is—"there is death and life," when you use it well or badly. (208)

They hid from the face of God by abandoning a pure understanding of God. Not in the manner of Cain; he "went away from the face of God" by banishing every idea of him, like the one of whom Scripture says, "A fool said in his heart, 'There is no God'";[27] all who deny providence hold this view. Instead, those who hid themselves were not without belief in divine oversight, but were only lacking confidence on account of the stain of sin, through a kind of contempt. The saints, by contrast, have a clear conscience and are in the presence of the Lord so as to say, "As the Lord lives, in whose presence I stand," whereas it is said of sinners, "They turned their back to me, not their face" as was required of them if they were to be sacred attendants and be like angels, who always gaze on the face of the Father in heaven.[28]

It is possible, however, to take in a different sense the clause, *They hid from the face of God,* if we interpret *face* to mean his only

24. Ps 30.5; Jer 2.23 LXX; Ps 118.24.

25. Jn 4.24.   26. Prv 18.21; Mt 12.37.

27. Gn 4.16; Ps 14.1.   28. 2 Kgs 5.16; Jer 2.27; Mt 18.10.

Son as his image and the exact imprint of his being; whoever sees him "has seen the Father."[29] So they were supposed to do everything to preserve the state of being *in his image* in which they had also been created. By preferring to be transgressors of the commandment, they forfeited enlightenment from God's image. It was right for them to take refuge *under the tree in the middle of the garden*, which was the tree of the knowledge of good and evil. The one who hides from God's face, in fact, so as not to practice virtue, but only to give the appearance, hides (210) hypocritically; the one who knows good and evil without distinguishing them and choosing the good, hides from God while basing his opinion on instinct and giving the appearance of virtue.

The Lord God called to Adam and said to him, Where are you? Adam replied, I heard your sound as you walked in the garden, and I was afraid because I am naked, and I hid. He said to him, Who told you that you are naked—unless you have eaten from the only tree I commanded you not to eat from? Adam replied, The woman you gave as my companion—she gave me fruit from the tree, and I ate it (vv.9–12). Being the fount of goodness, God calls us once more even after our falls, not canceling completely the knowledge of good from our reasoning, even if we have rejected virtue by sin. This is what God does with Adam also in the present case, *calling* him when he was hiding, and saying to him, *Where are you?* He had in fact been placed there by God to *till* and *keep* the garden,[30] receiving this place from him as his very own; but on forfeiting it through disobedience, he consequently hears from God, *Where are you?* The fact that the role entrusted to someone is called a "place" you can learn from the Acts of the Apostles, when in place of Judas, who betrayed Jesus, the apostles wanted to appoint a disciple, and offered a prayer to God as follows: "Lord, you know everyone's heart; show us one to take the place of this ministry."[31] It was logical for Adam as well, having transgressed the divine placement, to forfeit also the place corresponding to the function by being expelled from the garden.

29. Col 1.15; Heb 1.3; Jn 14.9. The Christological reference is fleeting.
30. Gn 2.15.
31. Acts 1.24.

The question *Where are you?* could also be an admonition: whereas I established you in virtue, now where are you? Ponder it, and be ashamed. There are some commentators, on the other hand, who consider the incorporeal substance as the primary substrate of the soul, and hence conclude that it is independent of any place, and that it was on experiencing a body by its behavior that it heard the admonition, *Where are you?* Are you in a place, when you should be free of every place by your incorporeal nature? Having failed to preserve it, and being attached to a body, are you in a place? The one who has his citizenship in heaven, on the other hand, and has his heart in heaven on account of storing his treasure there,[32] cannot be in a place, being above worldly things. It was therefore because Adam had been in this condition but had transgressed that he likewise heard, *Where are you?* You for your part, too, note the addition of *Lord* in this case to *God,* the text reading, *The Lord God said.* When in reference to creation the text read, in fact, *In the beginning God made heaven and earth,* and when there followed transgression, then it was that the name *Lord* also occurred; it is as Lord that he takes action against those who ignore his instructions. Retribution was required, you see, and it is appropriate for it to come from the master, who mixes retribution with goodness—hence the text, *The Lord God called.* David says as much in singing, "I shall sing to you of mercy and judgment, Lord";[33] he gives a demonstration of lovingkindness that combines showing mercy and giving judgment. (214) In fact, in his retribution he shows mercy: he inflicts punishment to our benefit.

Now, let us see also the reply: *I heard your sound as you walked in the garden.* When people who are in sin need only a brief sense of God for getting a thought of him in creation, where in his providence for all things he *walks* and bestows his order on each individual thing, then it is that they are converted and recognize that God surveys and manages all things, and thus cease their contempt. For example, when they observe the orderly progress of the sun, the movement of the heavens, the phases of the moon, and the regular rising of the stars, and

32. Phil 3.20; Mt 6.20–21.
33. Ps 101.1.

when they reason that the guide and controller of all this is the Creator of all things *walking* through it all,[34] they *hear the sound of God*, not uttered aloud but stamped on their thinking, to the effect that nothing escapes God—instead, everything falls under his management. And thus ashamed, they hide themselves; a sinner sins when he does not have God before his eyes.

From that sensation came also the statement, *I heard your sound as you walked in the garden, and I was afraid because I am naked.* It was the fear of one who has a realization that vice is shameful and punishable. He says that the cause of the fear is nakedness, which is that of someone who has lost virtue, which had been his covering, virtue being a divine garment. Paul also gives an exhortation in similar terms, "Put on Christ Jesus," and, "Put on compassion,"—that is, Bedeck yourselves in merciful behavior and life in keeping with Christ (216)—and again, "Let us put on the armor of light" to prepare ourselves for warring against the adversaries.[35] Since he had been deprived of these garments by his transgression, then, and was accused by conscience, he had not the assurance to look directly at God— hence his saying, *I was afraid because I am naked.* In other words, like someone who has done wrong and is under investigation, and hides himself from the ruler in fear of what has been done, so too Adam; only the one with no sin on his conscience keeps his assurance.

In reply, with the aim of correcting him, the Lord of all further goads his thinking by saying, *Who told you that you are naked—unless you have eaten from the only tree I commanded you not to eat from?* A loving question: God again replies to the sinner, suggesting reflection on the commandment. He should, in fact, have sampled all of them and not only the tree of the knowledge of good and evil; as explained before, human resourcefulness apart from the exercise of virtue is very harmful, but both together are beneficial. That was what God commanded, like a good physician providing a potion that is very conducive to good health, beneficial when mixed but harmful when taken

---

34. Nautin sees here a direct or indirect reliance on a lost work of Aristotle, which we know from Cicero's *De natura deorum;* SC 233.215, note 92,1.

35. Rom 13.14; Col 3.12; Rom 13.12.

unmixed, as explained in the case of so-called anti-venoms. In his instruction in the Gospels the Lord said something similar: "Be as wise as serpents and as guileless as doves."[36]

In reply Adam blamed the woman: *The woman you gave as my companion* (218)—*she gave me fruit from the tree, and I ate it.* Vice is fond of accusing others, and it is typical of sinners not to confess their sins readily, instead inventing reasons for their fall; some people who leave their lives in the hands of fate think they are forced by it even into sin, while others claim everything happens by chance and at random and believe these things happen likewise. The first-formed human being, on the other hand, having disobeyed the commandment, said, *The woman you gave as my companion.* Instead, he should have considered firstly that by receiving her from God he received her for what should have been his benefit, and then that he was given her not as a teacher but as someone to influence. This we also noted in passing in what went before from the reply of Eve to the serpent in saying to it, "We eat of every tree in the garden; but of the fruit of the tree in the middle of the garden God said, Do not eat from it or even touch it, lest you die."[37] In fact, God had given no instructions about touching it; she learned this from Adam's teaching her to be very circumspect in her weakness, and heard him say not even to touch it.

How, then, as teacher and guide was he led astray by his pupil? Some commentators quote in defense of Adam what was said by him, *The woman you gave as my companion.* In other words, in saying *you gave as my companion,* he understood that she would be expelled for disobedience, and (they claim) he did not go along with her transgression but wanted what was for her good. Frequently, in fact, teachers descend to the level of the more limited pupils so as (220) to lift them from there. And they confirm this view from Paul's words, which evoked Christ and the Church: "Adam was not deceived, but the woman was deceived and became a transgressor."[38] On the other

36. Mt 10.16. Didymus is evidently referring here and above to an explanation given in the lost earlier section.

37. Gn 2.2–3.

38. 1 Tm 2.14.

hand, interpreting the woman as the Church and Adam as Christ, an intelligent person would take the passage allegorically and consider whether the human race, from which the Church developed, by becoming guilty of transgression proved responsible for the descent of the Savior and his implementing the divine plan by which he became "curse" and "sin"[39]—not that he was these, but took them on for our sake.

The Lord God said to the woman, What is this you have done? The woman replied, The serpent deceived me, and I ate (v.13). Three persons are here nominated as blameworthy: the man, the woman, the serpent. The man for his part was in a position to allege in his defense that the woman was the cause of his eating from the forbidden tree, as a result of which he knew he was naked, while the woman blamed the serpent in the words, *The serpent deceived me, and I ate.* In fact, God asked them for the reason for the fall, but no such question was directed to the serpent; it could not level the blame for the crime at anyone else, being himself its author. The Lord in the Gospels, remember, also conveys this very fact when he says of him, "When he speaks a lie, he speaks according to his own nature, because he is a liar and its father," that is, the father of the lie, the devil having no father, as the spinners of fairy tales claim.[40] All those who practice evil except him do not do so "according to their own nature"; it is from his perversity (222) that they embark on it. He is the one spoken to thus: "You said in your heart, I shall ascend to heaven," and so on;[41] no one else suggested the arrogance to him, but only he to himself—hence no basis of defense is conceded him, either.

He asks, therefore, *Why have you done this?* Surely it was not so that you might be the cause of your husband's fall? *She replied, The serpent deceived me;* it happened through deception. When the actual commandment was adduced, in fact, he twisted the order as well as making them an inflated promise capable of

39. Gal 3.13; 2 Cor 5.21. Adam is not exonerated, and the blame is apportioned equally, but a positive aspect is lent to the Fall. It is noteworthy that there is no lengthy moralizing about the effects of the Fall.

40. Jn 8.44.

41. Is 14.13.

beguiling them: *God knows, you see, that on the day you eat of it, your eyes will be opened, and you will be like gods, knowing good and evil.*[42] She is now right to admit deception; sensing God's presence, she recognizes what has happened. It is customary with those who have been deceived, after all, to have an awareness of the fault after its happening; at the beginning, satisfaction smothers the awareness, and recognition does not occur.

Now, as to the term *the Lord God said,* there is need once more to say that the converse with God happened in the woman's mind. There is no mystery about this: when we sin and our reasoning is critical of the sin, we should think that God is present in our mind and is speaking. There, as we did before with the role of the characters, we are taking an allegorical interpretation; satisfaction, which is the serpent, first affects the sense, for which we understood the woman, and then likewise it ministers to the intelligence itself, for which we understood the man. (224)

The Lord God said to the serpent, Because you have done this, accursed are you beyond all the beasts and all the wild animals of the earth. Upon your chest and belly will you travel, and eat dirt all the days of your life (v.14). To both Adam and Eve God put the question, *Why did you do it?* He was told by them who was responsible, Adam blaming the woman, and the woman the serpent. Up to this point he had not yet asked the serpent; as the chief villain it could not transfer responsibility to anyone else. Hence, instead of the question, *Why did you do it?* he immediately imposed retribution in the words, *Because you have done this, accursed are you beyond all the beasts and all the wild animals of the earth.* It is clear, however, that it is not this serpent to which God applies retribution; it was not naturally able to proffer deceitful words that would encourage God to inflict retribution on it. Paul, for example, in writing to the Corinthians, realizing that it was not an irrational animal, said, "I am afraid that as the serpent deceived Eve by its cunning, your thoughts will be led astray from sincerity."[43] Paul in fact is comparing to the serpent's deception of Eve the deception committed by loose-

42. Gn 3.5.
43. 2 Cor 11.3.

living and cunning people who had appeared claiming that there was no resurrection of the dead and that the Savior had not been born of a virgin, and deceiving the neophytes in Christ at Corinth whose faculties of the heart had not been trained by practice to distinguish good from evil.[44] The comparison shows that instead of a serpent, it was a hostile force, which Scripture normally calls a devil; it is not referred to simply as "a serpent," as in the text referring to them, "Serpents, brood of vipers," but "the (226) serpent," a term suggesting the devil in person, who is responsible for evil in others as well; it is "at work among the sons who are disobedient,"[45] and does its work by implanting its own attitudes in them by a clever deception.

This is also the reason why it is the object of extreme retribution: *Accursed are you beyond all the wild animals of the earth.* In other words, as it was responsible for evil, it was also rightly subject to retribution beyond all those who from it have received their existence as serpents and beasts in their behavior and as animals of the earth, over whom the Savior gives power to his own disciples: "Lo, I have given you power to walk on serpents and scorpions, and on all the power of the foe." And to the person who abides in the power of the Most High it is said, "You will walk on asp and basilisk, and trample down lion and dragon."[46] Surpassing everything that has the savagery of vice, the devil under the name *serpent* consequently receives a condemnation beyond all.

Now, in addition to the retribution there comes the declaration, *Upon your chest and belly shall you travel;* since it worked its deception by giving the impression of having a superior understanding and having in the form that it adopted wonderful viands, the word presents its fall by saying that it would have dirt to eat, nothing divine or elevated. Instead, it would slither in the dirt, losing its control (conveyed by the word *chest*), no longer giving birth to anything divine or heavenly through the power to generate (conveyed by the word *belly*), with an interest in what is material and earthly. That this is the sense of *belly* you can learn from its opposite in the song of blessed David,

44. 1 Cor 3.1; Heb 5.14.   45. Mt 23.33; Eph 2.2.
46. Lk 10.19; Ps 90.1, 13.

"Your law is (228) in my belly," meaning not a material organ but a power of the soul. For instance, people engaged in repentance, of course, are aware that their understanding, which ought to partake of heavenly nourishment, has been brought down to the ground, and they say, "Our stomach has clung to the ground,"[47] since it has been rendered completely earthly by eating earthly things and giving birth to earthly things. In other words, as the belly is the receptacle of food, so too it is the workshop for what is formed. Those on the one hand who generate vile things travel by crawling on the ground, while on the other those who give birth to divine things exclaim, "In fear of you we conceived in the belly, we went into labor and gave birth":[48] the mind's offspring or its food, it is the same thing.

Now, it was right for the further remark to be made, *And you will eat dirt all the days of your life.* Not simply *life,* but *your life,* which you have chosen as a result of your own inclination. It is as if you were to say to someone not living as they ought, You will be a wretch all the days of the life you chose, your sins your nourishment all the wretched days you chose; by abandoning a proper life, each person leads his own life in his individual way. Resembling this is the statement made to the rich man, "You received your good things in your life, and Lazarus in like manner evil things."[49] Note that in the case of the wretch it called the indifferent things "good"; since he considered them good and put his trust in them, it also called them "your good things," whereas in the case of Lazarus the evil things were not called his, since it was not of his own will that he suffered, even if he bore it nobly. Job, too, when deprived (230) of pleasures, since he did not consider them to be his goods, knowing their nature and using them as given by God, did not say, "If we have received my good things," but, "If we have received good things from the hand of the Lord." In other words, the good things he chose were the virtues, whereas what accompanied them, indifferent in God's judgment, he used as he should, contenting himself with what was necessary. Hence his saying in a similar vein, "My door is open to everyone who comes."[50]

47. Pss 40.8; 44.25.   48. Is 26.18.
49. Lk 16.25.   50. Jb 2.10; 31.32.

I shall put enmity between you and the woman, and between your seed and her seed. He will watch for your head, and you will watch for his heel (v.15). When a naïve person associates with a villain, he suffers no little harm; the villain makes an approach and suggests what is harmful, and the naïve soul accepts it as something beneficial. A separation between them is therefore advisable, and a state of enmity and absence of communication, so that the naïve person is "wise" in response to the saving exhortation and says of the devil, "We are not ignorant of his designs."[51] We frequently witness, for example, a woman's friendship with a man arising with naïveté, and from this deception such people proceed to shameful behavior; so our anxiety is the result not of a hatred of the peace that is the fruit of the Spirit, but of a dissipation of that peace against which the Savior said he came to bring a sword, "I have come to bring not peace but a sword"[52] that divides and separates those longing for something helpful from those endeavoring to harm them. So in his goodness God plants *enmity* in those with whom peace and union are at war; when some in ignorance of (232) evil fall foul of it and learn that it is ruinous and damaging, they reap no little benefit.

Now, it is logical that he puts enmity between one *seed* and the other, and between the serpent and her. And since reference is not being made to a material serpent, its *seed* is not to be taken as something material, either, but as people bearing its stamp, form, and genesis, or thoughts that are at variance with the truth, and teachings foreign to it. Likewise, the *seed* of the woman is to be taken as virtuous people issuing from her, as she is a type of the Church, or the tenets of divine teaching, against which the malice of the adversary directs his endeavors. Now, in the Gospels as well there is a difference between *seed* and "child": when the Jews said, "We are seed of Abraham," the Savior conceded that, but denied their being children of Abraham when he said, "If you are children of Abraham, do what Abraham did"[53]—in other words, whereas the one who is a child is also *seed*, it is out of the question for a *seed* to become a child if aborted and not brought to term. This could also be

---

51. Mt 10.16; 2 Cor 2.11.   52. Gal 5.22; Mt 10.34.
53. Jn 8.33, 39.

taken anagogically; many people who made a beginning in the faith met with shipwreck, like Hymenaeus and Alexander, and were stillborn children.[54]

The whole of the phrasing is deliberate, too; the serpent is not put in parallel with the *seed* but with her, and the serpent's *seed* is not put in parallel with her but with her *seed;* in other words, extreme evil is at war with pre-eminent good, and the lesser with its equivalent. God in fact provides also (234) a way out so that we may be able to endure, not allowing any of us to suffer temptation beyond measure; Scripture says, "If the Lord had not been with us, they would have swallowed us."[55] In his goodness the Lord of all also draws attention to the schemes of the adversary and instructs us in resisting him; while the devil observes a person's advance and progress towards virtue, described as *heel,* the person observes the peak of the evil, for when this is destroyed, everything is destroyed with it.

Note, on the other hand, how the text changes from one gender to another: whereas all the following was spoken in reference to the woman, *I shall put enmity between you and the woman,* and so on, it now says, *He will watch for the head, and you for his heel.* In other words, the phrase *I shall put enmity* had to be spoken in reference to the weaker party so as to prevent further association as an occasion of deception, whereas in reference to the man, who according to the apostolic statement "was not deceived,"[56] it had to be said, *He will watch for the head.* After all, since he was strong and suited to fighting and guarding against the schemes of the adversary, he did not allow it to initiate deception as in the woman's case; as we said before, he followed her, as he said himself, *The woman you gave as my companion,* whom on account of her value to him he did not proceed to dismiss. It was not his fault, in fact, that he was expelled with her, as also the holy ones accompanied those made captive in

54. 1 Tm 1.19–20. Didymus's whole treatment of the lemma is allegorical (specifically rejecting *historia*), but with a particular use of typology and of anagogy.

55. 1 Cor 10.13; Ps 124.2–3.

56. 1 Tm 2.14. Didymus, though seeming to contradict what he said about the careful balance of woman against serpent, now sees the man involved because the pronoun in the LXX text is masculine.

Babylon; far from having done anything deserving of captivity, they proved physicians for the captives, like Daniel and Ezekiel and the three boys in the furnace. (236)

The statement made to the serpent, then, *He will watch for the head,* has this meaning: Even if you deceived the woman in her greater weakness, it is the man who will war against you by observing the peak of your evil, namely, impiety, something the wise person rejects. The devil, instead of reaching the head of the wise, affects their *heel,* which would be the outer limits of what contributes to virtue; often when he fails to attack anything of chief importance, he moves stealthily in regard to human necessities so as to cause a fall by those means. This is what is said also in the Psalms, "They will observe my heel," where "observe" means the same as *watch* in the present text; it has the sense of scrutinizing, though we are unsure if the terms occur in the sense of guarding, protecting, as in the verse, "You, Lord, will guard us and protect us," and "Holy Father, watch over them."[57]

He said to the woman, I shall greatly aggravate your pains and your groaning; in pain you will bear children; your yearning will be for your husband, and he will be your master. To Adam, on the other hand, he said, Because you listened to your wife's words and ate from this tree, the only one I told you not to eat from, accursed be the soil as you till it. In pain will you eat from it all the days of your life. Thorns and thistles it will yield you, and you will eat the grass of the field. In the sweat of your brow you will eat your bread until you return to the soil whence you were taken, because you are soil and to soil you will return (vv.16–19). It is not implausible (238) to take this text in a factual sense as well; obviously the woman is subjected to constant and unending *pains and groans,* suffering no little fatigue both in conception and in childbirth as well as in rearing the child, as the wife of blessed Job said, "Gone is your memorial from the earth, sons and daughters, pain and labor of my womb, for whom I suffered labor and distress to no purpose."[58] Obviously,

57. Pss 56.6; 12.7; Jn 17.11. Unable to check the Heb. for verification of the verb in question (where in fact it means "strike, bruise"), Didymus explains the odd use of "watch" by citing other biblical occurrences.

58. Jb 2.9 LXX. Though Didymus will proceed to treat the lemma also al-

too, she has borne everything for her husband, more so than for a master, in receiving orders from him, and the husband is worn out by hard work and anxiety, and spends all his life in sweat and toil; he is not without a share in that which pains his wife, and is beset by personal hardship throughout his life. He labors and grows weary in body and soul in other ways: he has no lack of concern for household matters, the rearing of the children, and often a range of worries about them either when affected by sickness or snatched away by death—all of which gives rise to extreme sorrow and immense hardship. And you could list many things obvious to everyone.

Now, let us give attention also to each of the items mentioned. Whereas it was said to the serpent, then, *Accursed are you,* this was not the case with Adam; instead, *Accursed be the soil as you till it.* And rightly so: far from transgressing by falling victim to sin, it was by following his wife, as we explained previously on the verse, *The woman you gave as my companion,* where we cited the apostolic statement, "For Adam was not deceived; instead, it was the woman who was deceived and became a transgressor."[59] (240) Rather, the threats were directed to the woman in person: *I shall greatly aggravate your pains.* In proceeding to add, *You are soil and to soil you will return,* he brings out what is characteristic of the body's being; the soul does not take its beginning from soil so as to be dissolved into it, the view of those who present it as corruptible.

Now, since in what went before the garden was taken allegorically by us as a divine place, a dwelling of blessed powers, the situation of the man and the woman should also be taken in a corresponding way. From blessed Paul, then, we have an introduction to an anagogical sense when he says, "This is a great mystery—I mean Christ and the Church." So the Church *in pain bears children;* hardship and *pain* are forerunners of virtue, producing a repentance that leads to salvation, and the Church *bears* them through the bath of regeneration, for while ease is a

---

legorically, he makes an effort first to establish the factual realization of the sentence given the woman and the man.

59. 1 Tm 2.14.

consequence of pleasure, hardship accompanies virtue.[60] This is what the Savior teaches in the words, "How narrow the gate and hard the road that leads to life," whereas "wide and easy the way that leads to destruction, and many there are who take it." Commendable, on the other hand, is the *groaning* coming from virtue: "Those who were groaning ..."[61] Her *yearning will be for* her *husband,* Christ, *mastered* as she is by him, in order that the offspring of virtue given birth by her according to his advice will achieve maturity in him; Paul says, "I joined you to one husband (242) to present you as a pure virgin to Christ."[62] The Church is blessed, in fact, when embraced by Christ, and each woman is also blessed when embraced by a perfect and zealous spouse who confines his control to what is proper. Therefore, let no one accept a corruption of marital relations and attempt to misrepresent the passage; the divine word is not to be made the subject of such distorted thinking, as Paul conveys in his exhortation, "Husbands, love your wives as Christ loves the Church,"[63] that is, without passion.

Since there was sufficient clarification given before this of the facts to do with the commandment forbidding them to eat of a single tree, they should now be omitted. I shall just make this one point: that it was only on hearing the word of his wife that Adam sinned, not with prior intent. Rather, he followed her, and it was on account of her that he was given the sentence, *Accursed be the soil as you till it ... Thorns and thistles it will yield you.* Is there anything that is a consequence of the body and not a source of pain, since it is from it that pleasures and cares stem? The Savior, in fact, explained what these *thorns* are that choke the seed sown by Jesus if the one receiving it does not admit it in depth, like the other saying, "Ground that

60. Eph 5.32; 2 Cor 7.10; Ti 3.5.

61. Mt 7.14, 13; Ex 2.23. As the treatment of the Genesis text is largely conducted in an allegorical sense, Didymus is able to signal the relatively infrequent adoption of an anagogical interpretation.

62. 2 Cor 11.2.

63. Eph 5.25. In speaking of corruption in marital relations, Nautin thinks Didymus is referring to an attempt to thwart procreation of children; SC 233.243, note 103,1.

drinks up the rain falling on it repeatedly, and that produces a crop useful to those for whom it is cultivated, receives blessings from God. But if it produces thorns and thistles, it is worthless and on the verge of being cursed, (244) its end burning." If you take care not to allow them to grow up, then, you will have *grass*, which is nourishing; what is planted is first grassy, as the Savior also says, "The earth produces of itself, first grass, then the head."[64] So the zealous person will find this spiritual grain only with care and effort; when people's hearts are carefully set on evil, virtue is difficult to pursue and grasped with effort, Scripture saying, "Many persecutions are necessary for you to enter the kingdom of heaven." A good person begins by eating *grass* for a while at the first stages of virtue, then the head when receiving major instruction that leads to maturity, thus being told, "Solid food is for the mature, for those whose faculties have been trained by practice to distinguish good from evil."[65] Virtue therefore requires effort, since people's hearts are carefully set on evil; hence, *all the days of your life in the sweat of your brow you will eat your bread,* something that would not be said to angels, since the practice of virtue is easier for them.

Now, there is need to take in accordance with allegory also the clause, *until you return to the soil whence you were taken.* When you rise again in a spiritual body, in fact, you will enjoy a heavenly way of life by being in the land of the meek, since "blessed are the meek because they will inherit the land," even if a person by his own faults has exchanged it for a barren land. In fact, of ourselves we are *soil* or we become heaven, something Paul in his wisdom teaches by saying, "Just as we have borne the image of the man of dust, we shall also bear the (246) image of the man of heaven," as the disciples were bidden to say in their prayer, "Your will be done on earth as it is in heaven." Now, this will happen when people, though walking on earth, have their citizenship in heaven.[66]

Now, it should be noted that, if some parts are treated allegorically, there is no need for everything to be taken uniformly

64. Lk 8.14; Mt 13.5; Heb 6.7–8; Mk 4.28.
65. Acts 14.22; Heb 5.14.
66. 1 Cor 15.44; Mt 5.5; 1 Cor 15.49; Mt 6.10; Phil 3.20.

to that level. Once it has been understood why the literal sense of the text is taken allegorically, it is not necessary for everything to be taken anagogically. For example, the clause, "You shall not muzzle an ox while it is treading out the grain," is cited to give due recognition to the teacher and the efforts he makes for his pupils; there is no need to state whether the ox has two horns and what is their elevated significance—that was not the reason for citing it.[67] Now, this point has been made to prevent anyone's requiring, when Adam has been taken anagogically as Christ, that everything literally referring to Adam be applied to Christ. He it was, remember, who became a *curse* for humankind, and the Church is represented by a symbol, which the woman was, in order that through his suffering and emptying he might prove to be life for the fallen; Scripture says, remember, "For our sake he made him to be sin who knew no sin, so that in him we might become the righteousness of God."[68] But he is not sin once and for all, since it could not be productive of righteousness; he also became a *curse,* so that we might enjoy a blessing. And just as Adam was not deceived, but followed the woman when she was deceived, so when humankind fell, "he emptied himself, taking the form of a slave."[69] In fact, if the human race had not become a transgressor, it would not have needed a healer, either, (248) for there would have been no wound, and it was this that required his coming among human beings.[70]

Adam gave his wife the name Life because she is the mother of all the living (v.20). Prompted by a far-sighted understanding, Adam realized that they would be removed from the garden because of their transgression, and foretold the future by calling his wife *Life, because she* would be *the mother of all the living.* In fact, it was from her that all descendants came. Not that we should form the idea that she was mother also of the brute beasts; even

67. 1 Cor 9.9–10; Dt 25.4. The passage is of significance for conveying some idea of the principles behind Didymus's selective movement between the literal level of a text and other levels (whether allegorical or anagogical, if these are distinct meanings).

68. Phil 2.7; 2 Cor 5.21.

69. Gal 3.13–14; 1 Tm 2.14; Phil 2.7.

70. The Fall turns out to be a *felix culpa.*

if the statement is general, it should not be applied also to beings not of her nature. Even if there is a saying, in fact, "I shall
pour out my spirit on all flesh," it is not logical to apply it also
to the flesh of brute beasts, nor, if it likewise says, "All flesh will
see the salvation of our God," is it fitting to form that idea in respect also of the flesh of brute beasts.[71] Likewise, in the present
case also Eve is *mother of all the living* in the sense that human
beings related by nature have her as their mother.[72]

If, on the other hand, she is taken in an anagogical sense as
the Church, who else could be *mother of the living,* according to
the Life who is our Lord Jesus Christ, who says, "I am the Life,"
than the Church, who receives life from him as from a fountain, from which those enrolled in her, Church of the firstborn,
share in divine life? Now, it is clear that if she is mother, Christ
also is father of the believers, "for from him all fatherhood in
heaven and on earth takes its name."[73]

*The Lord God made garments of skin for Adam and his wife and
clothed them in them* (v.21). It was fitting (250) that *garments of
skin,* in which there is reference to nothing else than their bodies, be made for the woman who was destined to be mother
of all and for her husband, a partner in that destiny. In fact,
if those bent on factual interpretation think that God made
garments out of skin, why does the further phrase occur, *and
clothed them in them,* when they were capable of doing so themselves? After all, they were not unfamiliar with coverings, having stitched together aprons for themselves from leaves. Now,
you can find that the body is frequently referred to as *skin* in
the divine teachings; blessed Job says, "I know that the one to
deliver me is eternal; he can raise on earth my skin, which has
endured these sufferings." It is obvious to all that Job said this
in reference to his own body, and it was he likewise who had
this to say of himself, "You clothed me with skin and flesh, and

71. Jl 2.28; Is 40.5 LXX.
72. In adopting *Zôê* ("Life") as the woman's name, the LXX is translating
the Heb. *havah* rather than simply transliterating it as *(H)eva,* so as the better
to reproduce the balance between name and function in the original; perhaps
likewise the best English version of the name would be "Life" to balance "living." When in Tb 8.6 such balance is not required, the LXX is content with *Eva.*
73. Jn 11.25; 14.6; Heb 12.23; Eph 3.15.

knit me together with bones and sinews." In fact, the clear and conspicuous proof that the *garments of skin* are the body is that Job also recalled the verb *clothe* as was used in the case of the first-formed as well.[74]

Now, the precision is worthwhile; whereas it could have been expressed this way, "God made both of them garments of skin," it was not put that way—instead, *God made garments for Adam and his wife.* In other words, clearly male and female have distinctive characteristics, other points of comparison, and many other features, so that one has the role of the man and to the woman belongs the beginning of reproduction. Previously, then, it was said that the human being was made *in the image,* which suggests immateriality; but since it found itself in a different (252) condition, where it had need of some instrument to use, it had to have a body as instrument, and in this case they became clad in skins. Related to this is the passage, "For a perishable body weighs down the soul," the perishable body suggesting this material one; and continuing, "and the earthly tent burdens the thoughtful mind,"[75] by "earthly tent" referring to what the soul uses for movement to other places when freed from this body, something intermediary that unites the intellectual substance with the material. This it is that "weighs down the soul," the tent "burdening" not the soul but "the thoughtful mind." The Apostle also teaches as much in saying, "We know that if the earthly tent we live in is destroyed, we have a building from God, not made with hands, eternal in the heavens, for in this tent we groan" (by "tent we live in" clearly conveying what was said above).[76]

---

74. Jb 19.25; 10.11. We saw Didymus reacting strongly, as here, to "literalists," *philistores,* against a factual account of the man and the woman stitching aprons together from fig leaves in Gn 3.7, an allegorical approach to their nakedness being the only permissible one. Elements in the garden were allowed only figurative status, though the man and woman were real. Clothing nakedness here again raises the temperature, Didymus explaining that Adam and Eve, if real, were immaterial when made in God's image; but if they were to be expelled from the garden, they must have had a material (*pachus*) element—hence the "garments of skin."

75. Wis 9.15.

76. 2 Cor 5.1.

If you were to ask, "If paradise is a place that surpasses all others, how is it that in it they were clad and thus expelled?" the necessary reply would be that the reality is not as claimed. When things happen simultaneously, you see, it is often convenient for one to be mentioned first and the other second, not to give the impression that reality is as claimed. You can find in the prophetic text an expression of this kind: "Lo, the Lord is seated on an airy cloud; he will come to Egypt, and Egypt's idols will be shaken."[77] Not that we should think that the Lord has brought his body from heaven so that he rides on it and comes to Egypt, an earthly place; instead, as soon as he (254) took a body he was in Egypt, though it is described in sequence to avoid confusing the facts. So just as we do not say in the case of the Savior that after first seating himself on the airy cloud he came into the world, but we call these events simultaneous, in this case too we do not claim that in paradise they had material bodies and thus were expelled; it was impossible for them to live there with that kind of body. The brigand, for instance, he introduced to paradise in his unclad soul, as he said to him, "This day you will be with me in paradise"[78] (his body remaining on the gibbet until consigned to the earth); at the same time as the one who was told, "You were a signet of likeness and a crown of beauty in the delights of paradise,"[79] there was no evidence of anyone with likeness to you living there. These texts show that material bodies could not have lived there.

God said, Lo, Adam has become like one from us in knowing good and evil. There is now a risk that at some time he may put out his hand and pick fruit from the tree of life, eat it, and live forever (v.22). The general run of commentators understand God to be making this remark to Adam in jest, a reference to God that is inapplicable; mocking someone's mistake is improper for a virtuous person, let alone God. Since, they claim, the serpent made a promise to the woman, remember, in saying, *God knows that on the day you eat* (256) *of it, your eyes will be opened and you will be like gods, knowing good and evil,* God said to Adam when he trans-

77. Is 19.1.
78. Lk 23.43.
79. Ezek 28.12–13, addressed to the king of Tyre.

gressed, *Lo, Adam has become like us,* speaking of him ironically. In our case, therefore, we abjure and dismiss such a notion on the part of God, and take the passage in conformity with the intent of the inspired Scripture. The devil is not evil by nature or in substance; instead, he was made upright and good, but underwent a change of his own doing and became a devil, Satan, and evil. Formerly he was good and upright when he belonged to the rank of the angels, but he left them and was thrust down to earth on account of the overweening pride he developed in himself. So he did not say to Adam, "Lo, you have become like one of us," but *like one from us;* he is the one that fell away from the heavenly beings, as the Psalmist also conveys by saying, "I said, You are gods and all children of the Most High, but you die like human beings and fall like one of the rulers." In other words, though ruler and god, not in substance but of God's making, he fell away, like those of whom it is said, "I gave birth to children and elevated them, but they set me at naught."[80]

Now, having said, *Lo, Adam has become like one from us,* the text went on to explain in what way: *in knowing good and evil.* In fact, this is the very thing, the only thing, that those people have who do not practice virtue, only a knowledge of good and evil, but they do not put the distinction into operation by choosing the good and shunning the evil. They treat things interchangeably, for instance, as do the wretches of whom it is said, "Woe to those who (258) claim that evil is good and good evil, classing darkness as light and light as darkness."[81]

Now, the phrase *from us* is the way God speaks to his angels, as a king to his bodyguards. The fact that it is known from Scripture that God associates with his creatures you can learn from what was said by the Savior to the disciples, "Rise, let us be on our way," which involves no little precision: "Rise" is said *to* them, whereas "let us be on our way" is done *with* them. In other words, since the Savior "committed no sin, nor was deceit found in his mouth,"[82] and hence he suffered no fall, either, he had no need of such "rising" as did the disciples to whom he

80. Ps 82.6–7; Is 1.2.
81. Is 5.20.
82. Jn 14.31; 1 Pt 2.22; Is 53.9.

said, "Rise" (leave human things), whereas he numbered himself with them in going on the way. Since it is not possible for human nature on its own to practice virtue apart from God's inspiration, hence he says, "Let us be on our way," for he is shepherd and way and staff,[83] which guide towards the divine. He said also to the brigand, remember, "This day you will be with me in paradise." It is also said when people have godless plans to build a tower, "Come, let us go down and confuse their language";[84] even if God does what he wishes by means of ministering angels—though I still claim that what happens is done by his ordinance—it is said that he comes down along with those he sent.

It says, then, *Lo, Adam has become like one from us in knowing good and evil,* and in his care and lovingkindness he appended to this a kind of condemnation; the threats and retribution he applies are for our good. (260) Now, what did he say? *There is now a risk that at some time he may put out his hand and pick fruit from the tree of life, eat it, and live forever.* Envy is excluded from the godly assembly; even more so and to a pre-eminent degree is it impossible with God. It is not from envy, then, that he forbids them again to take anything from the tree of life; what he forbids instead is its inappropriateness: just as the Savior gives the instruction, "Do not throw what is holy to dogs or your pearls before swine," and supplies also the reason in saying, "lest they trample them under foot and turn and maul you,"[85] so it is not good for the one who has fallen into sin and continues in it to partake of the tree of life, which would be contemptuous of it. Now, if the villain is excluded from such an education, through not having an opportunity to hear daily instruction, he will desire it on perceiving how vice-ridden he has been. If, on the other hand, he should not desire it, living with his evil thoughts would be better than contempt for the divine things if someone introduces these to him in an inopportune way; evil becomes chronic when contempt is shown for good, for it is from this that one comes to have no love for it. The term *forever* occurs in the sense of "throughout life," which is similar to what is said by Paul, "I shall

83. Jn 10.11; 14.6; Ps 23.4.   84. Gn 11.7.
85. Mt 7.6.

never eat meat, so that I may never cause my brother to fall."[86]

The Lord God sent him out of the garden of delight to till the soil from which he was taken. He drove Adam out and settled him opposite the garden of delight (vv.23–24). If (262) you were to ask how it is that, though the serpent was responsible for the transgression, and the woman was the first to be deceived, reference is made not to their being expelled but to Adam, who, we are told by the wise Paul, was not deceived,[87] our reply is that if the less guilty was expelled from the garden, much more those whose faults were greater; if the serpent had been expelled, it would still not be obvious that the woman and Adam deserved being expelled from the garden, whereas when Adam, who was not guilty of the major fall, was excluded, obviously also those who sinned gravely. Now, it can also be presumed of the woman that she too was cast out in Adam's expulsion; the name Adam means "human being," as is confirmed by the verse that says, "And God formed the human being, male and female, and called them Adam," that is, he called them "human being."[88] In reference to the serpent, on the other hand, it could be said that his being in the garden was not due to his worthiness to live there; instead, just as it is said in Job that "the angels of God came to present themselves before him,"[89] so should we understand the presence of the serpent.

God dispatched Adam from the garden, then, and clearly the woman as well. But what has been dispatched has the opportunity to return. In fact, he did not dispatch him without hope of return; rather, he was *settled facing the garden* by God so as to remember and be gazing at it.[90] (264) He was expelled *to*

---

86. 1 Cor 8.13. Didymus parallels Adam's exclusion from the tree of life with people's exclusion from church involvement, both (he believes) being for the individual's good.

87. 1 Tm 2.14 again, clearly an (oft-cited and) influential text in interpreting Gn 3 and assigning relative degrees of responsibility for the Fall (and forming attitudes to women).

88. Gn 2.7; 5.2, where the LXX is misreading the Heb. form for "human being" (with the article) as the proper name Adam (without the article).

89. Jb 1.6, where strangely the phrase "and the devil was with them"—basic to Didymus's point—is missing. For Didymus the serpent is the devil.

90. Nautin notes that in making this point Didymus is so dependent on

till the soil from which he was taken, to conduct his vessel in seemly fashion, restraining it and not allowing bodily impulses to over-run reason. This in fact is the motive behind God's *settling him facing the garden of delight,* placing in his mind a law (later pro-vided in writing) so that he might find virtue contained in its commands, put it into practice, and from it gain a realization of the divine and more pure life of paradise. Note how it was not said in the case of Cain, "God expelled him from his presence," but "Cain left God's presence,"[91] whereas in this case *he expelled Adam* as someone who in a fashion retained a breath of desire for paradise, though expelled for unworthiness. Likewise, he did not expel him as altogether a foreigner: *He settled him op-posite the garden,* still caring for him and not refraining from settling him. As explained before, however, he settled him to abide by laws, imparting to him a sense of law that forbade evil and was an introduction to good, and not concealing paradise from him. He did not take from him the knowledge of good, in fact, nor instill in him a forgetfulness of virtue by which he had lived in the garden.

He set the cherubim and the flailing sword of fire to guard the ap-proach to the tree of life. The names of the pre-eminent powers, so to speak, are not simply what we call proper (266) names, but rather are indicating offices—"rulers, powers, thrones, domi-nations," because of exercising rule and power and kingship ("throne" suggesting what is said in Proverbs, "A throne of gov-ernance has been prepared with righteousness"),[92] and they are called "dominations" on account of exercising dominance. Likewise, cherubim got their name from a particular attribute of theirs, "cherubim" meaning "abundance of knowledge"; so the name comes from this attribute of theirs. In the same way, to be sure, Abraham was given a name different from Abram, Sarah from Sarai, Israel from Jacob, and Peter, chief of the apostles, got his name as a result of advance in virtue, as did those mentioned; from a state of lesser virtue, indicated by

Philo as to adopt from him the word "facing" (καταντικρὺ) instead of "opposite" (ἀπέναντι) in the biblical text; SC 233.263, note 112,3. But see "opposite" several lines below.

    91. Gn 4.16.   92. Col 1.16; Prv 16.12.

their original name, they moved to a greater, and were appropriately given the name of this virtue. It is possible to see the virtue in the interpretations of these names. Abram, remember, has the meaning "father of a son" in addition to others,[93] whereas Abraham is "father of sons," the former suggesting an aptitude to teach but not yet capable of reaching everyone, as the latter suggests. Sarai with one "r"[94] means "smallness," which suggests an introductory stage, whereas Sarah[95] means "princess," suggesting maturity of virtue, which is something princely and very powerful. Jacob means "heeled," a name that suggests being ascetical and able to resist the passions, (268) whereas Israel was a new name given by God, who does nothing without purpose, suggesting a contemplative faculty and purity of mind by which one sees God, as happens after moral behavior, since Israel means "mind that sees God." What need is there to speak of the chief of the apostles when our Lord Jesus Christ clearly gave him his name in the Gospel on account of his confession? When he said, "You are the Christ, the Son of the living God," remember, he replied, "You are Peter, and on this rock I shall build my Church, and the gates of Hades will not prevail against it."[96]

So much for those matters; let us return to the text from the beginning: *He set the cherubim and the flailing sword of fire to guard the approach to the tree of life.* It is possible from this as well to refute those who even today think that paradise is on earth, by asking them how it is that a lifeless *sword* does the guarding, if taken in this fashion. After all, guarding—especially of God's paradise—belongs to something that is not only alive but also rational. How will they account for the *guarding of the approach to the tree of life* being entrusted to no one else than to the pre-eminently rational cherubim? After all, from those who do the guarding, you can conceive of the greatness of what is being guarded. Now, how is it that *sword* is in the singular and *cherubim* in the plural? Since their reply will amount to nothing, or trifling remarks not worth uttering, therefore, it is time for us, who consider the guard that was set to be worthy of the divine

93. Cf. Gn 17.5, 15; 25.26; 32.28.   94. Greek (one *rho*): Σάρα.
95. Greek (two *rho*'s): Σάρρα.   96. Mt 16.16, 18.

paradise, with God's help to make a clear and appropriate statement about it. It was an indication of the lovingkindness of the
(270) God of all, then, that to guard there was a single *sword*,
a symbol of punitive power, whereas there was "an abundance
of knowledge" to lead to divine virtue. God does not impose
punishment in accord with the sins, in fact, but gives many opportunities leading to salvation; that he does not punish as deserved the Psalm makes clear. "If you were to observe iniquities,
Lord, who could bear it? Because with you there is mercy."[97]
Instead of punishment, there are many stimuli to virtue: firstly, the general bestowal of ideas, and if they are preserved un-
changed, virtue is re-established; if they are covered over by a
multitude of sins, there are Patriarchs, Law, and Prophets, and
at the end of the ages the Lord, who has given us also the apostles—in short, there is nothing given by providence that does
not summon to salvation. The *sword* was also usefully set to that
end. Does not a divine paradise exist and the word of Scripture
containing as well as threats against those who refuse to follow
God's orders also countless forms of correction summoning to
virtue? In fact, they make ways for entry into paradise, and also
allay the harshness of the punishment.

Now, the fact that in the Scriptures the sword stands for
punishment can be confirmed from many instances: "All the
sinners of the people will die by the sword," not that everyone
dies by the blade—rather, the word *sword* conveys the imposition of future punishment of sinners. Also, "You Ethiopians fall
to my sword," to the same effect; and the statement in Exodus
by those (272) subjugated by Pharaoh, addressed to Moses and
Aaron, "May the Lord see and judge ... putting a sword in the
hands of Pharaoh," suggesting by the word *sword* the distress
caused them. In accord with these texts is the verse, "If you do
not divert his sword, he will wield it";[98] it is said to be averted
in the sense that, as a person turns from vice to virtue, it, too,
turns and allows entry.

The guard mounted by *sword* and *cherubim*, then, as mentioned before, would be for the better, in the sense that if de-

97. Ps 130.3–4.
98. Am 9.10, Zep 2.12; Ex 5.21; Ps 7.12.

sire to enter comes to anyone, guidance is provided by them. Whereas the *cherubim* suggest the knowledge of truth in which one who wants to enter must share, the *sword* implies painful access, for it is "with great tribulations" that one may achieve entrance to the kingdom, as Scripture says. Now, the fact that punishment imposed by God is *flailing* and does not necessarily reach its target is conveyed by the history of the Ninevites, who arrested wrath by repentance; the effects of the threat were averted from them.[99]

Aware of the sentence regarding the cherubim, that it is not possible to enter paradise independently of God's plan for them, the saints say, "Shine forth, you who are enthroned on the cherubim," mounted on them like a charioteer, and opening or closing the entrance by your decision,[100] because there are those outside who are obedient to your commands and long to enter. Others realize that it is he who delivers the verdict against the human being, *Soil you are, and unto soil you shall return,* and they beseech him in the words, "You who are enthroned on the cherubim, (274) let the earth tremble," so that when a change affects the earth, he may say to the brigand, "This day you shall be with me in paradise."[101]

99. Acts 14.22; Jon 3.10.   100. Ps 80.1; Rv 3.7.
101. Gn 3.19; Ps 99.1; Lk 23.43.

CHAPTER FOUR

OW, ADAM *knew his wife Eve. She conceived and gave birth to Cain, and said, I have gained a human being, thanks to God. She proceeded to give birth to his brother Abel. Abel was a shepherd of sheep, whereas Cain was a tiller of the soil* (vv.1–2). Following the expulsion from the garden and the making of the garments of skin, the text goes on, *Now, Adam knew his wife Eve,* where *knowing* has the meaning of experiencing and is taken to mean intercourse with a woman. In fact, he had known her in the sense of understanding, this being the sense used when he saw her, saying, "This is bone of my bones."[1] Of the knowledge by which *Adam knew his wife Eve,* there is mention also in the books of Kings: "Elkanah knew his wife Hannah"; likewise in reference to Rebekah, "She was a maiden; no man had known her,"[2] where it means that, since she had not been known by any man, she obviously had not been with any man. It was well put: "She was a maiden; no man had known her": if taken at face value, it would be a case of tautology, whereas the expression means that she was pure in body and mind. Likewise, at a more godly level, Mary also said, "How will this be for me, since I do not know a man?" Being innocent of contact with men, she would have been disturbed to see the angel unless he had removed her fear; and it was possible that being versed in the Law she wondered if the one appearing to her was one of the (276) fallen angels who were said to have coveted the daughters of men.[3]

She conceived and gave birth to Cain. What is described is a different way of human beings coming into existence: while Adam had been formed from dust, and Eve had been constructed by

1. Gn 2.23.   2. 1 Sm 1.19; Gn 24.16.
3. Lk 1.34; Gn 6.1–2.

being taken from the side of her husband, the one born now is the first to issue from both parents, whereas the birth of the Savior happened with only a virgin being involved. Such a comment, in fact, is not out of place, listing all the ways of human beings coming to be, since we maintain what was said before about the dust as an indication of bodily substance,[4] with the body being appropriate to life in the garden. Now, it is said in this case that she *conceived,* and it is clear that they came from seed; yet in not completely rejecting the doctrine of providence, she said, *I have gained a human being, thanks to God.* Although as parents they had served to assist in the birth, everything was carried out by God's action. The phrase *thanks to God* should be taken simply to mean "from God"; Joseph likewise said, "Is not their clarification due to God?"—that is, from God.[5] *She proceeded to give birth to Cain's brother Abel.* Philo takes it to mean they were twins (278) resulting from one conception; this is the reason, he claims, that to the clause *she gave birth to Cain* it added, *she proceeded to give birth to his brother Abel.* Whether he is right or not you can work out for yourself, though it is possible also that they were born separately at different times; if you are happy to accept the Book of the Testament, you will find also how much the one preceded the other chronologically.[6]

While the student will know all that Philo said in treating this passage allegorically, I should nevertheless present it as far as I can. The soul, then, when it has fallen victim to error and sin, generates vile offspring; but if the intelligence returns to sobriety, it enjoys a conversion, and then unquestionably begins to reject them and give birth to the first stages of virtue, a commendable development. Gradually, as progress increases, it arrives eventually at perfection. The reverse, however, is abhorrent, that after the beginning of virtue there is an increase in vice by the perversion of noble reason.

4. The ms is defective where Didymus's comments on 2.7 occur.

5. Gn 40.8, in reference to dreams.

6. "Book of the Testament": Didymus was the first Christian scholar to refer to this work by name; it claims that seven years separated the two brothers (4.1). This is also the first time that Didymus has acknowledged Philo by name as his source.

Now, it is also appropriate that their occupations are mentioned: *Abel was a shepherd, whereas Cain was a tiller of the soil,* which is worth noting as far as the facts are concerned when we take account of their order in the text. While it gave Cain pride of place in regard to birth, in fact, as chronology requires, it gives pride of place to the righteous one in regard to occupations; Abel's is noble and more honorable than what Cain pursued, as what is alive differs from what is lifeless on the basis of nature. (280) Philo was right to say on this that those due to have responsibility for others and of themselves should be trained beforehand in shepherding. Now, Cain was not called a farmer but a *tiller of the soil;* he was not as noble as Noah, who is called a *farmer,* not a tiller.

Now, Abel is a *shepherd* of animals in an allegorical sense, that is, of the senses, bringing them under control as a skilled pastor, imposing reason as a guide and organizer over the irascible and lascivious element. Cain, on the other hand, who was involved with the earth and earthly things, is not called a farmer—otherwise, he would have tried to achieve order in them—but only *tiller of the soil,* being fond of the body, and lacking reason and order. He might have said to himself, "Let us eat and drink, for tomorrow we die," which is applicable to him, whereas the one who does this with godly understanding in accordance with the maxim, "Whether you eat or drink or whatever you do, do everything for the glory of God,"[7] is a farmer, not a tiller of the soil. Now, as was said above, these men may be different kinds of soul which operate at different times.

In course of time Cain brought an offering of the fruits of the earth to the Lord, and Abel for his part also brought an offering of the first-born of his flock, and in fact the fattest of them. God took notice of Abel (282) *and his gifts, whereas to Cain and his offerings he paid no heed. This grieved Cain very much, and his face fell* (vv.3–5). The virtuous person ought to be so resolute and unhesitating as to be not only very ready for the practice of virtue, but also in the face of opposition from others to be willing to be put at risk by it, like blessed Susanna and Joseph, man of courage; when under pressure for adherence to self-control, they maintained their

7. 1 Cor 15.32; Is 22.13; 1 Cor 10.31.

persistence. The people urging them to commit sin, in fact, appeared capable of overwhelming them, but they did not yield, choosing instead to preserve a sincere desire for God, even if this involved dying. In this way they maintained a burning desire for purity, and the outcome proved even to the infidels their judgment and the salutary testing from God, who accepted their virtue.

Cain was not like that, however, being introduced as a procrastinator; *in course of time,* the text says, *he brought an offering of the fruits of the earth,* as if remembering God only on second thoughts. The divine Scripture conveys a criticism of this: "Do not refrain from doing good to the needy when it is in your power to help them. Do not say, 'Go away and come back; tomorrow I shall give you something,' when you are in a position to do good."[8] In reference to Abel, on the other hand, it did not say *in course of time*—rather, *Abel for his part also brought an offering,* and the text takes note of what he brought, suggesting their worth and value: *an offering of the firstborn of his flock, and in fact the fattest of them.* Insofar as Cain had made his offering with indifference, and Abel with sincerity, *God took notice of Abel and his gifts, whereas to Cain and his offerings he paid no heed.* Abel's sincerity (284) is manifest, in fact; he offered his firstborn, deciding to apportion to God the most precious, including *the fattest.* Cain should have done so as well by offering some of the first-fruits; offering first-fruits to God is particularly appropriate, as blessed David does spiritually in saying, "By night my spirit watches for you, O God,"[9] that is, nothing of mine surpasses recourse to you, while to you, O God, what is your due is apportioned before everything else. Now, a *gift* is here differentiated from an *offering* in that the *gift* is made of animals, but not the *offering;* obviously the former is more precious to the degree that living things are more precious than lifeless things.

Now, why was it, would you say, that *God paid no heed,* as a result of which Cain was *grieved* and *his face fell,* or how did Cain know that God did not accept them, and so he was *grieved?* You could reply on the basis of the Book of the Testament, where it

8. Prv 3.27–28.
9. Not David, in fact, but Is 26.9.

is written that fire came down from heaven and accepted the offerings that were properly offered, from which Cain probably realized that, whereas the fire did not descend on his, those of Abel were consumed by it.[10] This happened also in Leviticus: those who offered unauthorized fire on the altar suffered no slight retribution; and Elijah the great prophet in his contest with the priests of Baal proved his cause by fire descending from heaven on his offerings, holy man as he was.[11]

While the literal account provides this information, then, the anagogical sense would be as follows.[12] People who pretend to be virtuous and make a display of it, not from a sincere intention but for some other reason, (286) are procrastinators of a kind and dishonest, not offering first-fruits to God. The first-fruits of virtue, by contrast, come from free will, from where movement towards virtue arises. David conveys this in saying, "His delight was in the law of the Lord." Hypocrites, on the other hand, who have no delight in virtue, make a pretense of virtue for base gain, as has been said,[13] or for appearances. Being one of this group, Cain made an offering *in course of time*, whereas Abel offers firstborn animals and the fat ones without delay. The virtuous person in offering first-fruits, you see, thinks no action of his is fitting for God, as blessed Paul also said, "Not I, but the grace of God in me," and the Psalmist, "Unless the Lord build a house, they labor in vain who build it."[14]

Abel, therefore, having tamed the animal and irrational stock by reason and having made them well-bred, performed an offering to God befitting him and not his passions. This proves *grievous* to those using things improperly; in the manner of fire, conscience rebukes them and presents to them the fact, if vice still abides, of the impropriety of their behavior; it is from this that the *face* of their soul *falls,* and hence to their bodily demeanor also is imparted the depression. That the soul

10. The incident is not mentioned in Jubilees.

11. Lv 10.1–2; 1 Kgs 18.38.

12. While in some cases it would seem that Didymus distinguishes allegorical and anagogical senses of a text, here "anagogical" is used of an allegorical treatment.

13. Ps 1.2; Ti 1.11.

14. 1 Cor 15.10; Ps 127.1.

has a face this saying suggests, "A person's wisdom illumines the face," and, "With unveiled face we contemplate the glory of the Lord," whereas there is a reference to the physical face in the verse, "A glad heart makes a cheerful face, but when grief comes, it is clouded,"[15] (288) as happened to Cain when his conscience rebuked him.

The Lord God said to Cain, For what reason are you so aggrieved? For what reason has your face fallen? Is it not true that, even if you make your offering correctly but fail to choose the offering correctly, you commit sin? Be at peace: its movement will be towards you, and you will be superior to it (vv.6–7). The lovingkindness of the God of all is shown to be unmatched in dealing even with the fallen; far from allowing them to reach the depths of sin, he prompts them to come to their senses and be converted to virtue, as happens also in this case with Cain. God says to him in a message resounding in his mind, *For what reason are you so aggrieved?* You were responsible for it yourself; there was no one else who was the occasion of the sin. He suggests also the way he fell: *Even if you make your offering correctly but fail to choose the offering correctly, you commit sin.* In other words, all who think that providence extends to all people as they conduct their affairs render thanks appropriately by making an offering, whereas those who do so with such indifference as to keep the more valuable things for themselves and to offer the cheap things make a bad *choice*.

When Israel was guilty of this, the prophetic word said by way of threat and exhortation, "If you offer a blind animal in sacrifice, is that not wrong? And if you offer one that is lame or sick, is that not wrong? Offer it to your governor."[16] Also Ananias and Sapphira (290) in the Acts of the Apostles, when many people were making offerings for the needs of the indigent, for their part promised to give the price of a property, but kept one half and offered the other, thus making a bad *choice*, for which the chief of the apostles was moved by the Spirit to censure them, "While it remained unsold, did it not remain your own? And after it was sold, were not the proceeds at your disposal? How is it that you have contrived this deed in your heart?"[17]

15. Eccl 8.1; 2 Cor 3.18; Prv 15.13.   16. Mal 1.8.
17. Acts 5.4.

This is also what was said to Cain by God in this case: *For what reason are you so aggrieved? For what reason has your face fallen? Is it not true that, even if you make your offering correctly but fail to choose the offering correctly, you commit sin?* All those *commit sin,* in fact, who make an offering to God as to someone in need, unaware of what is said in the Psalms by God himself, "Surely I do not eat the flesh of bulls or drink the blood of goats?" and again, "All the wild animals of the field are mine, beasts in the mountains and oxen."[18] In other words, everything available to you is from me, whereas everything is mine; so the requirements are made, not because I need anything, but to teach you symbolically by this that there is need to practice virtue, not with indifference, but fully and completely.

Then, to prevent progress in evil, he bids him refrain from it lest it produce the worse result of an irritating wound. It is likewise said to Zion when influenced by disordered impulses (the meaning of the word, in fact), "Halt yourself, Zion."[19] In other words, since the rational animal is active in the practice of either vice or virtue, it is right that when it practices vice, it should put a halt to it so that virtue may thus (292) find its due place. This, to be sure, is also David's recommendation: "Desist from evil and do good."[20] So he says, *Be at peace,* go no further in evildoing, do not think in your depression that it is not right that your sacrifice has not been accepted. After all, it often happens that many people on falling into sin and hence not having God to assist them in what they do are disenchanted with providence—something that God discourages in Cain by saying, *Be at peace.*

He proceeds, *Its movement is towards you, and you will be superior to it,* his purpose being to teach that everything not properly offered to God is not offered to him; instead, it remains with the giver and *moves back to him* because of not finding a place in God. Likewise, those who offer alms "so as to be seen by peo-

18. Ps 50.13, 10.

19. Jer 38.21 LXX. Nautin, who despairs of tracing Didymus's etymology of "Zion" to his sources, concludes he is arriving at it from the drift of the Jeremiah verse; SC 233.290–91, note 124,1.

20. Ps 34.14.

ple" have their reward,[21] and get nothing from God, since they did not do it with a godly purpose.

The literal sense of the whole passage is therefore very relevant to behavior when taken superficially like this, teaching us to make offerings sincerely and not with indifference. Since in what went before, however, we applied previous verses to states of soul, we need to do it here as well.[22] The word of God, which abides in sentiments universally held and is present in the conscience, in caring fashion accuses the delinquent, as emerges in this case, too. Hypocrites, you see, insofar as they give evidence of esteem for virtue, even if not making a choice of it, seem to be doing something worthwhile; but since they exercise their choice badly by directing to their own enjoyment the movement that stems from the depth of their heart while giving the external appearance of offering their gift through God, (294) they are not accepted. And rightly so: though purifying the outside of the cup and being clad on the outside in sheep's clothing, inside they are ravening wolves. In criticism of such people the Lord said, "Why do you resemble whitewashed tombs, which inside are full of the bones of the dead and all kinds of filth?"[23] Virtuous people, by contrast, who belong to God entirely and completely in thought and behavior, perform human actions—only out of bodily necessity, be it noted—with wisdom, and perform offerings to God *correctly* out of a concern for purity of body and soul. Abel was a type of these people, setting God as ruler and patron of his behavior. This, in fact, is typical of the virtuous person, whereas the behavior of the hypocrite returns to him, since God sees the depths of the heart and does not accept what is done by such a person.

Cain said to his brother Abel, Let us go out into the open country. When they were in the open country, Cain set upon his brother Abel and killed him (v.8). A slight growth in vice left unchecked goes to excess, and a sin hiding in the heart unimpeded by reason will translate into action, even if it seems to be stalled for a brief time. This very thing is reported in the Acts of the Apos-

21. Mt 6.1.
22. The verb used for "apply" is ἀνάγω.
23. Mt 23.25–27; 7.15.

tles: after hearing a lengthy discourse from Paul on the divine teaching, and becoming afraid, the governor was again affected by the passion of avarice, and said to Paul in affirmation of the Spirit's role in the Scriptures, "When I have an opportunity, I shall send for you," in the expectation (296) of getting a bribe from him.[24] Such a passion affected the vengeful Cain, too; after being corrected, he bided his time and nourished envy in his heart. He said to his brother deceitfully, *Let us go out into the open country;* he went out, gave free rein to his anger, set upon his brother, and did away with him. Some commentators also want to raise this question: What weapon did he use to do away with Abel? There is no problem in that; even if there was no iron, he could still have used stone or wood, as the Book of the Testament also suggests.[25] Scripture nevertheless refers to the killing, whichever way it happened, as a slaughter, as is suggested in the Epistle of John: "As Cain slaughtered his brother because his works were evil whereas his brother's were righteous."[26] Now, the clause *Cain set upon Abel* implies his attacking him and his voluntary assault.

So much for the factual sense; but since we claim that Cain represents hypocritical behavior in the anagogical sense, this would be the case here as well. The *brother* of the exterior, visible man is the man hidden in thought; the zealous person should attend to both, using reason properly and wearing clothing suited to his behavior, as the Psalmist also teaches in the first Psalm, "Blessed the man who does not walk in the counsel of the impious," and a little later, "It will produce its fruit in due season, and its leaf will not fall,"[27] by "fruit" meaning virtuous behavior stemming from disposition, and by "leaf" an external condition manifested in appearance, attire, and a smile. So when (298) the hypocrite is zealous about these things, but

24. Acts 24.25–26.

25. Jubilees 4.2 mentions the act in terms similar to Gn 4.8 without specifying the weapon. The question raised is typical of the *apora* (the word used here for "problems") raised by literalists in the Questions genre, like those of Diodore and Theodoret. Whoever may be his intended readership, Didymus is prepared to take account of such issues, as we shall see.

26. 1 Jn 3.12.

27. Ps 1.1, 3.

his reason is directed elsewhere, "he slaughters his brother" by setting his thinking at odds with his exterior. For him *open country* is the strategy adopted against those being deceived; he goes into it in deceiving them before he leads himself into sin. Now, the sophists are like that, adopting *open country* in their language and through it conducting their own *brothers* into impiety.

The Lord God said to Cain, Where is your brother Abel? He replied, I do not know; surely I am not my brother's keeper? (v.9) The loving God in his abundant goodness still has regard for those completely alienated from him, and by his regard he arouses them to awareness, as he does Cain here. First, he imparts to him messages from his conscience; then, by saying *Abel your brother,* he depresses him, as it were, by use of the name referring to his natural origin, and brings him to an awareness of his ignominy. He presents him with the enormity of his crime, that he has killed a *brother* and a *righteous* brother, killing the one whom God had made for assistance and help. This, in fact, is what the proverb says, "May you have a friend for all seasons, may brothers be at hand to lend help in time of need; it is for this that they are born,"[28] the proverb conveying the *raison d'être* of brothers. Divine providence aims to unify, and is always doing so. In the Law as well, of course, because affection between brothers and family members suffices for unity, he does not allow them to be joined in matrimony, urging them instead to take as brides others rather than sisters or relatives so as thus (300) to be joined also with others ... and affection. It was this that Cain trampled underfoot. You can in fact see also his hypocrisy when he foolishly says, *I do not know; surely I am not my brother's keeper?* In other words, in saying *I do not know* he shows his audacity in thinking he had escaped God's notice, and in *surely not a keeper* he conveys his hostility and cruelty, and thus his lack of thought, since it behoved him to be his *brother's keeper.*

God said, Why have you done this? The voice of your brother's blood cries out to me from the earth. And now you will be cursed from the earth, which has opened its mouth to receive your brother's blood from your hand. When you till the soil, it will not proceed to yield its strength

28. Prv 17.17.

to you. You will live in lament and trepidation on the earth (vv.10–
12). The loving God conveyed to the one who was unashamed
and thought he had escaped God's notice the lesson that this
was impossible, saying, *The voice of your brother's blood cries out
to me from the earth:* Do not think that your crime has escaped
the unsleeping eye of Providence. By the blood's *voice* he means
its being obvious, as also elsewhere, "Lo, the wages of the la-
borers who mowed your fields, which you kept back by fraud,
cry out."[29] While this is to be taken in a similar sense, *blood* is
possibly used here in reference to the soul. On the other hand,
you could say that if there was mention only of *blood*, he had
hidden the body. It mentions pouring forth, the fact that *the
earth opened its mouth to receive the blood,* even *your brother's,* the
purpose being to highlight the crime and shame the murderer.
(302)

He also rightly inflicts on him curses for such a crime: *And
now you will be cursed from the earth. When you till the soil, it will not
proceed to yield its strength to you.* In fact, the earth is often impov-
erished on account of people's sins and does not yield crops,
as Scripture says, "The land is in mourning on account of its
inhabitants."[30] It has, in fact, been allowed to produce crops for
those who keep their reason free of perversion, and by God's
lovingkindness it provides necessities for sinners; but in turn
its crops fail by his command to ensure conversion. In an anagogical sense, on the other hand, if we follow our previous remarks, God reproaches the hypocrite for perverting the vital
force of the soul, which is the *brother* of the exterior man, as was
explained. Hence it will also be *cursed,* no longer producing
fruit, instead even losing its tendency to productivity, by which
it is inclined to the beginning of virtue. Better, in fact, for it to
turn from vice before arriving at its enactment, so that fatigue
may develop and instill love of virtue, as Scripture says, "Egypt
felt fatigue, and both the trade of Ethiopians and the tall Sa-
bean men will cross over to you."[31] *You will live in lament and
trepidation on the earth:* this is his sentence, to be ever accused by
conscience.

29. Jas 5.4.   30. Hos 4.3.
31. Is 45.14 LXX.

Cain said to the Lord God, My guilt is too great for me to be forgiven. If today you drive me from the face of the earth and (304) *I must hide from your presence, and live in lament and trepidation on the earth, it will happen that anyone finding me will kill me* (vv.13–14). Even on those who have alienated themselves from God his word impresses itself, and from it they derive a sense of God as loving and kind. Nor would it be possible for this abiding conviction to be dislodged, even if they often resist it as a result of the depths of vice. On feeling the pressure of necessity, for instance, people who have completely forgotten God immediately have recourse to prayer and supplication, as can be seen also in the case of Cain. In his forgetfulness of God, in fact, he had set about murdering his brother and had replied to his question, *Where is your brother Abel?* with impudence; yet since perversion had not yet gone to extremes among human beings, and he realized from God's words, which he experienced as a reproach in his conscience, that God's eye is inescapable, he asked him not to reduce him to a complete state of alienation from him, as a result of which he would be *in lament and trepidation* and expect execution by anyone encountering him. The person who is convinced, after all, that he is deprived of God's supervising power finds everything frightening and lacks confidence in everything he does.

So much for our remarks on all the sophistry of Cain's reply. Let us also have an eye to the confusion in his reply, that of a villain who has no share in God's grace. *My guilt is too great for me to be forgiven,* which at first flush would suggest, My crime will be too great if you do not prosecute my iniquity, O God; while I am still subject to your care, there is no despairing. This is exactly what was said in the prophet as the word of God in the case of people deserving of contempt who have (306) been given up to a debased attitude: "I shall not punish your daughters when they play the whore, nor your daughters-in-law when they commit adultery." Since, you see, he wishes to convert sinners capable of being corrected, he says, "I shall punish their transgressions with a rod and their sins with scourges, but I shall not deprive them of my mercy."[32]

32. Rom 1.28; Hos 4.14; Ps 89.32–33.

Now, this is what he is saying in this case: "My censure will be too severe, Lord, if you do not apply retribution," as we have explained. Having sinned, and being guilty of perversion, he thinks that he is *driven* from the earth and expelled from God's presence. In another sense he would mean, "My crime is too grave for me to remain on earth if you, O God, do not deprive me of existence; if you *drive me from the earth* and *I hide from your presence* by being no longer in existence, this would be desirable for me. But if you do not *drive me from the earth* (to be understood), *I shall live there in lament and trepidation, and anyone finding me will kill me.*" In the case of the general run of people, when they realize the enormity of their sins, and because they have the idea that God himself will go in pursuit of them, they consider it preferable not to exist, preferring insensibility to existence—a fact that is clear from the statement by the prophet about those who betrayed Jesus, "They will wish they had been consumed by fire."[33]

If you were to take in another sense his saying, *If you drive me*, the word *today* comes from someone asking for "an opportunity to repent,"[34] for the present (the word *today*) to be delayed. His desire was for his own particular end, as we say, to be imposed by God (308) lest he be subject to death by anyone finding him. You might inquire who Cain feared would find and kill him when there was no one in existence beyond him and his parents.[35] Your reply to this would be firstly that with the thought of future descendants he was afraid that after being guilty of such a grave offense he would be done away with as loathsome by people in the future, since such awful guilt passes to posterity. Next, even if this did not happen, he presumed that divine powers would avenge the sacrilege, since they had probably seen him, the evil having not yet spread.

Now, as to the anagogical sense ...[36]

33. Is 9.5. Is Didymus thinking of Mt 26.24?

34. Wis 12.10; Heb 12.17.

35. Again the kind of literalist "problem," *aporon*, raised by an imaginary questioner; see n. 25 above.

36. The phrase is followed simply by an arrow, leaving Nautin to wonder whether the scribe is implying that treatment has been given above and prefers

The Lord God said to him, Not so: anyone who kills Cain will be subject to a sevenfold vengeance. The Lord God put a mark on Cain lest anyone finding him do away with him (v.15). God reserved for a heavier punishment than Cain supposed anyone who would find and kill him for being the murderer of his own brother, saying, *Not so:* being done away with by anyone is not the penalty that befits your crime. Such a person, in fact, *would be subject to a sevenfold vengeance,* which implies complete retribution, the number seven frequently in Scripture taken to mean completion. This is suggested in the saying, "The seven eyes are gazing on the whole earth";[37] since God is not a body, with his eyes numbering seven, (310) it is clear instead that he is conveying that his supervisory powers are complete and extensive. On the other hand, other commentators have said that just as the humanity of the Savior had seven indwelling spirits—"a spirit of wisdom and understanding, a spirit of counsel and strength, a spirit of knowledge and piety, a spirit of fear of God"—so each human being is complete before sin, and it is to this that the Apostle teaches we arrive when he says, "Until all of us come to completeness, to the measure of the full stature of Christ."[38] You have these spirits indwelling, but if you sin, you will be *subject to* them, and of them will be required a full and appropriate vengeance.

Now, it should be noted that the phrase *anyone who kills Cain* can be read as in the vocative, "O Cain, anyone who kills," or as directed to others in reference to him, "Anyone who kills Cain," a phrase that you would not be wrong to apply to certain powers. To these same ones he gave a *mark to prevent their doing away with him,* namely, an order from God himself; sentences of this kind are not imposed without permission …[39]

He put a mark, the impetus to repentance after the falls, as a result of which he would not be in danger of being done away with. After all, while it is a great good not to fall, after falls a

not to repeat it; SC 233.309, note 133,1, which refers to the Introduction, SC 233.19.

37. Zec 4.10.
38. Is 11.2–3; Eph 3.13.
39. At this point in the ms eight lines are missing.

second haven would lie in repentance, something God in his providence promotes through teaching to prevent our falling foul of the deceiver. Such a notion is suggested by the saying in the Psalms, "The light of your countenance, O Lord, has left its mark on us," (312) and you could say that the light of his countenance is the Son or the divine ideas. This, in fact, is the sense in which "fleeing before the face of the bow" will occur, God's face being within us, as was said; and the sequel confirms it, "so that those whom you love may be rescued." So in his goodness and kindness God gives "an opportunity of repentance"[40] also to those guilty of grave sins so that they may once more embrace virtue.

So Cain left God's presence and settled in the land of Nod opposite Eden (v.16). Instead of taking in a local sense the clause, *Cain left God's presence,* we claim that every sinner is removed from God, since we also take this view of entering God's presence, the Psalm saying, "Enter his presence with joy."[41] Now, anyone entering God's presence leaves behind everything foreign, sins and material things, and becomes other than worldly, so as in this way to gain a share in knowledge of God. So it is said here, *Cain left God's presence,* and we do not claim that it is a particular place, where God is, where Cain was and left. God is uncircumscribed, after all, and is not confined to places, even if a temple was later made for instruction in symbolic worship.

So Cain *left,* having rendered himself unworthy of *God's presence,* and being now heedless of him. (314) Of such people it is said, "God is not before him," and of the sons of Eli it is said, "The sons of Eli did not know the Lord";[42] even if they were faithful in attending the temple, in attitude and behavior they were foreign to it. The fact that Cain left in that way the sequel brings out: *and settled in the land of Nod opposite Eden. Nod* means "tossing," in fact; after all, where must the one who has forsaken the virtue of peace settle if not in "tossing," in the unstable and unsteady thing that vice is? *Opposite* was well put, vice being the opposite of virtue.

40. Pss 4.6; 60.4, 5; Wis 12.10; Heb 12.17.
41. Ps 100.2.
42. Ps 10.4; 1 Sm 2.12.

We recall, then, that when we treated of Adam's exit, we noted that God drove him out, since instead of leaving willingly, he retained a spark of desire for life in *the garden of delight;* hence he also settled him *opposite* it,[43] as it was also he who arranged their dwelling. In the case of people whose sins are not grave, in fact, since virtue is not far from them, some encouragement is given them with the promise of a speedy return, given by God. This is not mentioned in the case of Cain; instead of being settled or expelled, he took a headlong course towards vice with an ardent desire. Hence he also settled in "tossing," being invariably disturbed, since it was what he desired. The virtuous person, on the other hand, is steady as a result of a firm position, and so can stand with God, as the saying goes, "But you, stand here by me," and the statement by the Savior about those not tasting death, "There are some standing here,"[44] (316) who were his familiars. And to give encouragement not to be caught up in anything unworthy of teaching, Paul writes, "Stand firm, then, and do not submit again to the yoke of slavery"; and the Psalmist says with gratitude, "You set my feet on a rock," whereas of the villains always suffering the effects of evil it is said that the tossing of their feet "will not last." It is, in fact, a grave sin ever to be involved in evildoing, something the word does not want happening in Zion, "Halt yourself, Zion"; blessed David, who achieved it and intended not to fall victim to it, sings, "May the hand of sinners not shake me,"[45] that is, may the behavior of a sinner—the devil—not divert me from virtue.

Cain knew his wife; she conceived and gave birth to Enoch. He was the builder of a city, and named it after his son, Enoch (v.17). Some people wonder where Cain got his wife, there being no other people than Adam and Eve, and from this in their malice they come to the conclusion of incest with a sister. They should, however, not come to the conclusion of incest on these grounds; if there were others and he had still taken his sister, the argument would be persuasive; but as there was no one else, and this happened with a view to providing offspring, what grounds

43. Gn 3.24.
44. Dt 5.31; Mk 9.1.
45. Gal 5.1; Ps 40.2; Jb 8.15; Jer 38.21 LXX; Ps 36.11.

are there for a charge of incest, since there was no one else to take for intercourse?[46] With the Stoics as well this question is raised: if an incineration of the world took place, and only a sage survived as an ember of the human race (318) along with his daughter, and he understood that the world would be developed afresh on condition of progeny, would he be right to have intercourse with his daughter? They judged that it would be acceptable, there being no one else. This seems to be the case also with the daughters of Lot, which censorious people find fault with, but no one of sense does; they believed that no other man existed as a result of the burning of those cities, and being young they supposed that the whole earth had suffered the fate of incineration, and said, "Lo, our father is old, and there is no one to come in to us after the manner of all the earth. Come, let us get our father to drink wine."[47] As proof that they did so, not out of passion but to leave an ember of life, one had intercourse and urged the other to do so, which would not have happened so quickly if they had been in thrall to passion; instead, in the same way as the first had conducted herself the second also did with a view to more offspring. Cain is therefore not to be blamed for this, even if he sinned in many ways. It should be noted that it did not say, Cain knew his sister, but *his wife,* this term being appropriate to procreation.

You could raise the question of how, when five[48] people are named—the parents of Cain, himself, and his wife—the text says, *he built a city,* a project that requires a lot of people. The (320) questioner could also ask the reason why they built a city when a single cave or a very tiny dwelling would have sufficed for accommodation. In reply ...

To Enoch was born Irad, Irad begot Mehujael, Mehujael begot Methushael, Methushael begot Lamech (v.18). It gives the line of Cain, which extended to the seventh generation and was wiped out when the flood came, whereas the line of Adam goes from

46. We have seen Didymus formally addressing, instead of ignoring, factual problems, *apora,* raised by literalists. Here he declines to take an allegorical approach.

47. Gn 19.31–32.

48. Note from the FOTC editor: The text indeed says "five" (πέντε), although Didymus names only four. The fifth is Enoch.

Seth, who was raised up by God; it continued and is preserved to this day. From it, in fact, came the house of Noah and those who were saved with him in the ark. If, on the other hand, you wanted to take this anagogically, you could begin the anagogy with a translation of the names and conduct it without undue detachment. Philo also treated of these matters, from which the students could on inspection draw due benefit.[49]

Lamech took to himself two wives: the name of one was Adah, and the name of the other Zillah. Adah gave birth to Jabal; he was the father of those who dwell in tents and keep cattle. His brother's name was Jubal; he was the inventor of the harp and the lyre. Zillah gave birth in turn to Tubal-cain; he was a metalsmith working in copper and iron. Tubal-cain's sister was Naamah (vv.19–22). In olden times it was not thought unlawful behavior even for zealous people to have two wives; it was the time for procreation and (322) increase in the number of people. Lamech, then, had two wives, and had sons from both; they became originators of occupations, one being the original cattleman, and his brother Jubal invented the harp and the lyre. His son from the other wife was Tubal-cain, who was the original metalsmith working in copper and iron; his sister is also named. In this outline, then, the divine teaching brings out that human beings are living things endowed with free will and gifted with knowledge; they do not live only by the senses like brute beasts—instead, the faculty of reason is indicated by their being also inventors of skills.

So much for the literal sense, then; now for the anagogical.[50] A cattleman is different from a shepherd: while the latter pastures his flock with knowledge, the cattleman does not. The righteous man Abel was a shepherd, managing his own irrational forces—of desire, of impulse, of anger—in accord with right reason, whereas the cattleman has no share in knowledge, being pleasure-bent, acting on senses alone, controlled by them rather than in control. The statement would be rendered clearer by an example: the healer uses touch differently from

49. Whereas in fact Philo in the treatment familiar to Didymus does explore the etymology of these names, Didymus (in this work) forgoes that line of commentary.

50. Here "anagogical" proves to mean allegorical.

the person bent on pleasure; the latter is in a way a cattleman, whereas the healer is a shepherd, using sense by reason. It is the same also with smell and the other senses, which are used best by the one employing reason, since reason commands sense. When reason is dominated, however, the human being then gets a name in keeping with the passions, thus being called a lion on account of anger, a fox on account of duplicity, a serpent on account of earthly interests, and likewise in other cases a horse on account of pleasure-seeking—Scripture says, remember, "You have become lusty stallions"—(324) and other people mules on account of being completely sensual and generating nothing divine, Scripture saying, "Be not like horse and mule, which lack intelligence."[51]

That is what a cattleman is like, then, a scoundrel, dwelling not in a house but in a *tent,* an unstable thing, unlike those who live in tents for the sake of progress, so as to move from there into a house, saying as is said in the Psalm, "How lovely your tents, Lord of hosts; my soul longs and faints for the courts of the Lord." The one who progresses from tents, in fact, longs for courts, and sings, "I shall pass through every corner of the wonderful tent as far as the house of God."[52]

The other brother, by contrast, is *the inventor of harp and lyre,* and rightly his brother, since what deceives by bringing music to the ears bears a relationship to enjoyment of pleasure. Scripture says, remember, "Woe to you who rise early in pursuit of strong drink and linger in the evening, for wine will inflame them; they drink wine to the accompaniment of lyre and harp, but do not regard the works of the Lord."[53] The one who was the son of the other woman fashioned weapons of war from *copper and iron,* copper meaning "noise," as Paul also says in his letter, "I have become sounding copper." The same man is also an ironsmith in that he is a sophist, deceiving by means of effectively persuasive powers.[54]

Lamech said to his wives Adah and Zillah, Listen to my voice, wives of Lamech, give ear to my words: I killed a man for (326) *wounding*

---

51. Jer 5.8; Ps 32.9.
53. Is 5.11–12.

52. Pss 83.1; 42.4.
54. 1 Cor 13.1.

me and a young man for striking me. On Cain fell sevenfold vengeance, but on Lamech seventy times sevenfold (vv.23–24). I think that the verb *give ear* occurs only in the divine teaching, and it differs from *listening* when associated with the latter, where *give ear* refers to hearing from someone nearby, and *listen* to hearing anything at all, even if the speech is not nearby. In Isaiah, "Listen, heaven, and give ear, earth, because the Lord has spoken," the verbs are not interchangeable, as also in the verse "Give ear, heaven, and I shall speak" (the other translators saying "Give ear" for "Pay heed"), "and let the earth listen to the words of my mouth."[55] By this distinction they mean that when the Law was given by God, since they were close to the heavenly works, accordingly heaven is urged to "give ear," whereas when they had abandoned the virtuous way of life so as to be near the earth, then it was said, "Listen, heaven" (it was far from them), "and give ear, earth" (it was close to their occupations).

… Instead of Lamech's employing the verbs *give ear* and *listen* interchangeably, we took occasion to observe the difference between them that occurs in Scripture. Now, let us learn what his meaning is: *Listen to my voice, wives of Lamech, give ear to my words.* You would claim, then, that *voice* and *words* (328) are interchangeable; but if you were to focus on precision in these, you would say that he used *listen* of *voice* and with greater precision applied *give ear* to *words.* With this difference in mind, you could say that John was "a voice crying," taking *voice* as the literal sense of the Scriptures, and *word* as the spiritual sense.[56]

I killed a man for wounding me and a young man for striking me. It is said in the Book of the Testament that Cain was accidentally killed by Lamech: in building a wall he caused it to topple, and Cain, who was behind it, was accidentally killed. His being killed, then, was *a wound for me,* whereas its being accidental meant *striking me…*[57]

---

55. Is 1.2; Dt 32.1. The alternative versions could be found in Origen's *Hexapla,* or simply in his commentaries.

56. Mt 3.3, in reference to John the Baptist. Didymus employs the adjective μυστικός here for the "spiritual sense."

57. Jubilees 4.31 reports Cain's accidental death in these terms, but without the involvement of Lamech. The loss of thirteen lines at this point has

Now, Adam knew his wife Eve. She conceived, bore a son, and gave him the name Seth, saying, God has raised up for me another child in place of Abel, whom Cain killed (v.25). In previously clarifying the sense of the verb *know,* we said that Adam's *knowing* his wife Eve did not mean understanding her but having intercourse with her, as is the meaning here, too. She *conceived* and *bore a son, and she gave him the name Seth, saying, God has raised up for me another child in place of Abel, whom Cain killed.* Adherents of the heresy of Valentinus maintain the existence of different natures, (330) one of which is not susceptible of virtue, to which they give the name "choic"; another not susceptible of vice, to which they give the name "pneumatic"; and the third they say is "psychic," which is thought by them to be a kind of mixture of both. They take Cain as a symbol of the nature that is not susceptible of virtue, Abel of the pneumatic, and to Seth they apply the remaining one. While this is not the time to refute this impious heresy at the risk of prolonging our treatment, we note that Eve's comment was a kind of confirmation of Seth's character; instead of the zealous Abel, his name means "giving to drink," a symbol of a life-giving offer. In other words, there was need for the "offer-er" (the meaning of Abel) to have as a brother one who "gives to drink," so that there would be someone first and more mature to make an offering of spiritual sacrifices to God like a priest, and that Seth in second place should offer to God those he taught through giving to drink and teaching. He was in place of Cain, who was self-obsessed, Cain meaning "acquiring."[58]

A son was born to Seth; he gave him the name Enosh. He it was who hoped to invoke the name of the Lord God (v.26). Holy offspring of a holy person often reflect their being born from them according to the flesh and according to their soul. In this way Abraham became father of Isaac, Isaac of Jacob, and Jacob of

deprived us of Didymus's comment on the last verse of the Song of the Sword (vv.23–24), where the LXX has misunderstood the Heb. and transformed Cain into an object of vengeance, not one for whom vengeance is taken.

58. Didymus's option above not to imitate Philo in proceeding through these genealogies by providing etymologies of all the names is here shown to have been a wise one, since in the three exceptions made here he is wide of the mark in two cases. The Heb. text finds in the name Cain an assonance with the verb "acquired, gained" in 4.1. Seth loomed large in the gnostic myth.

Joseph, who at the same time were their offspring by human generation and proved imitators of their virtue. Esau, by contrast, was Isaac's son only according to the flesh, (332) being different from him in attitude, since he proved a scoundrel. Seth, then, born in place of the righteous one, was the righteous father of the righteous Enosh, and instead of a personal name was called "mankind"; such a name indicated the virtue of his soul, which preserved the quality of being "in the image" and the state of a true human being (Enosh in Hebrew meaning "human being"). At any rate, it also attributes to him what is proper to a human being: *He it was who hoped to invoke the name of the Lord,* this practice being appropriate to a virtuous human being, whose real hope is to resemble God as far as possible. *To hope to invoke the name of the Lord God* is characteristic of one who submits himself at the same time to the authority and the teaching of God.[59]

59. Just as Didymus did not respond to the significance of the Song of the Sword (4.23–24), which can be seen as reflecting an important development in the primeval history, so at this point the historical difficulty of the beginning of the worship of Yahweh, which Elohist and Priestly authors assign to the time of Moses, is also lost on him. Only in comment on 12.7 will he make the point; see pp. 190–91 below.

CHAPTER FIVE

HIS IS THE book about the origin of human beings. On the day God made Adam, in God's image he made him; male and female he made them. He blessed them and gave them the name Adam on the day he made them (vv.1–2).[1] By *book* here the text referred to the account of Adam and his descendants down to the present. Before the sixth day, then, when the human being was made, it was called "the book of heaven and earth,"[2] since it set apart that whole account of what was made before the human being, reserving another beginning for the origin of the human being. The treatment of his creation, on the other hand, it calls *origin* in the way it speaks also of Jesus: "The book of the origin of Jesus Christ"—according to the flesh, that is: his eternal origin is unknown to human beings, Scripture saying, "Who will recount his lineage?"[3]

Now, as we said that the six days did not refer to a multiplicity of days, so too with one; God does not create in time. While in fact the actions of human beings are measured by time, not so God's: "He spoke, and they were made,"[4] and we cannot discern (10) the interval between his wishing and the coming into being of what he wishes to exist. Instead, it was for the sake of order that there was mention of one person being first along with completed ones. We likewise at that stage have spoken of the human being made "in his image." Now, the clause *he blessed them* implies that they were good; a blessing falls on the good. Scripture says, "Such a one receives blessing from the Lord." It should be noted that *Adam* refers to both of them, but as we

---

1. Nautin's second volume opens with this chapter, Genesis 5, beginning on p. 8 of SC 244.

2. Gn 2.4.   3. Mt 1.1; Is 53.8.

4. Ps 33.9.

treated of the clause *male and female he made them*[5] previously, we shall not go over it again.

Now, there is nothing unusual about Enosh and Adam both meaning "human being." Among the Hebrews, in fact, the human being is given many names, as also among Greek speakers they speak of *anthrôpos, merops, brotos, phôs,* which are etymologically connected with nature and not convention, as was also explained before.[6]

Adam was two hundred and thirty years old and had a son in his own form and image, and named him Seth. The days of Adam after he begot Seth were seven hundred years, and he begot other sons and daughters. The days of Adam were in all nine hundred and thirty years, and he died (vv.3–5). People's (12) lives today are limited to a few years; it will be said later on the basis of the facts that things gradually took such a turn for the worse that it was even foretold by God: "My spirit shall not abide in these men because they are flesh; their days shall be one hundred twenty years." The Psalmist said, "The number of our years is seventy, and eighty if they are strong, and beyond that trouble and hardship,"[7] there being trouble and hardship after eighty years of life. At that time, however, people did not grow old quickly, giving the impression of being in their prime at a hundred and sixty. It also made sense, at least in the beginning, for people to live long in case, should they die prematurely, the human race should fail by descending from a single stock. Thus, in fact, enjoying a longer life, they gave birth to bigger families, though mention is made of only one on account of the firstborn being named in regard to descendants. If, on the other hand, you were to object, Seth was the third, not the first, to be born,[8] it should be said in reply that it was not proper to begin with Cain, criminal as he was, nor with Abel, who died childless, but rather as a result with Seth, who in a sense was firstborn.

While the phrase *in his own form and image* would seem to

5. Ps 24.5; Gn 1.27.

6. Didymus is perhaps referring to his comments on 3.24. His reference to Hebrew and Greek speakers betrays the fact that neither is his mother tongue.

7. Gn 6.3; Ps 90.10.

8. Again Didymus shows himself ready to deal with factual discrepancies raised by literalists.

be synonymous if taken at face value, the sophisticated person would reply that *in his own form . . . whereas in his own image . . .*

So much for commentary. If, however, you are fascinated by the number of years and the significance of the names, (14) Philo would supply a mystical meaning without detachment. So apply to him; it would prove helpful.[9]

Seth lived two hundred and five years and begot Enosh. Seth lived seven hundred and seven years after begetting Enosh, and begot sons and daughters. The days of Seth in all were nine hundred and twelve years, and he died (vv.6–8). The name of this Enosh has the same sound as the one before him, Cain's son. This Enosh lived nine hundred years, and died; his son was Kenan, who lived nine hundred and ten years, and died. His son was Mahalalel, whose life lasted ninety-five years;[10] his son was Jared, who lived nine hundred and sixty-two years, and died, having begotten Enoch.

Enoch lived a hundred and sixty-five years and begot Methuselah. Now, Enoch pleased God well for two hundred years after begetting Methuselah, and begot sons and daughters. The days of Enoch in all were three hundred and sixty-five years. Enoch was well-pleasing to God, and he was not found because God had taken him away (vv.21–24). The Apostle quoted the text about Enoch in the letter to the Hebrews, "By faith Enoch was taken away (16) so as not to see death."[11] His life is recorded at the number of days in a year, when he was then "taken away," which you could then intelligently take to mean that he had acquired perfection and fullness of virtue expected of human beings, and was then taken away to better things.[12] His transfer, however, was not like what

9. Again Didymus declines to enter into number symbolism and etymologies (dear to him in the Zechariah commentary; see FOTC 111), recommending that anyone so "fascinated" should have recourse to Philo, who could dispense such refinements—and without detachment, frigidity (φυχρολογ[εῖ]ν). Note from FOTC editor: Nautin (SC 244.15) translates "frigidity" as "dryness," *sécheresse*. Perhaps there is a connotation of "irrelevance": hence "without irrelevance" would mean that Philo's interpretations are vitally connected to the text.

10. Didymus does not cite the biblical text of verses 9–20, simply reducing them to the vital statistics (which he seems to have misread in the case of the age of Mahalalel, putting it at 95 instead of 895 years).

11. Heb 11.5.

12. With this exception, Didymus has kept his promise to eschew Philo's development of number symbolism and etymologies. In these cases he has

happens to other people; other people's bodies remain here, dissolve, and are separated from their souls, whereas of him it is said that he was "taken away," which we understand to mean either that he was assumed like Elijah or that he was snatched to a divine place in some other way.

Here we should proceed to study how the statement by Paul, "Just as it is appointed for human beings to die once,"[13] is verified. That is to say, if those men Elijah and Enoch were taken up so as to be in their very dense bodies till now and forever, the statement by Paul in his wisdom and holiness would be false about all people having to die. But it is not false. The text in hand, then, has a proper meaning, even if they did not share in the death that is now the fate of other people; instead, there is need to understand their mortality in the sense that their physical life has been elevated in a manner hidden from us. After all, if the Savior is the "firstborn from the dead,"[14] he would also be the firstborn of them, for it would be illogical for them to be exempt from such reasoning; otherwise, if their material life had not been elevated, as we explained, they would not have shared in the resurrection, either, and it is by that we shall all receive the body that is priceless after being worthless, glorious after being inglorious, powerful after being weak, and spiritual after being physical.[15] (18)

Now, if you care to read the Book of the Testament, you would find that it is said that he was snatched up into paradise; it would not be wrong to hear of that, even if from a book that is not beyond dispute.[16] There are, on the other hand, commentators who claim that the change is from one form of life to another, as the Savior said to the disciples, "You do not belong to this world, but I have chosen you," this choice causing a change from worldly things. They take as evidence of this another saying: "We know that we have passed from death to life,"[17] that is,

---

also avoided literalist questions about the enormous lifespans cited (which incidentally in the LXX differ in some cases from the Heb.).

13. Heb 9.27.   14. Col 1.18.

15. 1 Cor 15.43–44.

16. Jubilees 4.23 (at least in the sense of the Garden of Eden). So the book's canonical status is dubious, Didymus acknowledges.

17. Jn 15.19; 1 Jn 3.14.

we have moved from the death that follows vice and have trans-
ferred to the life that comes from virtue. This interpretation,
however, applies not only to Enoch but also to all the saints;
accept it accordingly if the former one is not to be adopted.

*Noah was five hundred years old when he had three sons: Shem,
Ham, and Japheth* (v.32). It should be observed that it did not say
how old he was when he began to have children, but that by the
time he was five hundred years old he had three sons. Now, it
was proper that record should be made, not of his daughters,
but of his sons, the symbolic significance being that the righteous person generates nothing female, as is recorded also of
Moses and Abraham; they had no daughters, either.[18] One is
declared blessed, for instance, when at heart one is the father
of healthy offspring, and is told, "You are blessed and will prosper. Your sons like (20) olive plants around your table; such will
be the blessing on one who fears the Lord." Daughters, on the
other hand, stand for material things; the tyrant Pharaoh, for
example, a victim of passion, did away with the male children
of the Hebrews to keep the females for himself.[19] Those who direct themselves to things here-below, in fact, are bent on doing
away with the soul's healthy offspring, and they find satisfaction in wealth and human enjoyment. What follows, for example, conveys that idea; when they became numerous, *daughters
were born to them.*[20]

18. It is in view of the opening verses of ch. 6 that Didymus has chosen for
comment this final verse of ch. 5 after omitting preceding verses, and that he
proceeds to develop his notion of the symbolic significance of the female.

19. Ps 128.3; Ex 1.12, 16. Didymus is again astray in this further comparison of male and female. While the Heb. *ben* refers directly to the male "son,"
the plural form, *benim,* as in Ps 128.3, has the sense of children of either gender. And the biblical text reports that Pharaoh's action was motivated by the
Egyptian apprehension about the captive people's rapid growth.

20. Gn 6.1.

CHAPTER SIX

HEN HUMAN beings began to be numerous on the earth, and daughters were born to them (v.1). *Numerous* can be taken in the sense of a large number, its particular and proper sense, and can also be taken to refer to the general run of people; in the book of Exodus as well it is said, "The children of Israel multiplied and became a mob."[1] There is a verse, "The general run of people say to my soul," in the sense of the mob, which does not offer sincere words. Paul also says, "We are not peddlers of the word of the Lord as are the general run of people,"[2] meaning the indifferent.

It was well said that they multiplied *on the earth;* they were common people with earthly attitudes, having much in common with the general run of people, not in heaven but *on earth. And daughters were born to them* was well put; the scoundrel generates the female and the indifferent. (22)

Now, when the angels of God saw that the daughters of men were beautiful, they took wives for themselves from them all just as they were inclined (v.2). The woman was prepared for the man by the Lord; hence the man who engages in intercourse without hope in God takes her for himself and not from God,[3] since in Adam's case as well God brought his wife to him. So the literal sense is also useful for teaching us not to do anything without God; the man interested in an honorable marriage looks not to wealth, not to noble birth, not to bodily charm, as long as

---

1. Ex 1.7.

2. Ps 3.2; 2 Cor 2.17.

3. Nautin interprets Didymus to mean that marital relations should occur only when conception is possible, and he points out that Origen's interpretation of Genesis was the same, referring to Origen, *Hom. in Gen.* 5.4; SC 244.23, note 151,1.

the woman is above reproach. The holy Abraham likewise dispatched his servant in search of a betrothed with orders for Isaac to take one conspicuous for her behavior; the Spirit inspiring the Scriptures in fact described her, "She was a virgin, whom no man had known,"[4] by "She was a virgin" highlighting her purity of soul, and by "whom no man had known" this same undefiled quality of body. In proof that not every marriage is from God, Paul writes, "Do not be mismatched with unbelievers," an appropriate requirement at the beginning of the preaching, although Paul also seems ... "If anyone has a wife who is an unbeliever,"[5] where it is clear that they had been together before conversion, and he had no wish that they be separated after conversion in case there should be an obstacle to the word.

In an allegorical sense, God joins to the man sound attitudes, piety, and wisdom in order that he may generate virtues; "for a man wisdom brings forth good sense," and Solomon says of wisdom, "I was enamored of (24) her beauty" and brought her to live with me. It is God who provides this wife; "the Lord gives wisdom."[6]

The people in the present text, then, *took wives for themselves,* not accepting that they were from God. Proof of their irrational desires is the fact that they had regard for their bodily charm, the import of the term *beautiful.* The question is raised by many people whether the angels had physical relations with the women ... or the passage has a different sense. Some say, then, that in thrall to passion and in love with their bodies demons had relations with the women; but the fact that they conceived is an impediment to such an idea, since human offspring do not come into being in that way. Others by contrast claim that angels lusted for their bodies and had intercourse with sensation, the divine plan allowing that once their desire was sated they would return to what they had left; this view is based on the allegorical interpretation of the *women* as sense and bodies, and from them they generated thoughts and actions identified as *giants.*[7] There are others, however, who claim that in the grip of

4. Gn 24.16.   5. 2 Cor 6.14; 1 Cor 7.12.
6. Prv 10.23 LXX; Wis 8.29; Prv 2.6.   7. Gn 6.4.

passion demons use vile people as instruments through which, as it were, they have relations with women and gain pleasure from their sin. (26)

The Lord God said, My spirit is not to remain forever with these human beings on account of their being carnal (v.3). God's *spirit* abides in what rises above material things, whereas what is at the level of the latter is called *carnal,* the word *carnal* referring to conditions that are material and experiential. There is, in fact, no reference to flesh in a literal sense; otherwise, no human being would have a share in the Spirit of God. In proof that there is a flesh different from this visible kind in which we are clad, Paul writes, "The mind of the flesh is hostile to God; it does not submit to God's law—in fact, it cannot, and those who are in the flesh cannot please God." In fact, if you were to take it as flesh of the visible kind, many people have been pleasing to God in it, including all the saints. Again, he says, "You are not in the flesh, however, but in the Spirit,"[8] meaning the flesh that is culpable; they were still in the flesh in living this life. Then in regard to the flesh in which we are clad, there is reference both to the irrational animal and the human being: "I shall pour out my spirit on all flesh," meaning human beings, "and all flesh will see the salvation of God." And the text of Scripture is also called flesh: "The flesh is useless; it is the spirit that gives life."[9] Taken at face value and superficially, in fact, Scripture does not give life; it would be like saying that while the person who draws geometric figures serves a purpose, the one who only draws without purpose would be less than one who portrays living beings. (28)

Since human beings became numerous, therefore, and were full of villainy, *My spirit is not to remain* in them; after all, "a holy spirit of learning will flee from deceit," deceit being the worst of passions in causing harm unexpectedly. The word *forever* means "as long as they lived like that"; it has the same force as "I shall never eat meat."[10]

So whether human beings were driven by demons to take daughters, or, as explained above, the angels had lusted in a sensual way, the spirit did not abide in them. All who come into

8. Rom 8.7–9.   9. Jl 2.28; Acts 2.17; Jn 6.63.
10. Wis 1.5; 1 Cor 8.13.

this condition through passion and sin, in fact, clearly had no share in the divine spirit, just as people who come to give aid are not deprived of the divine spirit. Now, if you are surprised that there is reference in *angels* to souls, there is no reason to wonder; both have the same intellectual nature, even if an angel has a light, fine body, and a human being a heavy, thick one. Pleasing God, in fact, is common to both, since they have a rational nature in common. If, on the other hand, you were to pose the question, "How did pre-existing souls have a desire for bodies of which they were unaware?" the reply would be that "desiring" is often used of the direction that actions take, but not what is truly desired. For example, we often chide people living badly by saying, "You desire to ruin yourself," not meaning, "You actually long for it," but, "You are doing the kind of things that lead to your ruin." So if you were to say that the souls desired bodies, it would have to be taken to mean that they were in such a condition as required (30) life in a body, since with such behavior they were unworthy of being in such a place.

They will have a life of one hundred and twenty years. Everything that God does and says, he does and says with true judgment. So, since he says by way of laying down the law, *They will have a life of one hundred and twenty years,* and since this obviously is not the case, we must hunt for a different meaning for the passage. Numbers in the Scriptures are not to be taken at face value but as having a certain rationale; they are often cited not in accord with factuality, but as having a certain rationale. The statement, remember, "I have kept for myself seven thousand men who have not bent the knee to Baal,"[11] is not factually true— so many would not have escaped the holy man's notice—but was taken in a sense suggesting that everyone who has risen above things of the senses and the world that was made in six days, and who has achieved a sabbath in an anagogical sense,

11. 1 Kgs 19.18. To this point, we noted, Didymus has declined to investigate the names and numbers in the genealogies in the text (or note discrepancies between Heb. and LXX, or the relatively lower ages than in other literatures). Now that the length of lifespans has decreased, he addresses the question, falling back on number symbolism.

is "kept" by God as a model and salutary example for others. Likewise, the number six is also taken for the creation of the world as a perfect number, as was explained in what went before. And the statement, "Six times he will be delivered from troubles," means rescue from "troubles" not on account of the number or so many times; instead, since one is subject to "troubles" for as long as one is amidst the affairs of what was made in six days, so the meaning is that they do not have the purification of rest, suggested by the seventh.[12] (32) It resembles the Savior's words to the disciples, "You do not belong to this world,"[13] having overcome the troubles in it.

Now, these preliminary remarks are intended to demonstrate that the number *one hundred and twenty* has not been cited to no purpose. Instead, this also should be noted, that in citing numbers Scripture joins to them what is appropriate, as in the six *days* of the creation of the world. Let us take an example: God, of course, did not make the world with six angels, or with six monads, or with six human beings; it was a question of time. Appropriately, then, there is mention of six *days* because time is involved in creation, and so it is proper for him to avail himself of a day instead of years or months or hours; the former are unworthy of God, and the latter suggests imperfection, for unless we know what a day is, we do not know how long an hour is. In this text, on the other hand, since there is reference to a life, he mentioned *years;* and ... the general run of people will say that it was to limit their life that God confined it to a hundred and twenty, whereas people previously were living for many years. But this is not to the point; they had the impression of living a greater number of years.

Let us see, then, the particular character of this number. Accordingly, it is said that this number is doubled when its parts are added together; if you add up its half, which is 60, its third 40, its quarter 30, its fifth 24, its sixth 20, its eighth 15, its tenth 12, its twelfth 10, its fifteenth 8, its twentieth 6, its twenty-fourth 5, its thirtieth 4, its fortieth 3, its sixtieth 2, its hundred-and-twentieth 1, that gives 240, which is double a

12. Jb 5.19.
13. Jn 15.19.

hundred and twenty. It has 15 factors, and 15 by mathematical progression makes 120. Now, 15 has clearly been taken for the most perfect degree; (34) six degrees of the same number ...[14] As well, the saying, "Give a part to the seven" (indicating the Old Testament) "and to the eight" (which symbolizes the resurrection and the New Testament), amounts to fifteen. Jews for their part, who accept only the Old, "give a part to the seven," not heeding the command to give it also "to the eight." The heretics, who set at naught the Old and "give a part to the eight," decline to supply it "to the seven." A person of the Church, in accepting both testaments, gives a part to each.

Since the number *one hundred and twenty* is doubled, then, it is a symbol of doctrine that promotes advance to the true life, which is respected with regard both to action and to contemplation, so that in doubling their life they enjoy this life that is conveyed by the number. Hence the saying, that the person who does not live by action and by contemplation is not alive, but is dead, like the woman who lives for pleasure.[15]

Now, giants were on the earth in those days. Later, when the sons of God mated with the daughters of men, and children were born to them, these were the giants of old, people of renown (v.4). While, in presenting giants, authors who are not of the faith do so from fairy stories, in sacred Scripture the term designates (36) strong men. In Isaiah, for instance, when God threatens to do away with their assets since they deserve it, he includes "a giant and a strong man" among what is being done away with. Scripture also gives that name to Goliath in testifying that he was a strong warrior. As well, when Moses made mention of the spies sent into enemy territory, they said of the place, "We saw sons of giants there," and then in commenting on their size they said, "And we were like grasshoppers before them,"[16] this being his testimony to their enormous size. If it was said before that

14. This is the kind of numerology that Didymus opted to forgo in treating of the genealogies in ch. 5 (see pp. 137–40 above), whereas in his Zechariah commentary he plunged right into them (see FOTC 111, pp. 31–32, 38, 102, 164, 200, 210, 318). For "seven" and "eight," see Eccl 11.2 and p. 176 above.

15. 1 Tm 5.6.

16. Is 3.2; 1 Sm 17.33; Dt 1.28; Nm 13.33.

demons used as instruments people in thrall to passion, you could claim that it was proof of their bodily condition that such big offspring were born to them, given the name *people of renown* from *of old,* the phrase *of old* suggesting that the tradition of their enormous size was of longstanding. If, on the other hand, you were to say that they were called *giants* on account of the vileness of their life, the view would not be unreasonable, since it was in their viciousness that they generated those subject to them and encouraged them to outrageous villainy.

Now, take note as to whether the term *later* in the passage indicates, in addition to time, what happened after the spirit of God was removed from them, God saying of it, *My spirit is not to remain with these human beings on account of their being carnal.* It was then, in fact, that (38) they were estranged from participation in it and, whether human beings or others as well, had offspring that were raised in opposition to God's will, be they only thoughts or also people.

Now, the Lord God saw that the vices of human beings were multiplied on the earth, and everyone gave himself up to pondering evil in his heart all day long. God reconsidered what he had done in creating the human being on the earth. God thought about it and said, I shall wipe off the face of the earth the human being I have made, everything from human being to cattle, everything from reptiles to birds of heaven, because I have reconsidered what I have done in creating them (vv.5–7). Even though the brute beasts did not act with free will, it was logical that they should perish along with the human being, for whom they were made to meet his needs, only an ember surviving from them along with Noah. It was also logical that human beings should perish when evil increased on the earth, because along with the evil they sinned by *pondering* it, not acting idly but *giving themselves up to* sinful behavior.

Let us give ourselves to examining the text by beginning from the opening: *The Lord God saw that the vices of human beings were multiplied on the earth.* Had he not seen their evil before? Obviously, however, he now sees with the intention of punishing them; when he does not wish to send punishment on sinners, Scripture says that he does not see them, sometimes that he is asleep, at other times that he wakes up. It is said, for instance, by one author, "He woke up to my iniquities"; (40) having experienced God's longsuffering in regard to many iniquities, he says when chastisement arrived, "He woke up to my iniquities." Some other holy person said, "The Lord woke as from a sleep, like a warrior drunk on wine";[17] after extended longsuffering he suddenly inflicts extreme retribution on those who need it, referred to as waking and drunkenness on wine on account of the suddenness and extent. It is characteristic of a good physician, you see, to treat the ailments in timely fashion, as is suggested by the clause, *The Lord God saw.*

Now, if the text proceeds, *Everyone gave himself up to pondering evil in his heart,* despite this not being true of Noah, there is no need for surprise; this is the expression to indicate the majority, as in the saying, "All your kin will be supplanters, and every friend will act with treachery."[18] On the other hand, it is possible that, since Noah was not human in every respect, having surpassed the human condition, this meant that he was not numbered among human beings, and was a god, as it is said, "Those to whom the word of God came were called gods." Similar to this is the saying, "I said in my astonishment, Every human being is a liar"; the one saying this was a god, as we explained, for if he had not been, and was a lying human being, ... the claim that "every human being is a liar" would no longer be true. But it is true, and the one who has surpassed the description "human being" as a result of virtue is not a human being, (42) as the saying goes, "For as long as there are quarreling and jealousy, are you not human and behaving as such?"[19]

In fact, evil was not committed idly by them; instead, *they gave themselves to it* deliberately, as is indicated by the phrase *in their heart.* Likewise, the phrase *from their youth* could be taken in two ways:[20] either that they were encouraged in evil from an early age, or that none of those on the model of a human being described above is an elder, even if so physically, because inclined to novelties and superficial distractions. Scripture says,

17. Lam 1.14 LXX; Ps 78.65.   18. Jer 9.4.

19. Jn 10.35; Ps 116.11; 1 Cor 3.3.

20. Nautin, in noting that the phrase does in fact not occur in the lemma, attributes the error to Didymus's disability; SC 244.43, note 159,2.

"For old age is not honored for length of time, or measured by number of years; understanding is grey hair for anyone, and a blameless life is ripe old age."[21]

This being said, it is worth interpreting the clauses, *God reconsidered what he had done in creating the human being on the earth, and he thought about it* and *I have reconsidered what I have done in creating them,* which has the same force as the verse, "I am sorry I anointed Saul king."[22] It should be said that this is to refer human feelings to God, where the words do not correspond to the sense; if there is metaphorical reference in Scripture to hands, feet, eyes, and ears, we should not think that God has a human form. Instead, we obviously interpret hands as his powers of action, eyes to mean nothing escapes him, and likewise every item in reference to a power of God ... even if (44) in another sense his eyes are those in the Church who have discernment, his hands people of action, and the rest similarly. What I mean is that, in the case of things of the senses, everything that is named, like wood, means only one thing, whereas in the case of God many terms are employed which it is possible to interpret as his different attributes—for instance, God is referred to as a spirit and a fountain, and likewise is said to have hands and feet. In no fashion, however, could such terms be applied to him if anything material were involved; a light and a spirit and a fountain have no hands.

We shall also adopt this interpretation of *thought about* and *reconsidered* in reference to one who is unchanging: in the way that people who wish to emphasize to those whom they are instructing about sin that they have gravely sinned and are unworthy of instruction say, "I have had second thoughts about having passed such things on to you," bringing them to acknowledge the sin, just so is God said to have *reconsidered,* not under the influence of feeling, but for the sake of highlighting the gravity of the sin. Not that he was in fact ignorant that they would be like that; rather, in his goodness he wanted to see if [they would be converted][23] by the laws inscribed on their

21. Wis 4.8–9.
22. Cf. 1 Sm 15.35.
23. Nautin suggests that some such term has been omitted in the text; SC

heart. We employ the figure to show that there is feeling, not in God, but in those who undergo a change in it. Take the case of a wise person ... if it transpired ... and hence disinherited, it would not be he who had had a change of heart about those who had changed if his assets go only to the righteous, this being his intention from the outset. (46)

The clause, *I shall wipe off the face of the earth the human being I have made,* was well put: he does not bring him to non-existence, nor wipe out his soul—but only *from the earth.* God's sole concern with the increase in evil was not to do away with human beings. Instead, symbolically he destroys the inhabitant of *the earth* because of his villainy; it was a villain who was the inhabitant of *the earth,* no holy one inhabiting or residing in it. A similar point is made, for instance, in Jeremiah, "Troubles shall flare up against the inhabitants of the earth," those who have taken root in the earth; the holy one had not experienced that when he said in thanksgiving, "They have almost made an end of me on the earth." And in the Apocalypse it is written, "Woe to those who inhabit the earth,"[24] not to mere residents; God's purpose is to wrench the human being from earthly things, even if attached to earthly things.

Noah, on the contrary, found favor in the sight of the Lord God (v.8). It is a wonderful and heavenly thing to *find favor in the sight of God.* It is achieved on the basis of being pleasing to him, whereas the one who is pleasing to men is not guaranteed to be pleasing to God. Take note, in fact, of what the blessed Paul says: "If I were pleasing men, I would not be a servant of Christ"; and the Psalmist, "The Lord scattered the bones of those who pleased men."[25] Those who enjoy favor with God, on the contrary, say, "He showed favor to us in the Beloved," as Mary hears it said by the angel, "Hail, full of grace, the Lord is with you."[26] It is grace, in fact, to have the Lord with you, and you have (48) the Lord with you when you can say as a result of virtue

---

244.45, note 160,3. The length to which Didymus is going to make his point about metaphorical expressions in the Scriptures could suggest that this commentary is an early work meant for readers unfamiliar with such (basic) matters.

24. Jer 7.20; Ps 119.87; Rv 8.13.   25. Gal 1.10; Ps 53.5.

26. Eph 1.6; Lk 1.28.

and good works, "If you desire proof that Christ is speaking in me." He it is, after all, who gives grace and peace, which is the prayer of the holy one, "Grace to you and peace from God the Father and our Lord Jesus Christ."[27] Now, God gives this gift only when we provide the basis for receiving it; it is said in Proverbs, "Grace and peace bring deliverance, so preserve them for yourself and thus suffer no reproach,"[28] for it is in the power of free will to preserve and practice them.

It was thus of his own doing that Noah *found favor in the sight of the Lord God;* he won grace for himself through the works of virtue, and for this he received grace from God. With those, in fact, who of themselves perform and achieve good works the God of all cooperates, and in addition he gives increase and leads to a great amount of good. Aware of this very fact, the Savior's disciples, who already of themselves had achieved the first step of faith in him, said to him in the knowledge that faith is also given by God, "Increase our faith." In other words, as "the utterance of wisdom is given through the Spirit" and "the utterance of knowledge according to the Spirit," so also "faith by the same Spirit."[29] It is impossible, in fact, to receive the faith given by God as a grace without our having the faith which depends on us, as is exactly the suggestion of "Increase our faith." Isaiah also, remember, speaking from the viewpoint of the Lord's humanity, or, if you like, from his own as well, says, "He has given me an ear to hear, and the teaching of the Lord opens my ears";[30] the hearing and the teaching given by God (50) open even these ears to hear the more divine meaning. This is the way we shall interpret as well the phrase "grace for grace,"[31] understanding that which is from God to be coming in addition to what depends on us.

Now, *he found* was well put, to show that by seeking as he should, he found, since those who do not seek as they should do not find; Scripture says, "Evil people will not seek me and will not find." Now, the fact that he sought properly is known from this, God's selecting him and making him a gift, as it were

---

27. 2 Cor 13.3; Rom 1.7.
29. Lk 17.5; 1 Cor 12.8–9.
31. Jn 1.16.

28. Prv 25.10 LXX.
30. Is 50.4–5.

placing his seal on him when he gave him the grace. After all, "it depends not on human will or exertion, but on God who shows mercy," and, "Unless the Lord build the house, in vain do its builders labor."[32]

Now, these are the generations of Noah. Noah was a righteous person, faultless by comparison with his contemporaries. Noah pleased God (v.9). The genealogy of the righteous consists not so much of people as of virtues; they are his distinguished offspring. This, to be sure, is what the Spirit in Scripture teaches;[33] when the passage comes to speak of the *generations of Noah,* it proceeds, *Noah was a righteous person, faultless by comparison with his contemporaries. Noah pleased God.*

Now, let us see what is suggested by the phrase *faultless by comparison with his contemporaries.* At first flush you would say that, with people of his time being given to unlimited evil, by comparison with them he was *faultless,* which is no great achievement if one is compared with hopeless cases. Perhaps it could be said that (52) he was perfect in differing from those who entered the ark with him; they were probably of his calibre through familiarity with the holy man. It could also be expressed in these terms: the *contemporaries* of the *righteous* have a similarity of behavior, as is suggested by the verse, "Such are the contemporaries of those who seek him." It is in fact after saying, "Who will ascend the mountain of the Lord, or who will stand in his holy place? Those with guiltless hands and pure hearts," and so on, that Scripture proceeds, "Such are the contemporaries of those who seek him," meaning that those who are adorned with the same virtue are *contemporaries.* The obverse goes to the same effect, "The children of this age are more shrewd in dealing with their contemporaries than are the children of light,"[34] the *contemporaries* of such people sharing the same condition and lifestyle.

32. Prv 1.28; Rom 9.16; Ps 127.1. The drift of comment on the verse, however, has been to the effect of requiring honest effort to lay the human basis for the divine gift.

33. Instead of the phrase "the inspired Scripture," Didymus speaks of "the Spirit in Scripture," *to syngraphikon pneuma,* where the stress falls strongly on inspiration.

34. Ps 24.6, 3–4; Lk 16.8.

We should likewise take *faultless* as pertaining to the human condition. Such perfection Paul said consists in knowing in part when he refers to what is perfect, "But when perfection comes, what is partial will come to an end."[35] All perfection achieved by human beings is partial in comparison with the perfection in the age to come. Let us take an example for clarification: the person who is *faultless* in the basic letters of the alphabet is faulty by comparison with the one acquainted with rules of grammar. The Apostle himself says, "We know in part and we prophesy in part," but goes on to say of himself and his ilk, "Let those of us who are faultless be of the same mind," and, "We speak God's wisdom among the faultless." In other words, by comparison with the age to come, as we said, which will be knowledge "face to face,"[36] our life here is imperfect, even if it succeeds in reaching the summit. (54)

Now, references to Noah as *righteous, faultless,* and *pleasing to God* should be taken together, even if there is an order in the words. That is to say, it was because he was *righteous* and *faultless,* in fact, that he was *pleasing to God,* his being *pleasing* presupposing his being *faultless* and *righteous.* It was not because he was *pleasing* that he became *righteous* and *faultless*—instead, because he emerged as *righteous* and *faultless,* he was shown to be *pleasing to God.*[37] Now, there is no need to be surprised that while Noah was of such a fine character, he is referred to as a human being. We have often observed that the term "human being" has many senses, not only a pejorative sense, as in the statement, "As long as there are quarreling and jealousy among you, are you not human and behaving like human beings?" And in reference to the devil's spreading wicked thoughts, Scripture says, "A hostile human being has done this."[38] In this case, on the other hand, in addition to his nature, there is reference also to the human

35. 1 Cor 13.10.

36. 1 Cor 13.9; Phil 3.15; 1 Cor 2.6; 13.12.

37. Whereas on the one hand Didymus has declined to delve into the significance of numbers and names in the manner of Philo, on the other he plumbs the meaning of particular words, like these epithets applied to Noah (again placing an accent on the role of human effort) and even the term ἄνθρωπος.

38. 1 Cor 3.3; Mt 13.28.

being in the proper sense of preserving the aspect of being "in the image."

Now, the clause, *being faultless he pleased God,* was also well put. In other words, having already attained perfection *he pleased God;* when one pleases God, one sometimes, not always, pleases also righteous men, not to mention others. After all, if there is commendation for the one who is pleasing to the righteous, it is only after pleasing God.

Now, Noah had three sons: Shem, Ham, and Japheth (v.10). He had three sons, and this is the number of those Noah fathered; it was not mentioned before this, either, that he had further (56) children.[39] The literal sense is clear; if, on the other hand, you were to consider the anagogical sense, you would say that anyone fathering two children would produce the symbols of a materialistic attitude (two being a characteristic of matter, in that it is divisible), whereas the father of three is said to be perfect in that as one he is self-sufficient and bears the image of the Creator because he is productive, and yet with the removal of the number one he forms a two, so that clearly by addition a three is formed. Now, if to human things, suggested by two, reason is added, they no longer remain material and human because they are sharing in integrity; there is need not merely to act, but also with integrity, if one is to win commendation. You could also apply this allegorically to the perfection of soul; there is need for some passion first to be engendered in the soul, then for a disposition to occur, and thus for a move into action.[40] Now, we are speaking of passion, not in a pejorative sense, but as a kind of imprint on the soul with a view to a virtuous impulse. These three stages also occur in reverse. Such, then, are the three offspring of the zealous person, leaving aside for the time being the propensity to indifferent things.

Consideration should also be given to finding some benefit in the meaning of the names: Shem means "perfect," Japheth "broadening" or "beauty," and Ham "audacious," "headstrong,"

39. Didymus is adverting to the mention of Noah and his sons earlier at 5.32. See p. 140 above.

40. Note from the FOTC editor: Nautin remarks that a Stoic influence is evident here; SC 244.57, note 165,2.

"heat," or "extension."[41] Now, what other offspring are so becoming to the righteous as perfection, broadening, or beauty, all of which are signs of virtue? Beauty along with broadening, in fact, causes one to leave the "broad way that leads to destruction."[42] If (58) the meaning of Ham as "audacious" or "headstrong," "heat," or "extension" is taken in an unfavorable sense, it could mean a wicked son with behavior befitting him, or in a favorable sense a perfect person; the virtuous are not subject to force, since "the violent take the kingdom by force." Such a person is also audacious against the hostile powers, and so forth, as blessed Paul says, "Our struggle is not against flesh and blood," and he is also headstrong and audacious, not being headstrong in the direction of evil but proving warm towards virtue and "ardent in spirit,"[43] as a result of which he is removed also from human things.

Now, the earth was corrupt in God's eyes, and filled with lawlessness. The Lord God saw that the earth was utterly corrupt, because all flesh had corrupted his way on the earth (vv.11–12). By *corruption of the earth* there is implied, not disappearance of such a fine element into non-existence, but the enormity of people's sins. By metonymy it refers by *earth* to people, as also the Psalmist says, "Let all the earth bow down to you and sing your praises," and again, "Praise the Lord, all the earth"; when it says, "Heaven and earth were completed," and, "Let the earth put forth,"[44] this is the element signified. (60) Now, so grave was the evil of people (referred to as *earth*) that God *saw* it, when in his great goodness he passed over even their serious sins; Scripture says, "If you, Lord, were to mark iniquities, Lord, who would stand?" It is not every day he inflicts his wrath, then, but only when the measure of sins becomes so extreme that it is said, as in the prophet Jonah, "The cry of evil has risen up to God," and in reference to Sodom, "The cry of Sodom and Gomorrah has become extreme, and their sins very grave,"[45] as is similar also in this case, *The earth was filled with lawlessness,* and so on.

41. The meanings have been arrived at by popular etymology by considering similar forms or partial elements of the proper names.

42. Mt 7.13.

43. Mt 11.12; Eph 6.12; Rom 12.11.

44. Pss 66.4; 96.1; Gn 2.1; 1.11.

45. Ps 130.3; Jon 1.2; Gn 18.20.

He saw, not that previously he was in ignorance, but as an indication of his ability to survey in the sense of imposing punishment, as in the clause, *God saw that the earth was utterly corrupt.* By *corruption* he refers to the evil and its punishment, Scripture often referring to it this way, as in the statement by Paul, "If anyone corrupts God's temple, God will corrupt that person."[46] In other words, whoever by licentiousness sins by causing corruption of God's temple will be found corrupted by retribution, corruption in this case implying retribution. Now, it is *corruption* to be given over to a perverse attitude; this is the ultimate penalty, in fact. We should not think, however, as do the Manicheans,[47] that it is the leftover, formless matter that produces *corruption of the earth* by circulating around it; people would in fact be blameless if the damage were caused by what could not be put in order by God. Instead, by *corruption of the earth* is meant depravity of morals, as was said before,[48] whereby human beings (62) *corrupt the way* of God himself, which they had received as the good path to blessedness. In such a condition are people who hear the words of Jesus without putting them into action.

Now, if by *flesh* it refers to the human being, as has often been said, we should examine whether the clause, *All flesh had corrupted his way on the earth,* does not suggest that each person had deviated from his proper intention. That *flesh* stands for the human being is clear from the statements, "I shall pour out my spirit on all flesh," and, "He is entering into judgment with all flesh."[49] All Noah's *contemporaries,* therefore, had become earthly and fleshly, and each had deviated from *his way* which he had received; as the way had been given them by God, it is said that it was received from him. So they had corrupted their way or God's way; both interpretations are possible.

God said to Noah, In my view the whole human race has reached its critical time, insofar as the earth is filled with lawlessness on their

46. 1 Cor 3.17.

47. The view that Didymus attributes to the Manicheans, Nautin claims, is in fact that of Hermogenes; SC 244.61, note 167,1.

48. The reference is perhaps to a section of the ms on Gn 2 now missing.

49. Jl 2.28; Jer 25.31.

account (v.13). Many parts of the Scriptures contain a factual reference that is very useful for the general run of people; living at the level of sense and appearances, these people do not attain to what is truly important and (64) beneficial. Let us take some examples. Jesus healed the man who was blind from birth; he ordered Lazarus, who had been four days in the tomb, to come out; and again he raised the man who had been completely paralyzed for thirty-eight years.[50] Now, in their physical enactment these things were also symbolic: the man blind from birth represents recovery of sight by a soul that had never enjoyed sight on account of its falling victim to sin and ignorance from a tender age; likewise, the man who was already foul-smelling and was despaired of through falling away from the blessed life was shown symbolically to have returned to that life through Jesus; the victim of paralysis who was healed represents the recovery of a soul that had fallen into numbness. Now, these latter events are more admirable and more important than bodily healing to the extent that the soul's being is more valuable than the body's, a fact unknown to the general run of people.

The one who gives this sort of explanation to them, therefore, does them a more useful service, and in the present passage the factual reference contains a considerable benefit for the general run of people that is more comprehensive.[51] What in fact is it saying? *The whole human race has reached its critical time on the earth,* just as Peter also says that the flood was held in check by "God's longsuffering" to allow an opportunity for repentance. It was demonstrated before, remember, that the construction of the ark took a hundred years so that on seeing it people should ask the reason and seize the *critical time* for repentance. Now, by *critical time* here we should not think of what some people call a horoscope; (66) fate does not determine events—rather, everything happens by God's decree.[52]

50. Jn 9.1–7; 11.39, 43; 5.5–9.

51. Didymus has here outlined his principles about the relative value of factual (he speaks of *historia*) and more elevated levels of meaning in a biblical text. Nautin (referring to Origen, *In Matth.* 10.9, 10.29–39, 11.4) observes that Didymus agrees with Origen that most Christians do not achieve knowledge of the deeper meaning of Scripture; SC 244.65, note 168,2.

52. 1 Pt 3.20. Though the former "demonstration" may refer to Didymus's

Hence the clause *The whole human race has reached its critical time on the earth* should be taken to mean that such a stage had been reached in people's sinning, so to say, that an imposition of punishment had to be applied, as Scripture says, "The sins of the Amorites are not yet complete,"[53] meaning that their sins are not yet so great as to deny them repentance. It is not, in fact, day by day that God vents his wrath, despite sins being committed; instead, he does so with a view to providing "room for repentance"[54] and giving to sinners a *critical time* for self-condemnation. When, however, the point is reached where there is no longer the *critical time* to repent, the *critical time* has been reached for them to suffer.

Now, once mention has been made of sin reaching its zenith, there is need to note that one person's being full of sin is not the same thing as a whole people's; in the general run of people you can find sins of all kinds. For example, one person is prodigal, another miserly, one bold, another timid, and again one is licentious, another foolish. In regard to an individual, on the other hand, you cannot find these opposite vices: excess and defect; while it is possible to find all the virtues in a person, since they are interrelated, but not all the vices, for the reasons given.

So much by way of digression; let us go back to the beginning. *The whole human race has reached its critical time.* No one has sins of such a kind that concession is allowed him; and just as a skillful physician sets a *critical time* for the patient to take food, even if it is at night, depending on the nature of the complaint, so too with this statement: (68) since human beings had reached the extreme stage of sinning that would result in the flood, it would happen because of the unforgivable sins they committed. Now, one should not think that the statement *the whole human race has reached its critical time* was a lie even if eight were saved in the ark; here the general statement has the sense of the majority. The reference in *the whole human race* is in the

---

remarks on fatalism above (SC 233.218), he does make this same point about the ark also in comment on 7.6. See p. 92 above and p. 170 below.

53. Gn 15.16.
54. Heb 12.17.

sense of the saying, "Where there are quarreling and jealousy among you, are you not human?"[55] Noah was not included because he surpassed the human condition. And so it was true that *the whole human race had reached its critical time,* when the word *human* refers to sinning.

The phrase *in my view* does not occur idly, either; it belongs to no creature to know the *critical time* when someone has done what deserves his being pardoned no longer. And it is necessary that no creature would know this; if one had the knowledge of hearts, one would not lend help, but would promptly turn from those in sin. In fact, it belongs only to unsurpassable goodness—goodness of essence, goodness that cannot be diminished—to see what is hidden and to know the *critical time.* If, on the other hand, one shared God's goodness in disposition, one would still be ignorant of the degree of guilt and reasons for the sins; God knows all this and is aware of the *critical time* for retribution—hence his saying *in my view* and *the earth is filled with lawlessness on their account,* which is rightly said since it is not for the sins of others that the punishment falls on them. Now, it is clear from this as well that fate did not impose (70) such a death on them; since *it is filled with lawlessness on their account,* the *critical moment* was *reached,* which would not have happened if they had not sinned.

Lo, I am going to destroy them and the earth. From this as well emerges the lovingkindness and goodness of God in foretelling what was to come, his purpose being to suppress the evil through fear of what was expected. This happened also in the case of the Ninevites when the prophet Jonah was told, "In three days Nineveh will be overthrown."[56] Consequently, then, he foretells this to the righteous man and gives instructions for the ark to be built, proposing its building as a more compelling incitement to repentance than any proclamation; and he promises to *destroy them and the earth,* since they needed it. After all, there have been many rebukes delivered by God to make sinners repent, for "he wishes that everyone be saved and come

55. 1 Cor 3.3.
56. Jon 3.4, the LXX replacing the "forty" of the Heb., probably under influence of the previous verse.

to the knowledge of the truth": "How many times have I wanted to gather your children together, in the way a bird gathers
its chicks under its wings, and you would not."[57] Pressure, in
fact, does not force people to be good, nor is it possible; good
of that kind is no longer good. Instead, when God, who knows
everything, does not succeed despite many admonitions in ob-
taining obedience from the admonished, these are the ones
mentioned in the verse whom he *destroys,* to their betterment in
his view. But *the earth* is also destroyed—that is, what is on the
earth, the sense here of *earth*—and rightly so: (72) when people perish, it is necessary that what exists for them perish with
them. And since an ember is left behind in the person of Noah
and those with him, similarly embers of the other living things
were also preserved.

    *Make for yourself, then, an ark of hewn timber. You will make cab-
ins in the ark, and you will cover it with pitch inside and out. This is
the way you will make the ark: three hundred cubits long, five hundred
wide, and three hundred high. You will gather material to make the
ark, and round it off a cubit from the top, making a door on the sides
and building two or three decks below the waterline. For my part, however—lo, I am about to bring a flood of water upon the earth to destroy
all flesh in which there is a breath of life under heaven: whatever is on
earth will perish* (vv.14–17). The literal meaning makes a lot of
sense:[58] Noah is ordered to make the ark *of hewn timber,* firstly to
avoid wasting much time dividing it into planks, and secondly,
and more to the point, so that the ark would be safer if made
from whole timbers. After all, it was going to hit mountains and
meet with no little swell, which it would not survive if not made
of whole timbers. Now, it was also helpful for him to order the
making of *cabins,* or separate spaces, and this for two reasons:
to avoid living mixed up with the animals he was due to bring
on board with him, (74) and to ensure the cohesion of the
structure which, being *three hundred cubits long, five hundred wide,*

----

57. 1 Tm 2.4; Mt 23.37.

58. For one who has just above declared a literal interpretation insufficient
and a spiritual meaning "more admirable and more important" (see p. 157),
Didymus spends a lot of time analyzing the Yahwist's description of the ark
and commenting on its appropriateness.

and three hundred high, would have been weaker if not bound together.[59] It was *covered with pitch inside and out* to prevent any water entering. It was also good that its length was greater than its width for better ease of movement, and comparable with the shape of vessels. If, on the other hand, you were to point out that it was square down below, this too would not be illogical, since it was made not principally for sailing but for safety, and would otherwise have quickly capsized if it had not been rectangular. It was *rounded off* precisely to ensure that the water slid by and the waves did not strike it like a rock of the same height. Orders were also given appropriately for *making a door on the sides* ...[60] It was appropriate to build *two or three decks below the waterline* to provide sufficient space to contain the animals that entered and what was needed for their food.

The statement, *For my part, however—lo, I am about to bring a flood of water upon the earth to destroy all flesh in which there is a breath of life under heaven: whatever is on earth will perish,* (76) on the one hand is meant as a spur, as was said before, and on the other it suggests that the creatures on the land and in the air would perish, perhaps those in the water surviving ...[61]

I shall establish my covenant with you (v.18). A covenant "on oath" does not seem to have been made by God with Noah, as Symmachus and Aquila render it.[62] In case he should be at a loss for words, the future was revealed to Noah so that he should retain hope regarding what was due to happen and also teach his contemporaries that "God imposed this because of sins, and you have been saved as a result of righteousness." The purpose was that the shame of vice might be revealed as well as the desirability of virtue—not that virtue's reward is pleasure, but that from this form of punishment there is no rest for the zealous person, even if not subject to it. Now, in this case *establish* suggests stability. (78)

59. It would have escaped Didymus's notice that the LXX ship is a hundred times larger than the Heb. one.
60. Two lines are missing from the ms.
61. Twelve lines are missing from the ms.
62. We have not seen Didymus making mention of the alternative versions available in a copy of the Hexapla. Nautin suggests that in this rare case he finds them in Origen; SC 244.77, note 174,1.

You are to board the ark, you, your sons, your wife, and your sons'
wives with you (v.18). In the Gospel the Savior said that "on the
day of judgment people will give an account for every careless
word,"[63] by careless word meaning ... containing nothing useful. Now, if people are bidden not to utter it, much more is it the
case that the divine sayings contain nothing of the kind, only
containing useful things ... in the present text. When Noah
was boarding the ark, God placed his sons with him, and his
son's wives with his wife, whereas when the time came for dis-
embarking on dry land at the conclusion of the flood, the statement is conveyed in these terms: "And God said to Noah, Leave
the ark, you and your wife, your sons and your sons' wives with
you."[64] In other words, when the destruction of humankind was
imminent, it behoved righteous men to show fellow-feeling and
thus to refrain from marital intercourse. He therefore separated wives from husbands in the words, *You are to board, you, your*
sons, your wife, and your sons' wives with you, whereas when it was
clear that procreation was once more assured, he returned his
wife to Noah, as we explained, in the words, "Leave the ark, you
and your wife, your sons and your sons' wives." The fact that
God, as is his wont, did not say this without purpose, but deliberately, we can assert and adduce the Gospel in support, where
it is said by the Savior, "No one can serve two masters: either he
will hate the one and love the other, or be devoted to the one
and despise the other. You cannot serve God and mammon,"
service of mammon meaning avarice, and in every vice (80) ...
It is in fact impossible to serve both vice and virtue; "everyone
who commits sin is a slave to sin,"[65] and all ... to hate evil; those
who love ... evil is hated.

"Either he will hate the one and love the other"—the virtuous person who hates evil loves God—"or be devoted to the
one and despise the other," which ... is a precise statement: one
has devotion, not love, for vice. No one, in fact, acts through

---

63. Mt 12.36.

64. Gn 8.16. Again Didymus reveals his attachment to the literal sense of
the text, just as he has shown his interest in the factual character of the Yahwist's ark.

65. Mt 6.24; Jn 8.34.

love for ... but is drawn to have devotion, nor are they said to hate God, only to despise. Hence the proper term ... in each case, love for God and hatred of vice by the zealous person, and in turn the villain is guilty of being devoted to vice, while God is despised by such a person.[66] No one would, in fact, claim that someone despised sin or hated God, even if, by way of blame, villains, on account of being inclined to vice, are said to hate God, as in the verse, "Lord, did I not hate those who hate you?" Strictly speaking, in fact, he does not do so; he is only said to be drawn to hate him, as was mentioned. Despising requires such precision and analysis in the light of the further statement by the Savior himself, "Everyone who acknowledges me before others I also shall acknowledge, and everyone who denies"—he did not say "in me"—"I also shall deny him."[67] In other words, anyone confessing God does so in Christ; and anyone denying him does not do so in Christ; so it is necessary that the confession be in him ... directed not to such people but only to those who pretend in words to confess him; "they profess to know God, (82) but they deny him by their actions," and, "This people honors me with their lips, but in their heart they are far from me"[68]—in other words, the one who is confessed is in the one who confesses, and the one who confesses is in the one who is confessed. But in case you think the same is true of the saying, "I am in the Father and the Father is in me,"[69] in the one case in the one confessed ... whereas the other ... which is indicated in the clause, "Whoever will acknowledge me," the clause "I also shall acknowledge him" ... for God does not share in man ... from God who acknowledges.

Likewise, then, ... it was said also in reference to Noah's sons, himself, his wife, and their wives, but as we did well to

66. While again we note Didymus's precise textual analysis, it is the subtext that has become the text that is being analyzed, not the lemma. And as often with Didymus one subtext leads to a series of others before he returns to the lemma.

67. Ps 139.21; Mt 10.32–33.

68. Ti 1.16; Is 29.13; Mt 15.8.

69. Jn 14.10. Much of Didymus's argument arises from the occurrence of "confesses in" (= "acknowledges") in the Greek text of Mt 10.32.

observe ... *You are to board the ark, you and your sons with you;* it was not he who was saved on account of them, but they on his account and through assistance from him. This is confirmed by what follows, when God says to Noah, "Because I have found you to be righteous in my view by comparison with your contemporaries";[70] his greatness of soul is indicated by the text's saying not simply "righteous" but "in God's view."

Of all cattle and of all flesh two by two of them all (v.19). Anyone knowing the properties of numbers, and aware that in the Scriptures seven is mentioned as having many privileges, while two is proper to matter, (84) as mentioned before, will realize that the number seven is applied in what follows for the clean animals, and two in this place for the unclean. And if one were to raise the further question of how two is understood if the Law had not yet been given regarding clean and unclean things, you could give the explanation that to the righteous the arcane provisions of the Law were perceived in advance. And if that person were at a loss to explain how a single person had such control of so many animals as to make them board the ark, let him be told that the fulfillment of the order with God's cooperation was given to the righteous man, and the taming of wild beasts by God is not beyond belief. And if the images of all animals in something like a sheet was revealed to Peter, chief of the apostles,[71] why is it beyond belief if, in view of the world's being destined to be reborn, he cooperated in bidding the righteous man make them board so that from them there could later be offspring?

You will bring them into the ark to keep them alive with you; they will include male and female. Of every kind of birds, of every kind of cattle, and of every kind of reptiles of all kinds on the earth, two by two, all of them will come aboard to you, male and female, to be kept alive with you (vv.19–20). Now, (86) it should be mentioned that by

70. Gn 7.1.

71. Acts 10.11–12. The question of the numbers of animals brought aboard the ark is complicated by the two traditions represented, one (the Priestly) staying with two, the other (the Yahwist, in 7.2) varying between seven and two in the case of clean and unclean respectively. Didymus wants both to utilize number symbolism as well as to defend factuality.

kind is meant species, *kind* sometimes being used for species. And ...[72]

Now, for your part take a quantity of all the foods you will eat, and load them on board with you; they will serve as food for you and them (v.21). ... not only of himself and those with him was confided to the righteous man, but responsibility also for the brute beasts; it was right that he should have concern for the lives of his cattle. The clause *load on board with you* has this sense: Gather the foods where you are living, and where the other creatures have no access; if they were lodged in those places, they would have no hesitation in falling upon the food and causing a shortage ...[73]

Noah did all that the Lord God instructed him; this is what he did (v.22). It is a great compliment if, after your executing a command with understanding, someone who can be trusted to make a right judgment says (88) that you discharged the task entrusted to you, this being the way virtue proceeds. It is in fact ... not in the way ordered ...

Every action discharged without the proper intention is incomplete, even if its performance is complete. The righteous man, by contrast, is confirmed as having done ... The Savior, in fact, also teaches this in saying, "Show mercy, and you will have mercy shown you," but he means that mercy should not be shown to the sound of trumpets, that is, not to make the indigence of the needy an occasion for pomp and circumstance. "Be perfect," he says, remember, "as your heavenly Father is perfect";[74] God shares what he has without receiving from anyone else. For your part likewise, be zealous in sharing, as blessed Paul also recommends, "It is a more blessed thing to give than to receive."[75] It is not the one who receives who imitates God, in fact; God is in receipt of nothing from anybody, instead being the source of all good things. So the one who imitates God gives.

---

72. At this point seventeen lines of the ms are blank.
73. At this point thirteen lines of the ms are blank.
74. Mt 5.7; 6.2; 5.48.
75. Acts 20.35, a dominical saying.

CHAPTER SEVEN

HE LORD GOD said to Noah, Board the ark, you and all your house, because I have found you to be righteous in my view by comparison with your contemporaries (v.1). It thus appears that only these eight people composed *all the house;* they did not include a servant, either because at that stage there was no one reduced to servitude or because they did not have any such. (90) By *house* in this case, then, he refers to the family of eight, the word often being used in this sense, though strictly referring to a building. You would find the same to be true of a city; in the Gospel, for instance, it is said, "They brought him"—Jesus, that is—"to the crest of the mountain on which their city was built," in which case the word "city" means what was constructed and built, whereas in the statement, "When Jesus entered Jerusalem, the whole city was in turmoil," it means the group of people contained in the city. Likewise in the sentence, "Jesus began to reproach the cities in which most of his deeds of power had been done, because they did not repent";[1] repentance does not occur in inanimate or material things. The word "house" signifies a building in the statement, This house ... assembly or gathering when it is said ... the royal official, the prison guard, and the house ...

It proceeds to give the reason for boarding the ark, *because I have found you to be righteous in my view.* It did not say simply *because I have found you*—Abel also being righteous as well as Enoch, who hoped "to invoke the name of the Lord God";[2] instead, *because I have found you to be righteous in my view by comparison with your contemporaries*—of that time, that is. It does not

1. Lk 4.29; Mt 21.10; Mt 11.20.
2. Gn 4.26.

specify the fact that it was on account of his virtue that his children, who shared in it, were also saved; but by *contemporaries* it suggests, as was mentioned, a similarity of behavior, (92) as we cited in what went before, in addition to which is the reference to people of the same behavior as *contemporaries:* "An account will be required of your contemporaries for all the righteous blood shed on the earth."[3] Among his righteous contemporaries, if we take those who were righteous with him, he personally was found *righteous in my view,* not every righteous person being *righteous in my view;* his sons and their wives were righteous only in the view of Noah. It is instead such a great thing to be *righteous in God's view* that it is said, "The stars are not pure in his view," nor the other lights, and in the Psalms it is said, "No living being will be found righteous in your sight," and again another saying goes, spoken in the person of all the righteous, "All our righteousness like the rags of a woman in her period."[4]

From the cattle that are clean take on board with you, seven by seven, male and female, and from the cattle that are unclean two by two, male and female, and from the birds of heaven that are clean seven by seven, male and female, and from the birds that are unclean two by two, male and female, to raise offspring throughout the whole earth (vv.2–3). It was logical for him to give orders for taking clean animals on board *seven by seven;* since people, including those in the ark, would have need of them for both food and sacrifice, they accordingly took a larger number so that (94) from them there might come a more numerous offspring proportionate to their needs, whereas in the case of the others ... so great a need he gave orders for them to be taken on board *two by two.* Now, if there is need to call on natural science ... one would say as before that since a unit of two is divisible and is appropriate to matter, the number two suits the unclean. Proof that two is to be avoided is the Savior's calling the two into "one new humanity":[5] one from the circumcision and one from the nations, *taking* them *on board* together in unity of life according

3. Mt 23.35–36.

4. Jb 25.5; Ps 143.2; Is 64.5 LXX.

5. Eph 2.15. On the reasons behind the numbering of animals in chs 6 and 7, see note 71 on p. 164 in the previous chapter.

to the Gospel, which the saints of old enjoyed, now that there was no difference between Hellenism and Judaism. After all, it was only skills that gave rise to images and hence to idolatry, and only from the time of the Law that Judaism arose. So the premier way of life lived by human beings—namely, Christianity, even if not so called—existed in accord with the generally held ideas, which the Savior also ... proclaimed: "In everything do to others as you would have them do to you."[6] Now, this forms part of the generally held idea: what you do not want to experience you should not do to your neighbor. And it forms part of the generally held idea for this reason: for a person not to be defenseless before God. Later, however, when the generally held idea was distorted, the written form was given, not in opposition to it, but ... human beings to it, Scripture saying, for example, "He gave the Law as a help." Likewise, the Gospel has also been proclaimed throughout the world lest anyone claim not to have been reminded ... generally held ideas.[7] (96)

So much for the literal sense, then. On the other hand, it should also be said that the clean animals ... to be taken on board *seven by seven* ... saying it was logical in the historical sense to have a greater number because the people intended to use them for sacrifice and food, and further that, because of the significance of numbers, the number is much celebrated in Scripture ... the seventh day, I mean, "God rested" ... It is, in fact, as the ungenerated that the experts ... seven, being virginal and without father or mother, which is its meaning. All the numbers in the decade generate or are generated by a factor of 2 or 3 except 7; for example, 1 generates 2, 2 generates 4 after having been generated by 1, 4 generates 8 after itself having been generated by 2, 5 generates 10, 6 is generated without generating, whereas 7 is neither generated by lower numbers nor generates higher numbers below 10; and when multiplied by 3, 2 generates 6, and 3 generates 9. 7 also has another peculiarity:

6. Mt 7.12. Didymus has several times (e.g., twice in comment on 3.6–8) stated this Stoic principle, held also by Origen, of commonly-held ideas implanted by God. In this case he has chosen one such moral axiom, the so-called "Golden Rule," found in Old and New Testaments, rabbinic commentary, Aristotle.

7. Rom 1.20; Is 8.20 LXX; Mt 26.13.

if you make a series of 7 numbers beginning with 1 and double them, you get an even number that is a square: 1, 2, 4, 8, 16, 32, 64, which is a square, since 8 times 8 is 64, and also a cube, since 4 times 4 times 4 is 64. Further, a series of 7 numbers starting from the monad and tripled amounts to 729, which is itself a square and a cube: 1, 3, 9, 27, 81, 243, 729, which as was said is a square as well as being a cube—a square, (98) since 27 times 27 equals 729, and a cube, since 9 times 9 times 9 equals 729. While the square symbolizes solidity, the cube ... What has been said about numbers is not without point, the truth being that no detail in the divine writings is superfluous.

To what has already been stated there is need to add that a remnant as an ember was necessarily preserved in the ark, the danger being that if another beginning was made, a heresy about two creators would have emerged. You see, even if, despite the provision of such convincing proof, the heretics come up with different divinities,[8] much more would they have done so if they had discovered persuasive proofs for their wicked argument.

After seven more days I shall send rain on the earth for forty days and forty nights, and I shall wipe off the face of the earth all the life I have made (v.4). This prediction was also made in God's loving-kindness for correcting ... by hearing of a flood coming in seven days, just as in what went before we cited also the preaching of Jonah, which itself (100) was conducted for the conversion of the Ninevites, something that actually happened. *For forty days and forty nights* such a deluge occurred high and low as to rise above the mountains fifteen cubits.[9] Now, even if the number for the duration of the flood has significance, let us examine how to take the clause, *I shall wipe off the face of the earth all the life I have made.* Some commentators take *the life* ... in the belief that after the incineration of the former world, as the Stoics think, this one came into existence, and that the same things were held in potency in matter from that world corresponding to this. They were too casual, however, in substantiating their

8. Didymus is referring to dualistic theories about creation and the Scriptures proposed by Marcion and gnostic myths.

9. Gn 7.20.

teachings; it is impossible for there to be identity in the movements of souls of the world already made and those of the one
to come without any difference.[10]

Noah did everything the Lord God commanded him (v.5). A person's testimony is to have done *everything the Lord God commanded,* as was said in what preceded. Blessed David was also accorded such wonderful approval, since it was of him that God said
he found "David son of Jesse to be a man after my own heart,
who will carry out all my wishes."[11] (102)

*Now, Noah was six hundred years old when the deluge came upon
the earth* (v.6). … the goodness of God in allowing the making
of the ark to take a hundred years, a fact that emerges from
Noah's being five hundred years old when he began it[12] … was
done wisely by the one establishing everything, so that on seeing the novelty of the construction, hearing and learning the
reason for it, people might desist from evildoing. If they had
heard and repented, the flood would not have been sent. That
it was out of longsuffering and with the purpose of summoning
people to repentance that this happened Peter, the chief of the
apostles, confirms in writing in his letter about the Savior: "in
which also he went and made a proclamation to the spirits in
prison, who in former times did not obey, when God waited pa-
tiently in the days of Noah during the building of the ark." Let
us note in this as well that it said that while many sins had been
committed *upon the earth,* God in his wish not to inflict … in
his patience did it to provide "an opportunity for repentance."[13]

Likewise, after the transgression he gave the Law as a deter-
rent, and to the prescriptions he added the support of threats.
You will also find this in the …[14] Israel, "the Lord's portion and

10. Nautin observes that while Origen had propounded the Stoic view, he
voiced the latter reservation stated by Didymus; SC 244.101, note 185,2.

11. 1 Sm 13.14; Acts 13.22.

12. A somewhat vulnerable conclusion from Gn 5.32.

13. 1 Pt 3.19–20; Wis 12.10.

14. Though the lemma does not explicitly refer to God's intentions in
having the ark built before the flood, Didymus reintroduces the theme, and
begins a series of other texts to complement it, starting with the parable of
the infertile vineyard and its punishment in Is 5.1–7, a subtext which then
becomes the text to be elaborated with others.

son of God," transgressed his commands despite God's doing everything for them. What in fact does he say in Isaiah? "The beloved had a vineyard in a choice position on a hilltop," referring by "hilltop" to the kingdom, and by "choice position" meaning the teaching in Law and Prophets. "I planted a vine *soreq*" (which means "chosen")—(104) in other words, he had planted his people to be a "royal priesthood" and chosen vine. "I also built a tower" to repel marauding foes; the tower is the word of teaching that both stands guard and repulses the onset of foes. After it is built, the people are told, "If the ire of the ruler rises against you, do not leave your post."[15] He makes a wall and encircles it with a fence, suggesting the safety provided by the angels. Despite all that was done, it continued to be equally fruitless. Hence he says, "What more shall I do for my vineyard that I have not done for it?" I left nothing undone, and hence since they cannot cite anything that had to be done, I shall say, "I shall tell you what I shall do for my vineyard": I shall take away what I have given it, "I shall break down its wall, and it will be trampled down; I shall remove the fence, and it will be exposed to robbery." In other words, it helps to withdraw the protection of the angels from those who gained nothing from it, the purpose being that they may see the troubles they incur and long to be converted. Hence he also says by way of rebuke, "I shall instruct the clouds not to send rain on it," a reference to the prophets and the ministers of the spiritual rain, of whom it is said, "Let the clouds rain down righteousness."[16] After all, it did not use this rain properly, producing thorns instead of grapes; hence Israel became a ruin through its failure to accept such wonderful benefits. Likewise ... the flood was sent because the people in their headstrong ways refused to receive benefit. (106) ... the end of the world will result from a dearth of virtue, as the Savior also said, "When the Son of man comes, will he find faith on the earth?"[17]

Noah, his sons, his wife, and his sons' wives boarded the ark with

---

15. Sir 17.17; 1 Pt 2.9; Ex 19.6; Eccl 10.4. The rare Heb. term *soreq* occurs in the LXX of Is 5.2 for "chosen," as Didymus says.

16. Is 45.8.

17. Lk 18.8.

him on account of the floodwaters. The birds, the clean animals, the unclean animals, and all the reptiles of the earth, two by two, embarked with Noah on the ark, male and female, as God had commanded him (vv.7–9). It is obvious that when certain signs of the flood had emerged and had become apparent to Noah, such as the land's dampness and the like, Noah embarked on the ark without a great lapse of time. Now, matters dealing with the entry of his sons with Noah and of their wives with his wife were mentioned before; it was not fitting for them to enjoy marital intercourse when such punishment was befalling everyone. Hence for the time, in order that they might abstain from it, he separated the couples, restoring it on disembarkation from the ark. It also says that the animals boarded together, mentioning the clean ones first in order of rank; and you can insert here what was said before when Noah was ordered by God to make the animals embark on the ark, to avoid our repeating the same things.[18] (108)

After seven days the floodwaters came upon the earth in the six hundredth year of Noah's life on the twenty-seventh day of the second month (vv.10–11). On account of the flood being sent after such a number of days, certain commentators have made the observation that it was by reason of the perfection of the work that it was mentioned, a perfect flow of water having occurred, which happened for the salvation of the world. The removal of sinners from the earth, in fact, and the beginning of a virtuous life for the human race is something perfect. Just as it is the practice of a good physician not only to excise an ulcer from the body, but also to make flesh grow in the place of the ulcerated part, so it is God's role to destroy sinners in order for those living in accordance with righteousness to make a beginning. In fact, there later came Abraham, Isaac, and Jacob.

If, on the other hand, you preferred to have recourse to anagogy, you would say that since the number seven is a symbol of rest, the person unwilling to remain in it through a rejection of

18. Didymus does not reopen the question of differing numbers of clean and unclean animals cited in v.2 (from the Yahwist author), figures at variance (with the Priestly author and) with a gloss inserted here in the Heb. text, apparently to reconcile the two. But he will address the discrepancy later.

that rest, of which the Savior says, "Take my yoke upon you and learn of me, that I am meek and humble of heart, and you will find rest for your souls,"[19] is subject to the deluge of sin and the punishment inflicted because of vice. Now, this happens in the six hundredth year that was not complete, a symbol that the victims of the deluge were imperfect even in things of the senses because they were not using them as they should; six hundred is related to six, being made up of six times a hundred. (110)

If there is need to explain, on the other hand, the occurrence of the flood on the *twenty-seventh day,* this could be said.[20] Not every threat is carried out; it is up to us whether it is fulfilled or canceled, as happened even in the case of the Ninevites. So since this number is a symbol of enactment—3 times 3 times 3— accordingly confirmed punishment was sent on that day against those who were unconverted, disposed immovably to vice.

Now, it says that the flood happened *in the six hundredth year,* touching on its limit. This is customary with Scripture, as the Savior says, "For just as Jonah remained in the belly of the sea monster three days and three nights, so will the Son of man be in the heart of the earth three days and three nights."[21] If, in fact, you took this in its entirety, claiming that he remained there the whole of the three days and nights, you would be wrong; he was crucified at the sixth hour of the preparation day,[22] which it counts as a day, referring to the day by its limit (obviously including also the night, since the preceding night is calculated in the whole day, custom dictating that the nights are counted with the following days). After that day came the night to complete it and the day of the sabbath, then the night and the limit of the day of resurrection, for it touched also on this. Thus, by touching on the limits of the first night-day of preparation and of the Lord's day, plus the complete night-day of the sabbath, it is stated that he spent three days and three

19. Mt 11.29.

20. Didymus hazards a guess on the basis of number symbolism—as guess it may be: our Heb. in fact reads "seventeenth."

21. Mt 12.40.

22. Jn 19.14 (Mk 15.25: "third hour")—that is, Preparation Day for the Sabbath.

nights in the heart of the earth. Now, we have said this as a digression to show (112) to those interested that Scripture normally uses these ways of touching on time limits.

On that day all the fountains of the deep burst forth, and the sluice gates of heaven broke open; rain fell on the earth for forty days and forty nights (vv.11–12). This number is provocative; the children of Israel spent this number of years in their journey, Moses himself did not eat bread for forty days, and the Savior also fasted for this number of days[23]—facts which give grounds for thought to people not idly bypassing the divine writings. This is the reason why the flow of water lasted for such a number of days.

Now, in citing the text about the *sluice gates of heaven* you could wonder about God's sending the rain by calling into service the water of the sea, how the flood happened when the arrangement is that the rain comes from the sea and falls on it again. It could be said in reply, firstly, that *the fountains of the deep* were spilled and provided the source (it is recorded that when he withheld them, *the fountains of the deep were shut off*),[24] and then there is nothing improbable in God's increasing the quantity of the water, just as in the Gospels he had increased the number of loaves from five to five thousand.[25] (114)

On that day Noah boarded the ark with Noah's sons Shem, Ham, and Japheth, Noah's wife and the three wives of his sons, and all the wild animals, species by species, all the cattle, species by species, every reptile moving on the earth, species by species, and every bird, species by species. They boarded the ark after Noah, two by two, of all flesh in which there was the breath of life. And those that entered, male and female of all flesh, went in as God had commanded Noah (vv.13–16). It is clear that the flood did not happen all of a sudden; instead, he also provided a kind of sign, as was said before as well, so that the brute beasts might enter the ark in orderly fashion without confusion, and to ensure in the event of a sudden downpour that no damage was caused to the ark by the onset

---

23. Dt 2.7; Ex 34.28; Mt 4.2.

24. Gn 8.2. The question deals with an apparent interruption to the normal cycle of rainfall and evaporation—a further question of *historia* that interests Didymus.

25. See Mt 14.21.

of the waters. Boarding was done in order: first Noah, since it was due to him that the others were saved; next the others, and then the brute beasts. It should be noted that this happened by divine power, since it would have exceeded human control for the savage beasts to board unless it happened with God's cooperation. *Species by species* was well put: they could not have lived together, their natures being different. The clause *in which there was the breath of life* was added by contrast with the dead.

You could make the point: how is it that there was no mention of the clean animals, but only the unclean; *they boarded the ark, two by two,* a clear reference to the unclean? It could be said in reply that it is obvious that with the embarkation of the unclean animals the clean also (116) went on board. After all, if the lesser went on board, clearly the greater did. Also, *two by two* could be taken to refer also to the clean ones, in reference to their all embarking in couples.

The Lord God shut the ark from the outside. The deluge fell forty days and forty nights upon the earth, the water deepened and picked up the ark, and it was lifted above the earth. The force of the water grew stronger, and it spread widely on the earth, and the ark floated on the water (vv.16–18). It was in accord with the facts for the ark to be *shut from the outside* by God's power, there being no human being on the outside. You see, he had "covered it with pitch inside and out,"[26] except for covering the door with pitch on the outside, since it was not yet closed. So to prevent its being said that there was an entry for the water through the door, he went on to mention God's security, which was manifold and ingenious. It was just as well that the water *picked up the ark* steadily and not all of a sudden, for reasons we gave before.

The water continued to spread further and further on the earth, and covered all the high mountains under heaven. The water rose fifteen cubits (vv.19–20). It is an idle claim of some commentators that people survived on the high mountains; the text made a point of saying that (118) *the water rose fifteen cubits* over the high mountains. From this it is clear that that claim is baseless, especially since it is at variance with God's will; God had ordered Noah on account of his righteousness to build an ark by saying

26. Gn 6.14.

that he was going to "destroy all flesh,"[27] so that nobody outside the ark would be saved. In reference to the water's *rising fifteen cubits,* if you wanted to dwell on the number, you would see that it is employed in many places in Scripture: there were fifteen steps to the Temple,[28] and the word instructs us to give "a part to the seven and to the eight," which is taken to mean that those who accept the Old Testament along with the New apportion a part to the seven and to the eight.[29] You could plausibly claim that those who are contemptuous of the mystery contained in the number have fallen victim to the deluge of vice; vice is likewise signified in the Scriptures by a flood of water, as in the verse, "Why do you plot against the Lord? The end ..." If, in fact, you were to reason that when the torrential affairs of this life (taken in the sense of a deluge) are multiplied "as the love of many grows cold," the end will come,[30] you would by close attention understand the passage.

It was the death of all flesh moving on the earth—birds, cattle, wild animals—every reptile moving on the earth, every human being, (120) *everything that had the breath of life and everything on dry land died. All life that was on the face of the earth was wiped out, from human beings to cattle, reptiles, and birds of heaven—they were wiped off the earth* (vv.21–23). The literal sense is clear; it conveys the destruction of all living things except those in the ark, since the brute beasts also perished because they had been created to serve human needs. At a spiritual level, on the other hand, everyone perished, punished by water, for having lost their character as *image* and instead bearing "the image of the man of dust," the result being that they were divided into the differing behavior of wild animals, reptiles, and other brute beasts, as some people are called "brood of vipers," others "snakes and scorpions," and still others "dogs" as in the saying, "Beware of the dogs."[31] In short, because they had adopted various forms of vice, it was

---

27. Gn 6.17.
28. Ezek 40.49 speaks of ten steps.
29. Didymus had cited Eccl 11.2 to this effect in comment on 6.3—not quite the intention of the adage, "Don't put all your eggs in one basket." But he has to find a symbolic value for fifteen from somewhere. Cf. p. 146 above.
30. Na 1.9; Mt 24.12.
31. 1 Cor 15.49; Mt 3.7; 23.33; Phil 3.2.

right that they should be done away with in the destruction of vice, signified symbolically by the water. These people were also earthly in having lost "the image of the man of heaven";[32] and they perished *on dry land* since vice contains nothing life-giving.

Noah alone survived and those with him in the ark. The water was at flood level on the earth for a hundred and fifty days (vv.23–24). It (122) was right that Noah should be saved for having no share in vice, and those with him for being his disciples. He rose above the flow of water taken allegorically of *fifteen cubits*, having mounted to the Temple by the steps, and having fulfilled what was conveyed in that number according to the previous explanation; Scripture says, remember, "Floods of water will not succeed in quenching love."[33] ...

32. 1 Cor 15.49.
33. Song 8.7.

CHAPTER EIGHT

OD WAS *mindful of Noah and of all the wild beasts, all the cattle, and all the birds that were with him in the ark.*[1] *God sent a wind upon the earth, and the water subsided; the torrents of the deep and the sluice gates of heaven were shut off, and the rain from heaven stopped. The water gave way and flowed off the earth; the water gave way and diminished after a hundred and fifty days* (vv.1–3). The phrase *was mindful* we should take in a way befitting God, not as though God had forgotten him, but in the sense in which he refers to the impious, "I do not know where you come from; depart from me, workers of iniquity, I never knew you,"[2] the word "knew" suggesting here, "I never took you to be ours." He *was mindful* without having forgotten, since the holy person is ever before God; rather, he was mindful of him in the sense of appointing him head of the human race, and was likewise mindful of the others as well. (124) Some people wonder where the floodwater went after the wind came that made the water *subside,* which would have resulted either from God's will or from divine power encountering it. A further contribution to its subsiding was the closure of the deep and the termination of the downpour.

The ark came to rest in the seventh month, and so on (v.4). The text is clear; let us look at the meaning. The ark can be the Church,[3] which saves those attached to it by thoughts and deeds

1. Mention of the reptiles has been omitted in Didymus's text.

2. Mt 7.23; Lk 13.27.

3. Having dealt with one question about the *factuality* of the water's subsidence, Didymus declares the *text* free of problems, and proceeds to the "meaning," *dianoia,* in the sense of an anagogical interpretation, on which he is suitably tentative. He proceeds in similar fashion with the following verses, declaring them to offer no problem at a literal/factual level before moving to another level that he calls "anagogical."

of virtue; it also rests on high, never taking a low position, and hence "the gates of hell do not prevail against it." She is presented "in splendor" to Christ "without a spot or wrinkle or anything of the kind," since Christ is also on high, as is suggested by the verse, "Lo, he comes, leaping upon the mountains," which are the prophets, Moses, and the unseen powers. She therefore rests on a rock, which is the unbroken word of piety; Scripture says, "God's foundations are on the holy mountains," which are the city of God, for "God founded it forever." Scripture says, remember, "They looked forward to the city that has foundations, whose architect and builder is God." (126) The mountains would also be the ninety-nine sheep that stayed put and did not fall victim to error.[4]

If, on the other hand, you wanted to treat the number in a systematic way,[5] you would say that it conveys the stability of the divine Church, being a square and also a cube: 3 times 3 times 3 equals 27. Now, *Ararat* means "testimony of descent." God testifies to the person who takes refuge in the Church by his way of living, and he is unaffected by tempests; Scripture says, "If you pass through water, rivers will not engulf you," and again, "We went through fire and water, and he led us out to refreshment."[6] It was well, too, that the deluge finished in a year; when the true Sun enlightens and illuminates our thinking, all disturbance to our soul will cease.[7]

Noah opened the window of the ark, and so on (v.6). Here, too, there is no obscurity in the text. If, on the other hand, you were to consider the anagogical sense, you would focus on mention of the *opening,* noting that a knowledge of times befits the righteous and is for their benefit and that of others: sometimes it is appropriate to close, sometimes to open. Thus, it was when

4. Mt 16.18; Eph 5.27; Song 2.8; Pss 87.1; 48.8; Mt 18.12.

5. The verb is τεχνολογέω. The lemma as quoted did not proceed to say "on the twenty-seventh (Heb., seventeenth) day of the month the ark came to rest on the mountains of Ararat ..."

6. Is 43.2; Ps 66.12. The etymology that Didymus finds for Ararat is a popular one only.

7. If Didymus is suggesting that the deluge lasted a full year's cycle of the sun, he would need to make some such comment on 8.13 (which in fact implies a shorter period), where he is less precise.

the Savior had opened (128) that it was said by those in the company of Cleopas, "Were not our hearts burning when he opened to us the Scriptures?" You will also consider if the verse, "Open to me gates of righteousness," bears on the passage, and you will consider in the same context the order given in Isaiah, "Open, you rulers," and likewise the closure in the statement, "Do not throw holy things to dogs."[8] In other words, when one closes or opens properly, one is then an imitator of Noah.

He sent out the raven, and so on (v.7). Not all who are subject to the Church behave identically: some are *doves,* others *ravens,* speaking symbolically of their ways and habits. While a dove is a sign of pure life, being listed among the clean animals and offered in sacrifice, this is not true of a raven. To be taken in the same sense also is the story about ravens feeding Elijah; it means that when a teacher changes someone impure so that he changes his ways, he enjoys nourishment from the one who is helped. This person—I mean the kind of one who has the manners of a raven—even if appearing to be subject to the righteous one, goes off to do battle with temptation, and does not return.[9] Now, do not be surprised if the righteous person sends such a one into an exercise of testing, since the divine saying also says, "My child, if you enter the Lord's service, prepare your soul for temptation."[10] That is why he did not return: he was unstable and incapable of sustaining the tempest under pressure. (130)

He sent out the dove, and so on (v.8). The introduction and foundation of the true way of living is enthusiasm for testing; hence the one who lives like a *dove* is *sent out* into the arena. There is a saying in regard to zealous people: "If you lie down among the lots, a dove's wing covered in silver, and its back in the color of gold." To such a soul the word says, "My beautiful, my dove."[11] Hence such a soul is stable, and even if it is amidst temptations

8. Lk 24.32; Ps 118.19; Is 13.2 LXX; Mt 7.6. Didymus's mode of interpretation involves flipping through one's mental concordance and citing a range of verses where an individual word occurs.

9. 1 Kgs 17.6.

10. Sir 2.1.

11. Ps 68.13 (a most obscure verse, cited here by a loose association without clear relevance); Song 2.10, 14.

and is sent away from those who are of help to it, it returns un-
changed to its benefactor, especially when it is conscious that
the end of the testing has not come for it to take possession of
the land. It is not appropriate to be under pressure indefinitely;
hence the righteous person also extends his hand to lend help
and assistance. Now, this is the anagogical interpretation we offer because of the clarity of the text.[12]

He waited a further seven days before sending it out again (v.11). It
was appropriate that he sent out the dove again, and that it returned with an olive twig in its mouth; the zealous person does
everything for a reason. So it brought back to the righteous one
actions attentive to light, a sign not to rely on oneself but rather
to yield to the teacher, *towards* (132) *evening,* now close to the
end. When sent out a third time it did not return any more;[13]
after making such great progress it then proved to be independent of a teacher. Such is the anagogical sense, the text offering no obscurity.

In the six-hundred-and-first year, and so on (v.13). Since the text
is clear, the sense is to be discussed. When the person who has
retired on high for good works sees vice coming to an end, he
removes the *covering* that comes from testing because he has
surmounted it. Cessation of the deluge on the twenty-seventh[14]
conveys the meaning of stability, the number being a square
and a cube.

*The Lord God said, Disembark from the ark, you and your wife,
your sons and your sons' wives,* and so on (v.15). We noted above
that at the beginning of the deluge it was appropriate for the
text to read, *Embark on the ark, you and your sons, your wife and
your sons' wives with you,* but now, *Disembark from the ark, you and
your wife, your sons and your sons' wives.* While it was necessary,
remember, considering the destruction of all humankind, that
in some fashion they not indulge themselves in unrestrainedly
enjoying marital intercourse, (134) he is now properly bidden

12. Where Didymus speaks of "anagogical," we would rather use the term
"allegorical."

13. 8.12. The mention of "light" is related to the olive tree; interpretation-
by-association can rest on tenuous connections.

14. 8.14 speaks rather of the drying out of the earth on the twenty-seventh
day of the month.

to disembark with his wife, and his sons with theirs, for a begin-ning … had to be made.[15] Now, it was appropriate that whereas he was told to disembark, he was instructed to *bring out* the ani-mals, since he was entrusted by God as their king and master. It is noteworthy that *all* disembarked, none having been harmed.

Noah built an altar (v.20). Even though Noah had made a con-tribution to salvation by building the ark, covering it with pitch for security, and doing the other things, far from taking credit for it himself, he built an altar to give thanks. Now, we were previously correct in saying that he was right to have more of the clean animals embark on the ark, his intention being to sacrifice some of them … Even though there was not yet a re-quirement by Law to offer sacrifice, he was a righteous man and thought it right to offer the first-fruits in gratitude to the giver, just as Abel also had offered the first-fruits of his labors and possessions. Now, the mention of his offering at the altar some of *all* the animals should be taken sensibly; there are three kinds offered in sacrifice … from the animals: calf, sheep, and if … also dove[16]—so these amounted to *all.* You can also find in the Scriptures (136) cases where a general reference is made and should be taken in context; the verse, "All flesh will see the salvation of God,"[17] should be taken to mean not all but what is capable of doing so, namely, human nature.

Now, the animals mentioned above are clean in view of the statement in the Law …[18]

15. Cf. above, p. 162.

16. Lv 1.5, 10, 14. Didymus is back to scrutiny of the literal sense of the text.

17. Is 40.5 LXX.

18. Ten pages of the manuscript (chapters 9–11) are missing at this point; much of the material in chs 10–11 is genealogical, anyway, and may have elicited relatively brief comment. Therefore, we resume at the calling of Abram in chapter 12.

CHAPTER TWELVE

HE LORD said to Abram, Go forth from your country, from your kindred, and from your father's house to a land that I shall show you. I shall make you into a mighty nation, I shall bless you and magnify your name, and you will be blessed. I shall bless those who bless you, and curse those who curse you. All the tribes of the earth will be blessed in you (vv.1–3). It was not by chance that God bade Abram leave his own land and kindred; instead, he saw in him something that made him worthy of being henceforth an object of his care, namely, faith in him. It was not fitting that the one with faith in God should abide among wretches (his own father being an idolater); often association with evildoers proves harmful to people of zeal, especially when they have lately become so. This is surely the reason that the Savior also (138) proclaims, "If anyone wishes to come after me and does not hate his father and brothers and sisters, and even his wife and children, he cannot be my disciple." Now, the Lord did not say this to provoke hatred of one's family; rather, if any of them proved an obstacle to virtue, they were to be hated for virtue's sake. When the disciples did it, they said, "See, we have left everything and followed you."[1]

This, then, was the order given in this case to the patriarch, too, God promising to show him a land for him to live in, to make him a great nation, bless him, magnify his name, and show him to be so blessed that those blessing him would enjoy blessing from him, and those cursing him would incur a curse from him. In addition, he promises that by the promise to him all the tribes of the earth would be blessed in him. All this was not of a human kind, as we saw from the anagogical approach

1. Lk 14.26; Mt 19.27.

to the text, which we adopted from the outset. Every sinner has the devil for father, according to the statement, "Everyone who commits sin is of the devil"; just as the one doing God's will becomes his offspring—Scripture says, remember, "Everyone who does right has been born of God"—so "everyone who commits sin is of the devil,"[2] its father, and has kinship with those born of this father.

God, then, bids him abandon it, calling it *land,* there being nothing heavenly in the adversary, the devil, but everything earthly, the purpose being that having thus set aside the "image of the man of dust," he may adopt the "image of the man of heaven." In a Psalm there is a similar reference to the (140) church of the nations that reads, "Hear, O daughter, see, incline your ear, forget your people and your father's house, because the king has desired your beauty, and he is your Lord."[3] In other words, since she has already begun to move from idolatry, the word prompts her with a prophetic glance and calls her "daughter" to urge her both to "hear" and to "see" (the word of God being something heard and at the same time seen) with a pure heart, and further "incline her ear" so as thus to "forget her own people and her father" by renouncing him. He proceeds to mention the reason, which we said the patriarch had, "beauty" of soul; nothing so beautifies the soul as virtue. There is therefore need to forget all these "earthly" things, which fall into the divisions mentioned above. He tells the zealous man to go *to a land that* God *will show* him, not something visible, even if the visible has corresponded to it by way of a symbol, but something invisible; after all, "hope that is seen is not hope."[4]

Now, what is the meaning of making him *a mighty nation* after we take it literally? Clearly it happened in actual fact; but in becoming a *nation* he is in reality *great* when adorned with virtues. Now, it is obvious that when further progress is made in a soul, it acquires a greatness that is not human but heavenly, a *blessing* that is not simply offered but conferred, (142) a *name* that is *great* and celebrated as a result of the accompanying virtue and the adornment that follows the spiritual blessing. After

2. 1 Jn 3.8; 2.29.   3. 1 Cor 15.49; Ps 45.10–11.
4. Rom 8.24.

all, "a good name is better than riches" … and "a sound reputation fattens the bones."[5]

Not content with blessing him, he proceeds to say, *and you will be blessed,* having become worthy of blessing on account of your greatness and progress towards perfect virtue. He also blesses *those who bless* him, not with a mere protestation but by the choice and election with which he was selected; similarly, those hostile to him will fall under a *curse.* This is clear to anyone reading the facts, where it emerges that all who received him gladly were blessed, while all who treated him improperly fell under a curse, as Abimelech did.[6] It is possible, on the other hand, that this refers also to the unseen powers, since holy angels bless the man of zeal and are blessed, while the devil and the demons curse him and fall under a curse. Yet another development is *all the tribes of the earth being blessed in him,* since they cease to be tribes of the earth when they imitate him in his saintliness, and they no longer think in terms of earthly things. The man of zeal is committed to this, the blessing of *all the tribes of the earth in him* through imitation, even if not all willingly make their approach, having separated themselves from him.

Abram went, as the Lord had told him, and Lot went with him. Abram was seventy-five years old when he departed from Haran. (144) *Abram took his wife Sarai, his brother's son Lot, all the possessions they had acquired, and every person they had acquired in Haran, and they set forth to go to the land of Canaan, and arrived in the land of Canaan* (vv.4–5). It is a great testimony to the patriarch that he set out just *as the Lord had told him,* and Lot also is a recipient of commendation for accompanying Abram. Now, the passage testifies also to the age at which he left and the fact that he took *all the possessions they had acquired* in Haran, *every person they had acquired,* and thus *arrived in the land of Canaan.* In itself it would have been grounds for high commendation that he did not stay put, that he did not yield to family ties, friends, other people, everything encouraging him not to abandon his own country, and that he overlooked all of that in obedience to the divine command. Further, as we remarked above, that he set forth just

5. Prv 22.1; 15.30.
6. Gn 20.2–18.

as the Lord had told him; it frequently happens that a person carries out the command, but does not do so as prescribed by the one giving the command. In this case things were done just as God bade, the reason for the action being given by God and the deed accomplished in keeping with the intention of the bidder. This is not true of those who give alms so as to be seen by people, performing the action but falling short in the way they do it. This was not what the blessed Paul meant in saying, "Be imitators of me": instead of simply giving the direction, he went on, "as I also am of Christ," not in appearance but in reality. Likewise the Savior in saying, "Learn of me that (146) I am meek and humble of heart,"[7] encourages the listeners to reflect in order to learn the manner and the performance and the reasons of meekness and humility.

The patriarch takes also his possessions, not as though attached to them—he was not even attached to his own son—but taking them to meet his needs. So much for factual reference to what was needed; in addition we should mention his taking from Haran also *the persons they had acquired,* that is to say, he took with him as servants those he had acquired in keeping with his own manners. After all, as the proverb goes, There is no slacker in the house of a wise man.[8] The anagogical sense, on the other hand, contains much benefit for the person capable of unraveling the meaning. Haran, then, means "holes," and as such is a symbol of the senses, since the senses have holes, as it were, for their location. God's wish is for him to stand aloof from the senses. What has been prudently acquired in these things the holy person collects for his own benefit with a view to perfection in spiritual things, or the perfect in the company of the mighty—does he not have an ornamental garment, a smile on his lips, and a stool for his feet?[9] Now, he brought also his wife, whose name appropriately means "my rule";[10] the wise

7. Mt 6.1–2; 1 Cor 11.9; Mt 11.29.

8. The maxim, Nautin assures us, can be documented from both Philo and Origen; SC 244.146–47, note 213,1.

9. Sir 19.30.

10. Didymus finds in Philo the above proverb and etymologies (popular in the case of Haran, as of Lot below); SC 244.147–48, notes 213,2; 213,3; and 213,4.

man is with wisdom, either ruled by her or exercising rule from her, with her for his partner, as Solomon says, "I brought her to live with me"—wisdom, that is—"and fell in love with her beauty," (148) and "for a man she brings forth good sense."[11]

He also brought his nephew Lot, on whom we would reflect as follows. Abram is a son of God because of his righteousness—Scripture says, remember, "Everyone who does right has been born of God"[12]—and hence is a participant in the divine mysteries that are invisible and supernatural. Such a man has as a brother one who partakes of the senses in a wise manner, which contributes to perfection. His son is Lot, which means "decline, redeemed"; insofar as he is son not of the wise man but of the one involved in things of the senses he is "decline" because slightly detached from things of the senses, whereas to the extent that he is subject to the holy man and a follower of his he is "redeemed" because accepting this introduction to understanding divine and supernatural things. This was the man and the manners that Abram took, himself a wise recipient also of things of the senses; a "decline" is commendable when moving in the direction of the good and shaken away from its opposite. In those terms, in fact, a prayer is also offered by the Psalmist in the words, "Let all the earth shake before his face"; when this happens, the earth no longer remains earth, since his face enlightens people on earth to make them heavenly. To the same effect is the verse, "He is enthroned on the cherubim; let the earth tremble," so that it may undergo a change in his regard. This is actually the way that those accompanying the patriarch himself made their departure by changing for the better, arriving in Canaan, which means "made ready"; the neophyte who begins to abandon things of the senses ought to make himself ready for acceptance of more divine things.[13] (150)

Abram traveled the length of the land to the place at Shechem by the lofty oak. Now, the Canaanites inhabited the land at that time (v.6). The text begins by stating that as a recent arrival in this land he

11. Wis 8.9, 2; Prv 10.23 LXX.

12. 1 Jn 2.29.

13. Pss 96.9; 99.1. Thus, by the use of allegory and a couple of popular etymologies, some moral capital can be made out of Lot's name.

necessarily inspects its outline by *traveling its length* and probably also its breadth to learn its extent. The text indicates, in fact, *to the place at Shechem,* and the fact that *the Canaanites inhabited the land.* Of necessity, however, we must move to the anagogical sense. The holy one moved from things of the senses, though he had partaken properly of them as well, to a more divine level, and became involved by studying the length, which gives the impression of contemplating also the loftiness of divine things. This is the same as blessed Paul also ... "breadth and length and depth, and to know the surpassing grace of God."[14] All this he contemplates, then, evidence of the rest being based on the greater part.

Now, he comes *to the place at Shechem* where there was a spring by which Jesus seated himself when wearied by having a body of the same substance as our flesh. You could plausibly take this to mean that following his important attention to the true doctrine of God (suggested by *length*) he arrived also at the meaning of the Incarnation, according to the statement by Jesus, "Abraham longed to see my day; (152) he saw it and rejoiced."[15] He comes to Shechem, which means "shouldering," as he deserved all this for his virtuous actions; the shoulder, from which derives "shouldering," is a symbol of work, as Scripture says, "Put your heart into your shoulders," and in reference to one of the patriarchs, "He bowed his shoulder to the burden." In this sense, in fact, it is also said of the human being whom the Savior assumed, "His government was on his shoulder," that is to say, he exercised government as a result of hard work, but his work was not from vice to virtue ("he committed no sin," remember) but maintaining perfection. Likewise, even in respect of his humanity he was king, since God the Word enjoys a kingship that is eternal, inherent, and substantial, and that is not the result of work or effort.[16]

---

14. Eph 3.18.

15. Jn 4.6; 8.56. Here Didymus speaks of Jesus's body as ὁμοούσιος ("of the same substance") with our flesh, and of "the true doctrine of God," θεολογία.

16. The "plausible" allegorical interpretation of Shechem turns into a digression on the basis of a false etymology (based on an identical Heb. word) as related to "shoulder," which after a tissue of nominally associated texts (Jer

He comes also to *the lofty oak.* Many of the trees and plants designate certain spiritual realities, like those Isaiah mentions, "You will go out in joy and be instructed in happiness; the mountains and the hills will exult with joy in receiving you, and all the trees of the field will clap their branches," which implies nothing material, only the departure of noble people, who take their leave not with grief but with joy. So while a wretch says, "How harsh death is," it is said of Abraham that he lay down and joined his fathers, "brought to a fine old age." When the righteous pass on, therefore, "the mountains and the hills," the angels and the righteous, will receive them "with joy," rejoicing on account of the one sheep, and with (154) them "all the trees of the field will clap" in rejoicing, meaning those rational ones in paradise. He goes on to say, "A cypress will spring up in place of weed"—in place of a thorny plant without fruit, a useful and sweet-smelling one, which is what the penitent is—"and a myrtle will spring up in place of a bramble," stench being changed into fragrance.[17] Since we have taken trees in a spiritual sense, then, it is necessary to adopt such an interpretation also of the oak to which Abram came, under which he sat and was accorded a vision when he also received the promise about Isaac. It is therefore due to work and effort that he advances upwards, and shares in fragrance and insight into lofty and divine thoughts.[18]

You will consider also whether we may take the observation, *the Canaanites still inhabited the land,* to mean that the one who is making progress is not immediately liberated from everything, but retains something of his former habits—the sense

31.21; Gn 49.15; Is 9.6; 1 Pt 2.2) is found wanting. "God the Word" is not a phrase found widely in Didymus.

17. As occurs in Didymus, it is not so much the lemma that receives comment but a loosely-related Isaian text (55.12–13) that better illustrates the commentator's point (trees symbolizing virtues), to which other texts are joined: 1 Sm 15.32 (words of Agag, king of the Amalekites), Gn 15.15 (where Didymus's text reads τραφείς, translated here as "brought to," instead of ταφείς, "buried").

18. Typically, Didymus gives a spiritual meaning to the "lofty" oak tree in the lemma instead of being in a position to see the Heb. term either as the proper name Moreh or as having the meaning "oracular." He identifies this tree as the one under which Abram was sitting at the opening of ch.18.

of *still*[19]—which you could understand of continuing imperfections in the holy one.

The Lord appeared to Abram and said to him, I shall give this land to your seed. There Abram built an altar to the Lord, who appeared to him (v.7). It is logical that God would manifest himself to the one who obeyed his commands, to confirm him in sound hope of what was awaited, his promise to him being to give the land to his seed.[20] It was also logical for (156) the holy man, grateful as he was, to build an altar to the one making the promise. So much for a paraphrase; it is worth giving an interpretation, on the other hand, of the clause, *God appeared to Abram,* since God is invisible, as the words of the Gospel say, "No one has ever seen God," and, "Not that anyone has seen the Father," and Paul says of God, "No one has ever seen or can see him,"[21] which indicates he is invisible by nature. There are in fact some visible things we do not see, but we can see them, even if this does not happen, since they are visible by nature; but what is invisible is not seen, not on account of its not being seen but on account of its invisibility. So it is clear that seeing is twofold, by the senses and in thought: in the former case one grasps visible things; in the other, invisible, which presupposes a pure mind, by which God was seen by Abram.

Now, the text contains a further observation: it does not say, "Abram saw God," but *God appeared to Abram.* In other words, as far as our created nature and its limitations go, it is an impossible achievement; but as far as God's lovingkindness goes, it is possible, since through his goodness he allows himself to be understood. If, on the one hand, "saw" occurs in place of *appeared,* as in Isaiah, "I saw the Lord enthroned," and so on,[22] we should learn from what happened to Abram that this happens if God allows himself to be seen. On the other hand, the fact that "seeing" is sometimes employed in the sense of "understanding"

19. By (unconsciously) replacing "at that time" (τότε) with "still" (ἔτι)—a rare error in recall for a blind commentator—Didymus bypasses the celebrated rabbinic conundrum as to how the author could draw the implied comparison.

20. Below we shall see Didymus getting full value from this textual datum, the use of "seed," not child.

21. Jn 1.18; Jn 6.46; 1 Tm 6.16.

22. Is 6.1.

Paul (158) mentions in his letter to the Romans: "Ever since the creation of the world his invisible powers have been understood and seen through the things he has made." And Moses, expressing his belief that God, of whom he had some notion, is invisible, said, "Show yourself to me so that I may have a clear sight of you," and again, "He manifests himself to those who do not distrust him."[23] In other words, if that which was seen were of a visible nature, it could be manifested to unbelievers too, whereas this statement says, "He manifests himself to those who do not distrust him," since their mind is illuminated by a divine light.

The case is the opposite with things of the senses: we see them first, and then, when the impression from our senses reaches the mind, we understand them. Things of the intellect, on the other hand, make themselves available for knowing; the mind does not take the initiative except for preparing itself for knowledge, and instead responds to what is seen. Now, in some cases knowledge of God comes also from knowledge of creation, as Scripture says, "For from the beauty of created things comes a corresponding perception of their Creator,"[24] just as *God appeared to Abram;* the word *God* is generally associated with creation, as in the verse, "In the beginning God made heaven," and "God said, Let there be light," whereas the title *Lord* is cited at the time when the Law was given.[25] In similar fashion, at any rate, it was on contemplating God in the orderly arrangement of the universe that he forsook the error of polytheism learned from his father, and in consequence God offered himself to the holy man for understanding after the audible teaching that came to him in the words, *Go forth from your country and from your kindred.* Now, by the soul's hearing is to be understood obedient acceptance of suggestions, (160) and by its eye the solid application and grasp of teachings following on prog-

23. Rom 1.20; Ex 33.13; Wis 1.2.

24. Wis 13.5. This deuterocanonical book is clearly part of Didymus's canon, whereas at this stage of his career other works like the *Epistle of Barnabas* and *The Shepherd of Hermas* do not appear here (although they do in the Zechariah commentary).

25. Cf. pp. 41–42 and 134, above, which differ from the comment here.

ress. It should be understood, in fact, that the same things can be known in different ways: as a neophyte; when progress has been made; and in a proper way at an advanced level, thanks to understanding of God.

He promises also to give the land to his seed, that land of which the Savior said, "Blessed the meek, for they will inherit the land," and in the Psalms, "Wait for the Lord and keep to his way, and he will exalt you to inherit the land"—obviously not this land that we tread and cultivate, since he was its king, but the heavenly one, which is perfect knowledge of God. It is this that "the righteous will inherit and occupy forever,"[26] whereas this will not be the case with the land of the senses. This is the land, then, that God promises to give to the holy man's *seed*, which here means "child." A difference often exists, in fact, between *seed* and "children": if you are someone's child, you are also his seed, but it is not because you are a seed that you are also a child; it can happen that the seed does not take shape, come to term, or achieve resemblance, as Scripture says.[27] Now, just as in bodily matters there is a seed that does not become a child, and a child that is also a seed, so too in matters of the soul and the mind; the Savior, remember, says to the people claiming that "we have Abraham as our father," "If you were Abraham's children, you would be doing what Abraham did," for from that you become a child. He said they were not Abraham's children, calling them his seed in the words, "I know that you are seed (162) of Abraham."[28] Hence it is clear that the seed is not also a child; they are seed only in the sense of descending from him and enjoying the fruit of upbringing from him, but not imitating his behavior, although it would have been possible for them to capitalize on the affinity and become children. Here, then, since a promise is given to the *seed*, we take *seed* to mean child. In the Psalms, for instance, it is said,

26. Mt 5.5; Ps 37.34, 29.

27. Ex 21.22.

28. Jn 8.39, 37. It is an index of Didymus's reluctance in this work to adopt a Christological dimension (and thus a further clue to its relatively early composition?) that he does not pursue Paul's similar discussion of "seed" versus "seeds" (σπέρμα, σπέρματα, though both in the dative) in Gal 3.16, where the point is made that Jesus is the real heir of Abraham, not the Jewish people.

"His servants are seed of Abraham, sons of Jacob, his chosen ones." The fact that it suggests sometimes that the seed is not a child Paul confirms in writing, "... but not all his children"; not all who descend from Israel are Israel, but that one is of whom the Savior said, "Behold an Israelite, in whom there is no guile," and not those of whom it is said, "Consider Israel according to the flesh."[29]

So much for the difference between *seed* and child; it is now time to return to the text. *Abram built an altar,* then, moved by gratitude and intending to offer sacrifices spiritually, even if he performed a symbol of what Scripture says, "to offer spiritual sacrifices acceptable to God" and "sacrifice to God a sacrifice of praise" and "offer a sacrifice of righteousness, and have hope in the Lord." Now, "it was necessary for the sketches of the heavenly things to be purified with these rites, but the heavenly things themselves need better sacrifices than these."[30] So this altar is built by one who is progressing and following the one calling him to leave country, kindred, and father's house, becoming thereby worthy of seeing God, who himself deigned to appear to the holy man. (164)

He moved on from there to the mountain to the east of Bethel, and pitched his tent there by the sea with Ai to the south (v.8). While there is no obscurity in the literal sense, the anagogical sense suggests that he passed to a more elevated stage and condition. It is indicated by the *mountain,* and not simply *to the mountain* but "the house of God," the meaning of *Bethel,* which is not a single mountain but described in the Song as one among others: "My nephew is like a gazelle or a young stag on the mountains of Bethel." There are, in fact, many mountains and hills in the house of God, as emerges from the verse, "Here he comes, leaping on the mountains, bounding on the hills";[31] at each stage you can mount a hill, and from a hill to a mountain, with a view from the lower mountains to the higher, as is known at the early stage of the virtues and in the virtues themselves. There is a single mountain above them all, however, our Savior and Lord,

29. Ps 105.6; Rom 9.7; Jn 1.47; 1 Cor 10.18.
30. 1 Pt 2.5; Pss 50.14; 4.5; Heb 9.23.
31. Song 29 LXX; 2.8.

of whom it is said, "At the end of the days the mountain of the Lord will be visible." It is different from the other mountains, so that the holy one says for our instruction lest some of us be mistaken, "Why are you suspicious, curdled mountains?" Then, to teach about the pre-eminent mountain, he says, "God's mountain, fat mountain, curdled mountain, fat mountain. Why are you suspicious, curdled mountains, the mountain in which God is pleased to dwell?"[32] which designates the Lord incarnate. (166) The enfleshment is indicated, in fact, by this statement, as also in Job, "Did you not pour me out like milk, and curdle me like cheese?"[33] Only the Savior was born of a virgin, remember—hence the expression. Surely the expression is used of no one else, nor does anyone else have this existence. Hence Job did not say, "I was curdled," but, "You curdled me like cheese." In other words, what the Spirit did, the deposit of sperm effects in other people, as God had bidden. Its being "fat" is also the result of the presence of the Spirit and "the power of the Most High."[34]

While it is on a common basis that everyone, including the very temple of the Savior, owes existence to God's creative work, the Lord is a special case, for he used it as an instrument for the Incarnation. Just as the whole earth is God's creation, and yet the Temple was special in view of God's pronouncing oracles from there, so too in the case of the aforementioned. Now, the fact that the place where God pronounces oracles is called his house Jacob confirms in saying, "How fearsome is this place! It is nothing but the house of God, and this is the gate of heaven." We should therefore pay no heed to many people calling themselves Christ, as the text says, "Many people will come in my name and say, I am the Christ." There is, in fact, only one mountain in which "God is pleased to dwell";[35] his good pleasure to dwell there made it so, not man.

Abram was therefore on fire to advance in understanding to this mountain. When it arrived, of course, remember, it testified to him in these words: "Your ancestor Abraham rejoiced

32. Mi 4.1; Ps 68.15–16.
34. Lk 1.35.
33. Jb 10.10.
35. Gn 28.17; Mt 24.5; Ps 68.16.

that he would see my day; he saw it and was glad,"[36] enlightened by the true light which was accorded him after his earlier progress. (168) Now, it was well said that this mountain was *to the east,* enjoying lights from all quarters; whichever view you take from this mountain is luminous. It is called, remember, wisdom, word, life, truth, righteousness, sanctification, redemption; they are all dawning lights, not multiple in their essence, having a single subject, the Son of God, but different in their operation. With the house of God totally illuminated, the holy man came *to the east,* guided by the virtues. Now, you could say also that the *east* represents the various teachings of religion, through which Abram passed to pitch his *tent,* which he used in his progress (as *tent* suggests) whereas the house of God is permanent; Scripture says, "I shall pass throughout the locality of the wonderful tent as far as the house of God."[37]

So having passed throughout the locality of the tent, he pitches it in the house that abides forever, after which there is no further ascent. This is also said in another Psalm, "How lovely are your tents, Lord of hosts! My soul longs, indeed it faints, for the courts of the Lord." In other words, the person who has not yet reached the halls has the tents as objects of his love, advancing and looking towards perfection while saying, "My heart and my flesh will rejoice in the living God," when they are in that condition after which there is no further stage, because those who reach it are blessed. The Psalm says, "Blessed are all who dwell in your house," not staying but dwelling; this (170) is true of those who live in tents and are in progress, whereas dwellers have come to God's house, where they are blessed in praising him "for ages of ages."[38] This suggests the goal for everyone, where he *pitched his tent* after moving by stages and then achieved perfection. At this point will arrive the person who obeys the exhortation, "Guard your steps when you go to the house of God, and draw near to listen," this being the way to

36. Jn 8.56.

37. Ps 42.4. With regard to "to the east": "east," "dawn," is in the plural (ἀνατολὰς), as often.

38. Ps 84.1–4. The progressive commentary and precise distinctions, of course, are made on a subtext, not the lemma.

succeed in dwelling in the house, and say, "That I may dwell in the house of the Lord for length of days."[39] We should realize that in this is a symbolic reference to the divine way of life, even if the person of Abram still had room for perfection, not yet having had a change of name.[40]

Now, he pitched his tent *by the sea,* steady and unshakeable as he was, owing to his perfect grasp of virtue so as to be able to say, "Who will separate us from the love of Christ? Will hardship, or distress, or persecution?"[41] and so on, which you would not be wrong to refer to as *sea.* In other words, wherever the holy person is, even if in perfection, there is lying in wait for him the tempest or the instability of created nature, which the perfect soul checks, preventing the operation of vice by remaining in control of it. This is fortunate, a result of goodness and living in virtue, since even the evildoer has the power of virtue, even though by his own choice he turned to vice and keeps no guard over himself as does the good person.

Now, the same person also pitches his tent *with Ai to the south,* the right way to arrive at the mountain of the house of God, totally illuminated by the *east,* (172) a reference to the virtues of each sort, and with nothing to fear from what is opposite, since the sea's billows do not overthrow his house, firmly built as it is.[42] This is because he has put the words of Jesus into effect as a result of being in festive mood (the meaning of *Ai*), the greatest festival being the perfection of virtue. This in fact is what the Psalmist also said, "A sound of rejoicing and loud confession from those in festal mood"; the one who rejoices at the coming of the Spirit, not like the sinner who repents but like one giving thanks, is in festal mood. The term "confession" is used to mean thanksgiving, in fact, as in the statement, "I confess to

39. Eccl 5.1; Ps 23.5.

40. Unfortunately, the ms concludes just as Didymus is about to comment on the change of name in Gn 17.5. See p. 222.

41. Rom 8.35.

42. Didymus, though not neglectful of the literal and factual sense of the text, is not a geographer, the allegorical meaning (based often on false etymologies) more to his liking. Oddly here his text reads "Ai to the south" (which Nautin also oddly renders "north"), whereas the LXX (including the Antioch form) speaks of "east."

you, Father, Lord of heaven and earth," for Scripture says, "The wrath of a human"—obviously of one rejoicing—"will praise you, and the remnant of your wrath will fete you."[43]

There he built an altar to the Lord and called on the name of the Lord (v.8). Having duly moved to the mountain in the sense explained and to "the house of God," and being illuminated from the east and trampling down the adversaries so that no one need fear them any more, he erected an altar in thanksgiving. On this he performed the sacrifice of praise and righteousness in keeping with what was previously said about spiritual sacrifice, which is the collection of the virtues. *And he called on the name of the Lord,* which, if you were to take it at a surface level, would mean that he called the altar that he (174) built "the Lord's." It is possible, on the other hand, to say in a more spiritual and elevated sense that *he called on the name of the Lord* not by a simple phrase but in action, his mind engaging with God by practicing the virtues for no other reason than the good itself. This, in fact, is the sense in which the Savior intends to teach us to pray by saying, "Our Father," and instructed us to do so not in utterance but by showing ourselves to be children and no longer idly calling on God as Father. This is what we also heard ... "No one says, 'Jesus is Lord,' except by the Holy Spirit,"[44] which does not happen with those saying so only in words and in an idle manner. Abram therefore undertook the building of the altar for the Lord from the virtues, for him and for no other.

Abram arose and traveled until he pitched camp in the desert (v.9). There being no obscurity in the text, we should speak of the meaning. Even if one is perfect, there is no being rid of enemies, even if one is an "infant," like the Corinthians, to whom Paul wrote in the words, "No testing has overtaken you that is not common to everyone; God is faithful, and he will not let you be tested beyond your strength, but with the testing he will also provide the way out so that you may be able to endure it." To the Ephesians, on the other hand, he writes as to adults, and numbers himself among them, "For our struggle is not against

43. Ps 42.4; Mt 11.25; Ps 75.10 (Didymus again picking up details of the subtext for comment).
44. Mt 6.9; 1 Cor 12.3.

blood and flesh"[45]—not "was"; (176) rather, our struggle "is" not. In other words, at one time it "was," when he supposed he was "of the flesh, sold into slavery under sin," referring to those in such a condition, to whom he would have had to say, as he himself writes, "I punish my body and enslave it, lest after preaching to others I should be disqualified."[46] He conducts this battle with the use of heavenly weapons, since it is against spiritual and heavenly beings.

It is the role of the mature person, then, to do combat like Abram, keeping close to the house of God in the sense explained, and being like it as Scripture says, "Those who trust in the Lord are like Mount Zion."[47] Being in this condition, then, and aware that the hostile cohort was not far from him, *he pitched camp,* as did Jacob on the point of meeting Esau, who was very hostile and jealous of him: "he saw God's camp," for it was necessary that God should prepare the athlete to be brave by showing him that he has allies. Elisha, too, when on the point of being attacked by the king of Syria, had a divine army around him, which frightened the prophet's servant in his ignorance, but later emboldened him when his eyes were opened.[48]

It was good, too, that he pitched camp *in the desert.* The Savior, for instance, was likewise tempted in the desert; and in Isaiah you have, "Like a tempest in the desert it travels from the desert on its way from land," which suggests temptation. So Abram pitched camp *in the desert;* it is outside cities that for the most part temptations happen on account of there being none of one's fellows to lend help; (178) Scripture says, "A brother helped by a brother is like a fortified city,"[49] and as I said, the Savior was tempted in the desert. Hence the meaning is something like this: the soul experiencing temptation sees itself as a *desert,* as deprived of assistance, something of God's doing in the scheme of things. After all, if he had revealed to them the outcome and the fact that they would overcome temptation, the achievement would not be great, nor would they have uttered

---

45. 1 Cor 3.1; 10.13; Eph 6.12.   46. Rom 7.14; 1 Cor 9.27.
47. Ps 125.1.   48. 2 Kgs 6.15–17.
49. Is 21.1; Prv 18.19. Interpretation-by-association again.

prayers or done anything else. Instead, it is shown to them in due course that God is also ready to assist in case they should in the circumstances lose heart. While this is the case with human beings, in the Savior's case it was after the temptation that angels appeared to him, doing so with a view to serving him, in case people of evil disposition should claim, on the angels' appearing before him, that the victory belonged to the angels. What else, on the contrary, is the service of the angels than attending on souls obedient to God? Their presence was not for the purpose of giving support. He chided Peter, at any rate, for his intention to fight for him, "Do you think that I cannot appeal to my Father and he would send me more than twelve legions of angels?"[50] So he had no need of assistance.

There was a famine in the land. Abram went down into Egypt to sojourn there because famine raged in the land (v.10). The text being clear, the following deals with the meaning. God's wise ones are superior to earth, and do not belong to it. There was a famine in it, then; for people of earthly interests there is often a famine of hearing the word of the Lord, (180) and if they are worthy of it, it is later restored in due course. Hence Abram also went to *sojourn* in Egypt, not to live there, his intention being to make allowances for the victims of famine, not to dwell there. Those in the company of Daniel were in Babylon, remember, not for their sins but to help those who had been deported to live there because of their sins; God has pity on sinners to the extent that they agree to repent. And just as physicians are sent where there is serious injury or disease, not to contract it themselves but to cure the sufferers, so the holy ones come to Confusion[51] and to Babylon without residing there. After all, they had done nothing to deserve it, something that was the fault of the inhabitants.

When Abram was on the point of entering Egypt, Abram said to his wife Sarai, I am aware that you are a very beautiful woman. So it will happen that when the Egyptians see you, they will say, She is his wife, and they will kill me and take you for themselves. Consequently

---

50. Mt 26.53.

51. A reference to Babel in Gn 11.9, on which Didymus's commentary is not extant. Nautin points to an etymology of Babylon; SC 244.181, note 226,2.

say, I am his sister, so that things may go well for me on your account, and my life will be spared thanks to you (vv.11–13). As far as the literal sense goes, he shrewdly counted on the Egyptians' pleasure-seeking while believing that God, who was leading him out of his own country, would not ignore his being married. He suggested to her to say to them that she was his sister (182) so that if this was the first and only thing said, they would not entertain the idea that she was his wife, and thus he would deceive them. In fact, marriage between brother and sister was practiced in Egypt and in his own country, as he said later, "She really is my sister";[52] so it was a clever ploy for her to be told to say this first and this only. As the laws against adultery were probably observed by the Egyptians, Abram reasoned that they would kill him to avoid appearing to be adulterers.

So much for the text. As to the meaning, people who go from virtue to vice are said to go down into Egypt; Scripture often says, for example, "Woe to those who go down to Egypt."[53] Here it does not say, "He went down," but, "He *entered,*" his going down being an entry; every zealous person makes allowances for the fallen, not falling but rescuing them from their fall. Just as one becomes a Jew to Jews without being a Jew, and outside the law to those outside the law without being outside the Law,[54] so one goes into Egypt without adopting Egyptian ways. Hence, while others go down there, he *enters;* it was not their vicious ways that brought him down, but execution of the divine plan. The virtuous person *enters* Egypt many times in adopting a foreign culture so as to make something useful of it, as was the case also with blessed Paul in citing the verse from Aratus, "For we too are his offspring," so as to develop the thought, and the phrase, "To an unknown god," and the saying, "Cretans are always liars." He likewise exhorts people also to "take every thought captive to obey Christ."[55] (184)

---

52. Gn 20.12. Didymus (who is interested in salvaging Abram's reputation) claims that the patriarch's remark was correct as far as it went, mentioning a blood connection without proceeding to a marital one.

53. Is 31.1.

54. 1 Cor 9.20–21.

55. Acts 17.28, 23; Ti 1.12; 2 Cor 10.5.

Having entered Egypt, as we said, he was restrained by virtue from saying that she was his wife; the man of zeal and maturity does not tell his inferiors that he has been assigned possession of virtue lest he arouse envy in them. Instead, he said that she was his sister, thus giving her second place to the union he had with virtue so as to make allowances for the weak, who might thus desire to receive her as something held in common. Often, for example, when we want someone to understand, we share ideas such as providence in order that afterwards they may accept it for themselves. The evangelical teaching, then, is the gracious spouse of the man of zeal; but he does not keep her for himself, speaking of her among the perfect, and sharing her with everyone, as Paul says, "I would like everyone to be as I am."[56] When they have become so, in fact, they will know that learning is the partner of the perfect; "for a man wisdom brings forth good sense," and I (says the perfect one) "fell in love with her beauty"[57]—wisdom's, that is. The wise person, however, wants to share what is his with everyone, for in this way they will not be envious.

When Abram entered Egypt, the Egyptians noticed that his wife was very beautiful. Pharaoh's courtiers saw her, (186) *sang her praises to Pharaoh, and brought her into Pharaoh's household. On her account they treated Abram well; there came into his possession sheep, cattle, and asses, slave boys and girls, mules and camels* (vv.14–16). The patriarch's clever stratagem did not fail; far from his being outwitted, a way was devised for the holy man's marriage not to be defiled. Instead of the Egyptians laying hold of her as though a woman overlooked, the courtiers noticed her, earmarked her for the king, and brought her to him as a trophy, the result being that they also treated Abram well for her sake.

Abram *entered Egypt* in an allegorical sense, then, as a perfect man to the imperfect, so as to bring them benefit, making allowances, having a hold on virtue, as I said, not as though having been assigned possession of it, but giving everyone a glimpse of it as his sister by way of considerateness in order that they might thus be able on seeing it to love it. Now, notice that

56. 1 Cor 2.6; 7.7.
57. Prv 10.23 LXX; Wis 8.2.

the *courtiers saw her;* in the ranks of the Egyptians, understood allegorically, there were some who were purer and who enjoyed a great aptitude to recognize virtue. They did not stop at recognizing her: they also *brought her* to their ruler, that is, to reason that guided them along with praise of her. This, in fact, was the intention of holy Abram in gently guiding them ...[58] (188)

58. Nautin reports that the next page of the papyrus is blank; SC 244.186. In fact, comment is missing on all the following text preceding Gn 15.12.

CHAPTER FIFTEEN

OW, AT sunset a trance fell upon Abram, and, lo, a fearful gloom fell on him (v.12) ... on contemplating them as though divine visions, Abram was frightened by a fear that becomes one who is perfect. Note, on the other hand, that it was *at sunset* that *a trance fell upon him*, the text suggesting progress in that the day of the present condition had passed him by so that for him further progress should succeed. There had come upon him the blessing of which it is said, "I shall fill him with length of days,"[1] a promise that is not altogether to do with longevity, suggesting rather progress in illumination.

A trance came upon him, then, a *trance* not like derangement but wonderment and the change from visible things to invisible. The Apostle says, for example, "For whether we are beside ourselves for God, or whether we are in our right mind for you," suggesting not that we are insane for God, but that even if we are transported by contemplation beyond human things, we do so for God, as David also says, "I said in my trance, 'Everyone is a liar.'"[2] In other words, being beside himself and having become divine, he says of other people that they are liars, while he himself is no longer human on account of a share in the Holy Spirit, and is different from those of whom it is said, "For as long as there are quarreling and jealousy among you, are you not human and behaving like human beings?"[3]

When Abram was beside himself, then, *a fearful gloom fell on him,* the result not of darkness but of obscurity, not (190) readily understood; it was a deep fear that does not affect shal-

---

1. Ps 91.16.   2. 2 Cor 5.13; Ps 116.11.
3. 1 Cor 3.3.

low people. Now, for proof that "darkness" is often used in the sense of "obscurity," Scripture says, "He made darkness his hiding place";[4] and in truth the contemplation and grasp of supernatural teachings instill panic and a godly fear, even in outstanding people when they attempt it.

Abram was told, You will surely know that your descendants will be inhabitants of a land that is not theirs, and people will enslave them and maltreat them for four hundred years. But I shall judge the people by whom they are enslaved, and later they will depart from there with great possessions (vv.13–14). The passage foretells the people's stay in Egypt; it was not their own land they occupied when enslaved to Pharaoh and gravely maltreated by Pharaoh and the Egyptians. Now, there is no discrepancy between this statement and the writings in Exodus; it says there, "After four hundred and thirty years the might of the Lord came out of Egypt," whereas here it says after *four hundred*. We should note, however, that it did not say that they left at the completion of the four hundred years, only after *four hundred years,* which gives room for the thirty.[5]

The promise, *I shall judge the people by whom they are enslaved,* reached its fulfillment according to the account in Exodus; he inflicted on them ten plagues, and at completion "they sank like lead in the mighty waters." (192) They also left *with great possessions,* as the facts prove,[6] and from this we learn that even if God *maltreats* anyone for a period, he is not indifferent about doing it—rather, he brings it to a good conclusion.

Give a thought to the question as to whether the passage touches on the sojourn of the saints.[7]

You, however, will go to your fathers in peace after reaching a fine old age. But in the fourth generation they will return here, for the iniquities of the Amorites will not have run their course until then (vv.15–16). A

4. 2 Sm 22.12.

5. Ex 12.41. It is not surprising if Didymus slightly misquotes the two texts. His concern for factuality is still manifest.

6. Ex 15.10; 12.35–36.

7. Nautin interprets Didymus's commentary as suggesting that the fall of souls may be alluded to in the verse "your descendants will be inhabitants of a land that is not theirs"; SC 244.193, note 231,1.

superficial impression would be that it foretells his departure from this life; but the anagogical meaning would be as follows. The wise man departs this life *in peace* whereas the sinner is confused in his thinking and his soul is disturbed; and as one is taken in death, so is one judged as well.[8] The one who ensures peace for himself here-below also departs *in peace*, whereas the one with disturbed and confused thinking will be judged for that as well. This point is made in Ecclesiastes, "Where the tree falls, it will lie." This is not the case in actual fact; a tree does not always fall and lie in that position, frequently being moved. The meaning rather is that the human being, which is represented figuratively by the tree, will be judged just as it is found.[9]

It was appropriate, then, that Abram, since he was pleasing to God, should *go to his fathers in peace* to share the same promise: (194) "Christ as first-fruits, then those belonging to Christ." For the righteous as well there are different promises and different dwelling places, there being "many dwelling places in the Father's house."[10] The man of zeal will therefore depart for his spiritual *fathers,* whose son he is by identity of behavior, even if in the flesh he should have evil fathers.

After saying this of Abram himself, he says of his offspring that *in the fourth generation they will return here,* indicating the land of their inheritance. Now, this is the reason why he says that the return will be after *four hundred years:* that *the iniquities of the Amorites will not have run their course until then,* and it is on account of the iniquities that they will then experience overthrow, in order that with their condemnation they may become occupants of their land. God inflicts punishment, remember, in a moderate and timely manner by showing longsuffering until the moment comes for retribution. The statement in the Gospel is similar to this and supportive of it, "Then Jesus began to reproach the cities in which most of his deeds of power had

8. Whereas the Antioch text of the lemma omits the phrase "in peace," Didymus finds it grist to his mill. But, unlike the LXX generally, both are reading a copyist's error: τραφεὶς (for ταφεὶς, "buried") in the phrase "reaching (a fine old age)," as noted before; see above, p. 189, n. 17.

9. Eccl 11.3.

10. 1 Cor 15.23; Jn 14.2.

been done, because they did not repent: Woe to you, Chorazin! Woe to you, Bethsaida! For if the deeds of power done in you had been done in Tyre and Sidon, they would have repented long ago in sackcloth and ashes."[11] You could respond to this by asking, "Why, then, were they not done there if they would have repented, whereas they were performed where they did not repent?" We would reply that the Son of God is Wisdom, and it was he who did them; since he knows what is hidden, and was aware that in repenting they had not been genuinely repentant, the deeds of power accordingly were not done there. (196) It is appropriate to say this of them as well: it would have been better for them not to know the truth than to know it and then relapse. Thus he did not work marvels in Tyre and Sidon, since their repentance would prove unstable. Since, on the other hand, those among whom they were worked had not experienced a movement of soul known to the judge that required the manifestation of signs, he worked them with the intention that they would have no excuse, and that the others would not come to greater harm in being accorded some untimely favor. It is a matter for pondering, however, whether this was also said by the Savior by way of hyperbole with a view to reproaching the eyewitnesses of the signs who had not repented, this being a form of teaching.

The longsuffering and goodness of the judge, therefore, are revealed in his waiting for the sins of the Amorites to run their course. It is after reproving, encouraging, and doing everything towards repentance that God inflicts punishment. This happened also in the case of Pharaoh; after being frequently corrected and winning pardon, he eventually brought condemnation on himself for his hardness of heart.

After the sun had set, flames appeared, and, lo, there were a smoking pan and fiery torches that passed between these cut portions (v.17). The clear import of the passage could be presented thus: at the setting of the sun *flames appeared* and there were seen *a smoking pan and fiery torches that passed between the cut portions;* (198) both of them were alight and illuminating the place so that the pa-

11. Mt 11.20–21.

triarch could see what happened and there could be a revelation in a more divine fashion of these symbols, which must be investigated. Now, it should be noted that a fire appeared not only at the making of a covenant; it was also with fire that the Law was given through Moses, but though they saw the fire and heard the commandments, they did not see the one who was speaking. The implications of this are as follows. Since the Law contains rewards and punishments, it was given in the midst of fire to indicate that to some people it brings burning, to others enlightenment, since fire has a twofold effect, enlightening together with burning; so the Law that was given burns those who forsake it and enlightens those who observe it. Likewise, *torches* and *smoke* also appeared on this occasion, smoke being the result and as it were the consequence of the lighting of a fire, whereas a *flame* is lit beforehand. We therefore say that faced with such difficulty, the person who distinguishes between what is to be done and not to be done requires enlightenment from God and fear (symbolized by the *pan*) so as to perform everything by right reason.

On that day the Lord God made a covenant with Abram, saying, To your descendants I shall give this land from the river of Egypt to the great river, the river Euphrates, the Kenites, and so on (vv.18–19). The covenant was forged with the passing of the torches between the cut portions, and with God's words, *To your descendants I shall give* (200) *this land*. It also describes the extent of the land. We should also understand by an anagogical interpretation explained before, however, what is the land given to the holy man's spiritual descendants. The Savior also promises it to those who practice meekness. This promise applies to the true children and not to all his descendants: "It is not the children of the flesh who are children of God—but the children of the promise are counted as descendants," for only the one doing his works is his child.[12]

Now, the phrase *from river to river* was well put; the promise applying to the holy man's descendants is virtue, which occurs

12. Mt 5.5; Rom 9.8; Jn 8.39. Didymus does not dwell on this covenant with Abram and prefers to take it anagogically.

amidst things in a state of flux. While things in a state of flux are not parts of it, they are its limits, for if one abandons virtue, one encounters them immediately. On the other hand, you might wonder whether this has also been said on account of the trials besetting the virtuous person, since he finds himself amidst people who cause distress but he overcomes them.

CHAPTER SIXTEEN

OW, SARAI, *Abram's wife, had borne him no children. She had, however, an Egyptian maidservant, whose name was Hagar. Now, Sarai said to Abram, Lo, the Lord has stopped me from bearing children; so go into my maidservant so that I may have children from her. Abram consented to Sarai's request* (vv.1–2). By the norm of allegory the Apostle interpreted these women as the two Testaments;[1] but since the events occurred also in a literal sense, it is worthwhile considering it as well. The purpose holy people had in living together was (202) not for pursuing pleasure but for having children; there is a tradition about them to the effect that they had intercourse with their wives only when it was a suitable time for conceiving, having no intercourse with her when she was suckling or feeding the baby or was pregnant, in the belief that intercourse was not appropriate at any of these times. Jacob also confirms the tradition; having established over a long period that Rachel was not in a position to have children, he had no further relations with her; but because she thought that if he had relations with her, she would have a child, she said, "Give me children; if not, kill me yourself." It was surely not that she was unaware that Jacob was not the creator; rather, she demanded intercourse in the belief that the holy man had desisted for the reason cited, that is, lest it be to no purpose. He replied to her, "Surely I am not in God's place for you, depriving you of the fruit of the womb?"[2]

Sarai, then, a wise and holy woman, realized for a long time that despite having intercourse she had not conceived, and abstained from relations with him. Since she knew that it was

---

1. Gal 4.22–26.
2. Gn 30.1–2.

right for him to have children, she gave him her maidservant as a concubine. This shows Sarai's self-control and absence of jealousy, as well as Abram's dispassionate behavior in opting for this at his wife's instigation, not from any impulse of his own, but allowing it for the sake of having children.

The literal sense is edifying, then, as we have explained. In an anagogical sense, on the other hand, it can be interpreted to mean that blessed Paul took the two women to be a type of the two Testaments. Philo also adopted this approach, though to a different effect, figuratively taking Sarai as perfect virtue and sound values, because she was a free spouse, of noble birth and a lawful partner. Virtue lives with (204) the wise person in accord with law in order that he may beget divine offspring from her; Scripture says, "For a man wisdom brings forth good sense," and to the reverent and holy man it is said, "Your wife like a luxuriant vine ... your sons like young olive plants around your table. This is the way the one who fears the Lord will be blessed."[3] While Sarai is interpreted as virtue that is perfect and spiritual, then, the Egyptian handmaid Hagar is said by Philo to betoken the preliminary exercises, and by Paul the shadow. In other words, it is impossible to grasp any of the spiritual or elevated ideas without the shadow in the letter or the introductory stages of initiation; it is necessary to produce offspring first from what is underlying. For example, they offered animal sacrifices in the shadow, they celebrated the Passover in a material way and performed circumcision on their bodies, by these means being guided to sacrifice "to God a sacrifice of praise,"[4] which is proper to the free woman. So when zeal in the wise person leads to greater things, virtue suggests by a divine purpose the employment first of the introductory stages and the production of offspring from them. After all, because the person initially embracing virtue cannot attain to perfection so as also to produce offspring from it, he is advised first to engage in preparatory exercises so as then to obtain it perfectly, if possible. (206)

3. Prv 10.23 LXX; Ps 128.3–4.
4. Ps 50.14. Heb 10.1 speaks of the OT as a "shadow," the thought also of the Galatians passage (see n. 1 above).

Abram's wife Sarai, after ten years of living with Abram in Canaan, brought her Egyptian maidservant and gave her as a wife to her husband Abram. He went in to Hagar, and she conceived (vv.3–4). As was said above, Sarai provides a particularly striking example of continence in offering to Abram her own maidservant without jealousy, having observed that *after ten years* she had not conceived. One also notes the wise man's dispassionate behavior in yielding to his wife with the intention of having children. The anagogical meaning, on the other hand, has already been explained, that in keeping with its purpose virtue recommends the adoption of introductory stages first with a view to producing offspring from them at first. There is nothing to prevent the results of initial stages being also children of virtue since they are produced for her; by recourse to them he promptly produced a *conception,* progress being a simple matter for a wise man.

She saw that she was pregnant, and her mistress was shown scant respect by her (v.4) … the purpose, as explained above, was for the wise man to go through the introductory stages of preparation and the shadow so that after being exercised in these stages he might advance to higher things. This being the proper order, in fact, it would be illogical after a knowledge of what is perfect for a reversal to occur to lesser things. (208) The Apostle, for example, writes to the Galatians, who, despite hearing the Gospel, still wanted to live by the shadow that was the Law. Though not being Jews, in fact, who had the shadow as a companion, the Galatians after coming to faith in the Gospel wanted to live like Jews, being deceived by a certain Ebion, who chose to live like a Jew despite becoming a Christian, and who persuaded others that he had been given this name by the apostles to indicate his poverty. "Ebion," in fact, means "poor," and he was called Ebion on account of the unsoundness and poverty of his ideas.[5] Now, the fact that the Galatians were pagans Paul states in the letter:

5. Cf. J. N. D. Kelly, *Early Christian Doctrines,* 5th ed. (New York: Harper & Row, 1978), 139, who mentions the Ebionites as a Jewish group within Christianity who took Jesus to be a fully human messiah: "Hippolytus and Tertullian connect their name with one Ebion, presumably the apocryphal founder of the sect; but in fact it derives from the Hebrew for 'poor,' no doubt recalling the humble title by which the original Jewish-Christian community in Jerusalem liked to be known."

"When you did not know God, you were enslaved to beings that by nature are not gods, but now you have come to know God, or rather to be known by God." So he reproaches them, as I said before; I need to quote the text, "Having started with the Spirit, are you now ending with the flesh?"[6] In other words, after making a godly beginning, it was not proper for them to go looking for mere types, for their looking was untimely; they should have understood why physical circumcision had been allowed and to what point it was of advantage to practice it. In fact, if they had understood, they would have had offspring from the concubine, and afterwards would have been able to understand the circumcision of the heart that is effected by the Spirit.

Guided by virtue, this holy man went into the servant girl who had been entrusted to him, as we explained, and who also conceived; but it was not appropriate for him to remain with her beyond the time necessary. Many people, in fact, with a view to perfect instruction make use of preparatory exercises, but remain with them, (210) producing behavior suited to a slave and *showing scant respect* for virtue. This should not be attributed personally to Abram, however, but to such a way of acting and to the sort of people adopting it. If, on the other hand, as we claim that virtue ... recommending introductory stages, you could object that in a certain manner they are her offspring and that such a man cohabits with virtue first, since the one subject to her follows her recommendations, the reply would be that some of the things that happen over time are prior to others, and some later, though sometimes they happen at the one time. Still, of those that happen together we form the idea that one is prior and the other follows, as with natural causes; virtue, for instance, is the cause of everything that is the result of her. Hence, even if these things are prior in time, she is prior by nature, as marriage precedes having a family, since it is on account of this that marriage ... virtue. And with other things it is by understanding the ...

The person who gives priority to other things, then, *shows scant respect* for virtue. If, for instance, you were to choose her not for herself but for some other reason, like praise or glory,

6. Gal 4.8–9; 3.3.

in some way you would show scant respect for the good, which of itself is not susceptible of scant respect. Note, on the other hand, that it is not said that Abram showed scant respect for her, which would not become him; rather, it is because this fault can assuredly happen with others that the passage made the point so as to suggest that virtue should not be continually shown scant respect in what precedes ...[7] (212)

Sarai said to Abram, I am being wronged on your account. I gave my maidservant into your arms, but when she saw that she was pregnant, I was shown scant respect by her. Let God judge between you and me (v.5). The phrase *on your account* can have two meanings, either "as a result of you" or "from the time when." The meaning "as a result of you" can be taken as follows: when someone decides for the sake of virtue and perfect wisdom to adopt preparatory steps and remains at that level, in some way one *does wrong to* virtue in failing to adopt what is necessary to lead to it. The meaning "from the time when" is to the same effect, the only difference being the aforementioned, that one really *shows scant respect* for virtue when one is anxious to produce offspring from the introduction alone and sets this as the goal.

Give attention also to the phrase *by her:* virtue is not simply *shown scant respect,* but *by her*—that is, when with a view to perfect wisdom one uses the preparatory steps beyond what is necessary, one thus *shows scant respect* for virtue. The clause *Let God judge between you and me* could mean at a literal level that it was spoken as a result of some human motivation of hers, and at a spiritual level in keeping with what preceded, it was said to the person remaining at the introductory level, namely, "It was not (214) on account of me that you bore imperfect children, but because you stayed at that level."

And Abram said to Sarai, Behold, your maidservant is in your hands. Treat her as you please (v.6). Literally understood, the words of the patriarch show his detachment and that he did not pursue pleasure when he received his wife's maidservant. Now he defers to Sarai and retreats when she wishes. In the anagogical sense, the zealous person, even if remaining at the introductory level while not being entirely unfamiliar with virtue, readily re-

7. There follows a blank section in the papyrus.

ceives rebuke from it and quickly shifts away from petty matters;
likewise, in submitting himself to virtue he follows its guidance
in his engagement with the introductory exercises and yields
the governance to it. The one who is eager to say, to do, and to
understand all these things with virtue as his aim is thoroughly
prepared to receive its corrections.

Sarai abused her, and she ran away from her presence. There is
abuse of the handmaid, which we have allegorically applied to
the introductory exercises, when in some fashion their abolition
occurs; the person bent on perfection no longer needs them.
This is surely the reason why she was right to *run away;* introduction is no longer required when progress and perfection have
occurred. (216)

*An angel of the Lord God found her at the spring of water in the
desert, at the spring on the Shur road. The angel of the Lord said to her,
Hagar, maidservant of Sarai, where have you come from and where
are you going? She replied, I am running away from the presence of
Sarai my mistress* (vv.7–8). From this it is possible both to recognize the virtue of Hagar and also to realize that she is not
despicable, since an angel converses with her and displays an
interest in her that is not idle. It is clear, in fact, that it was in
accord with God's will ... It is not unlikely that she was a woman of zeal, chosen as she was by the holy Sarai as a partner for
Abram. Her high-mindedness emerges also from her saying,
I am running away from the presence of Sarai my mistress, nothing
derogatory of her ... running away to do ... In what was said
before, Sarai was cited as virtue and spiritual understanding of
the Scriptures, and Hagar as introductory stage and shadow.
The person who comes to divine instruction, then, ought to be
so attentive to it as to understand it in the letter and move progressively to the level of the spirit.

For a child of Sarai, therefore, there is need of introduction
so as thus to attain to the more perfect things, as is said also
of the Israelites that "they were the first to be entrusted with
the oracles of God,"[8] given to them up to the moment of
correction. No one, you see, who remains at the level of the
letter or the introductory stage can lay claim to Wisdom her-

8. Rom 3.2.

self.[9] So the lover of Wisdom (218) who takes advantage of the introductory stages and remains there shows to some extent *scant respect* for virtue, whereas the one who thinks better of it sets aside the introductory stage so as to *run away from* it. Once progress is made, the former things are left behind, as was true with the Egyptian Hagar; the introductory stages are confirmed by the earthly examples.

She flees, then, and an *angel* finds her as she flees; an angel is not invisible ... the meaning of the further phrase *of the Lord*. They were said ... evil, as is said, "A company of wicked angels" ... "we are to judge angels."[10] So the angel finds her fleeing on account of the greatness of her virtue, and turns her about—in other words, the instructive word also redirects the introductory teachings towards virtue. It was also well said that she was found *in the desert* and *at the spring on the Shur road,* "Shur" meaning "restraint": she was not fleeing from the house, nor ... So it was not from the restrictions ... remaining at the introductory stage; hence the instructive word also turns such people about to show them the futility of staying put by asking, *Where have you come from and where are you going?* It is proper, in fact, that the virtuous person know the beginning and the goal, whereas the person who is beginning often stays put on the pretext of the enormity of virtue, to some extent avoiding the challenge of perfection, as is suggested by the statement, *I am running away from the presence of Sarai my mistress.*

As well, when the beauty of the spiritual law is presented, what is shadowy is put to flight; the sacrifices that are lightsome by comparison with those under (220) shadow have been transmitted and implemented. Likewise, what is only partial is abolished when there appears what is perfect. That person who *ran away from the presence* of the Savior heard him saying, "You must be born from above," and asked, "How can anyone in old age be born?" through understanding in human fashion what is divine.[11]

9. This is a hermeneutical (and ascetical) principle that Didymus derives from Philo.

10. Ps 78.49; 1 Cor 6.3.

11. Heb 10.1; 1 Cor 13.10; Jn 3.3, 4 (where ἄνωθεν can mean "from above" or "again").

Now, it is also good to be found *at the spring of water;* the neophyte is found in the process of purification, signified by the *water,* and a person in this condition is *deserted* by sin because freed from evil and clinging fast to virtue.

The angel of the Lord replied to her, Return to your mistress and submit to her control (v.9). The literal sense being clear, it implies allegorically that anyone performing an idle deed which they think is required of those respecting the shadow of the Law the instructive word brings back to the prior wish of.... The Lord, in fact, gradually suggested that the contents of the shadow in the Scriptures lost their force when he said, "What good to me is the multitude of your sacrifices?" and, "Surely I do not eat the flesh of bulls and drink the blood of goats? Sacrifice (222) to God a sacrifice of praise, and offer your prayers to the Most High."[12] It is therefore a wonderful thing to find oneself *under the control* of spiritual teaching, referred to as *mistress,* and to *submit* to it, not as to something lowly but as to a *mistress.* In this case, you see, what has been glorified is not glorified, since its glory is pre-eminent.

The angel of the Lord said to her, I shall greatly multiply your descendants, and there will be no numbering their multitude (v.10). It is not implausible that the person at an introductory stage of life should also be accorded a blessing, since his progress towards a proper goal will attain to perfection. Note, however, that on the other hand in the case of virtue (for it is from virtue that the genuine *descendants* of Abraham derive), it is God who leads him out and says, "Look up at the sky and count the number of the stars, if in fact you can number them," and proceeds, "That will be the number of your descendants."[13] In this case, on the other hand, instead of saying, "Your descendants will be like the stars," he says only, *There will be no numbering their multitude.* The reason is to prevent your being able to take the difference to mean that while the offspring of the perfect are lightsome, those of the introduction are not.[14] (224)

12. Is 1.11; Ps 50.13–14.

13. Gn 15.5 (a verse not appearing as a lemma in the ms in its present state).

14. Nautin reads this sentence to the opposite effect, in accord with the overall argument; see his translation at SC 244.223.

The angel of the Lord said to her, Lo, you are pregnant and will have a son, and you will call him Ishmael because the Lord has hearkened to your lowliness (v.11). At that time, having children was thought important … human beings, whereas virginity and the doctrine of virtue had not yet acquired influence with people. Hence they offered prayers for it and thought such events to be examples of blessing. So much for highlighting the literal sense; the spiritual sense may be expressed as follows. The person at the beginning of instruction about God and at an introductory stage is, as it were, pregnant … yet there is a promise of the instructive word to the effect that he will give birth. Instructors, in fact, often have the insight to know the efforts of their students and are not unaware of their natural gifts. That the issue from the womb is uncertain, however, you can learn from the Savior's words in the Gospel, "Woe to those who are pregnant and to those who are nursing infants on that day"; such situations are unreliable, as testing discovers. Hence, in its wish that such people be weaned, the word says, "Those weaned from milk, those snatched from the breast. Expect tribulation upon tribulation, hope upon hope"; people now enjoying stability expect "tribulation upon tribulation." On the other hand, there are immature people of whom Paul says, "I fed you with milk, not solid food, for you were not ready for solid food, and are still not ready."[15] (226)

He announces to her, then, that she will bear a son, adding, *You will call him Ishmael.*

He will be a rough man (v.12). There are many ways in which a person who is zealous, wise, and refined differs from one who is not. So we say that by comparison with one who is refined and knowledgeable, the latter is uncultivated and *rough,* and by comparison with one who is learned and cultivated, he is unlearned and ignorant. So since the offspring of virtue is a lifestyle in conformity with the law, the one not living a heavenly life by a lifestyle in keeping with "the city of the living God" is *rough,* … falls short of that condition and inhabits the country, not the city.[16] It was right, on the other hand, to describe

15. Mt 24.19; Is 28.9–10; 1 Cor 3.2.

16. Heb 12.22. The term applied to Ishmael in this lemma (and LXX) is ἄγροικος.

him not only as *rough* but also as *man*; a share in the word of
God does not come to the one at the beginning, but after some
progress ("gods" is the name given to those to whom the word
of God has come),[17] and then he will be a citizen of the heavenly city. Of such people, remember, it is said by the wise Paul
to the Hebrews, "To Mount Zion and the city of the living God,
the heavenly Jerusalem," in which they are enrolled. The Savior
for instance says, "Do not rejoice that the demons are subject
to you, but that your names are written in heaven."[18] (228) We
should not think that names composed of syllables are written
in heaven, but only names bearing on virtue; these names in
heaven bear an unforgettable inscription. While these people
are enrolled in heaven, those of the opposite disposition and of
an earthly mentality register their names only with the earthly
things themselves, Jeremiah rightly saying of them, "In turning
away they will be recorded on the earth."[19]

*His hand will be raised against everyone, and everyone's hand
against him; he will take up his abode in opposition to all his brothers.
Hagar invoked the name of the Lord as he spoke to her, You are God
who watched over me, for she said, I saw him face-to-face as he appeared
to me. Hence she called the well "Well where I saw him face-to-face." It is
between Kadesh and Bered* (vv.12–14). In what was read before, it
was an angel of God who spoke to her, whereas here she called
him *Lord* and *God*. You would not be wide of the mark to say
that the angel was transmitting not his own words but those
of God, like the prophets; to some extent when the angels also
transmit ... and foretell the future, they take the role of prophets ... The name "angel" suggests their activity, not their essence, and similarly that of prophet ... (230) The angel spoke
God's ... gave the name as a result of the one dwelling within,
as Isaiah prophesied, sometimes speaking in his own person
as one possessing the spirit within himself, sometimes in the
person of God without specifically saying, "The Lord says," as
in the statement, "I made the earth and humankind upon it,"
whereas on the Lord's part he announces ... "Hear, O heaven,
and give ear, O earth, for the Lord has spoken."[20] We cite this

17. Jn 10.34; Ps 82.6.   18. Lk 10.20.
19. Jer 17.13.   20. Is 45.12; 1.2.

to show that not all the words uttered are his; instead, since participation in God confers authority, and as a result of God's indwelling, the beneficiaries are called "gods." For instance, an angel speaking to Moses was also called ... "An angel of the Lord called to him, saying, I am the God of Abraham, the God of Isaac, and the God of Jacob."[21] In relation to ministry, then, they were the words of angels, but in regard to power, God's.

While this is the first explanation, ... there is also another for a neophyte to this effect: there are many gods and many lords in heaven and on earth, yet idols and demons are not gods, but only those to whom the one who made them came. If the word of God comes to people, these people become gods ... when the word of God ... is. It is said, for instance, of gods ... in the verse "The Lord, God of gods, spoke,"[22] meaning those who by a share ... God's word in this respect ... The one who appeared ... was called the Lord ... God, but *You are God who watched over me* ... (232) the pure authenticity of the vision, she went on, *I saw him face-to-face as he appeared to me,* that is, with eyes not of the flesh but of the mind, as is said, "Blessed the pure of heart, for it is they who will see God";[23] he manifests himself to those who do not refuse to believe in him. In his goodness, you see, God offers himself for understanding, since created nature could not see him if he had not made himself available for contemplation in proportion to each one's faith. The *well* the Spirit in Scripture also[24] ... says, *Hence she called the well "Well where I saw him face-to-face"*; in fact, *well* ... is the understanding of what is proper, since the word ... is often used of spiritual things: "Drink waters from your pitchers and from your wells of a spring."[25] The beginning ... Insights that sprinkle are referred to by "wells of a spring," the latter being a correct impression of God, while the "wells" are the divine words.

Now, it was also appropriate that the vision of the instructive

21. Ex 3.6, where in fact it is not an angel speaking.

22. 1 Cor 8.5; Jn 10.35; Ps 50.1.

23. Mt 5.8.

24. We noted Didymus using this alternative phrase, "the Spirit in Scripture," for biblical inspiration also in comment on 6.9. See p. 152 above.

25. Prv 5.15.

word was had *between Kadesh and Bered, Kadesh* meaning "holy," and *Bered* "bright light." It was thus between these, the holy, to whom it belongs ... and a bright light, a lightsome condition, by which divine instruction comes to be. Scripture says, remember, "Your bright lights shone on the world."[26]

Hagar bore to Abram a son, and to the son whom Hagar bore him Abram gave the name Ishmael. Abram was eighty-six years old when Hagar bore Ishmael to Abram (vv.15–16). It would be reasonable (234) to claim that it was with a view to establishing seriousness and legitimacy that the note is made, *Hagar bore to Abram a son.* The verse and its sequel are clear; let us look also at its anagogical meaning. When a person makes progress and gives birth according to the end set by the instructor, what is given birth is not to be despised. Thus, the verse applies the appropriate notion of generation to the one who teaches correctly and sows what is beneficial ... it said, *Hagar bore to Abram.* Now, the fact that this is so ... I provided from scriptural statement, which says, *and to the son Abram gave the name,* and added, *whom she bore him;* if it did not have the intention, which ... it would have been content with *and to the son Abram gave the name* without adding the clause *whom she bore him.*

So much for that. Let us see also what bears on the number of years of the patriarch; the text says, *Abram was eighty-six years old when Hagar bore Ishmael to Abram.* Both digits, then, ...[27] (236)

26. Ps 77.18, where, unbeknownst to Didymus, the Heb. term for "bright light, lightning" differs from his popular etymology of "Bered" (based, as often, on the first syllable).

27. The allegorical interpretation of the two digits is missing from our manuscript, as is true of that of the age of Abraham at the beginning of the next chapter.

CHAPTER SEVENTEEN

OW, WHEN Abram was ninety-nine years old, the Lord appeared to Abram and said to him, I am your God; be pleasing in my sight and prove yourself blameless (v.1). The number a hundred is made up of ten times ten. Now, these numbers that roll on themselves are called squares, a square being a stable figure. For example, ...[1] Likewise, then, God appeared to Abraham ... loving humanity to the extent of appearing and deigning to be his God in the words, *I am your God.* Now, he is God of the holy ones, not ... but also Creator of everything, of heaven and earth and all that is in them, in a special way becoming their God by reason of worship ... it is said, "O God, my God,"[2] the verse suggesting, "God of all things, you are also my God in that I am your servant."

In preparing him for combat he adds the requirement of courage, *Be pleasing in my sight* (238) ...[3]

And I shall make my covenant between me and you, and I shall make you exceedingly numerous (v.2). As ... *in my sight and prove yourself blameless* ... to make himself numerous ... according to the literal sense ...it was no wonder; other nations had become numerous ...

Abram fell on his face (v.3).[4] ... rejoicing and also multiplying as the patriarch also ...

God said to him, Lo, I am making my covenant with you. You will be father of a host of nations; you will no longer be called by the name Abram. Instead, your name will be Abraham, because I have appoint-

1. Several lines of the ms are fragmentary.
2. Acts 4.24; Ps 22.1.
3. Several lines are missing at this point.
4. Half a dozen lines are missing at this point.

ed you father of many nations. I shall make you extremely numerous (vv.3–6). Again, after he fell down, the Lord confirmed the promise by telling him that he would make a covenant with him; he would be *father of a host . . .*[5]

5. The ms goes no further than this point.

INDICES

INDEX OF PROPER NAMES

Where a name appears both in the text and in a footnote on the same page, only the page number is listed. Where a name appears only in a footnote on a given page, the note number is supplied in addition to the page number.

Abel, 12, 15, 114–18, 121–23, 125, 131, 134, 137, 166, 182
Abimelech, 185
Abraham, 9, 14, 21, 33, 70, 97, 134, 140, 142, 172, 188–89, 192–93, 194, 216, 219, 220n27, 221
Abraham (the name), 110–11
Abram, 19, 182n18, 183, 185, 187, 189–91, 193–202, 203–5, 207, 209–14, 220, 221
Abram (the name), 110–11
Ackroyd, P., 20n58
Adam, 12n25, 18, 20, 41–42, 84, 89–94, 99–101, 103–10, 114, 129, 130, 134, 136–37, 141
Ai, 9, 193, 196
Alexander (of 1 Tm 1.20), 5, 98
Alexandria, Alexandrian, 5n9, 7, 12n25, 21, 22, 50n77, 55n92
Altaner, B., xi, 4n6
Amorites, 158, 204, 205–6
Ananias and Sapphira, 119
Antony (hermit), 3
Apostle, the. *See* Paul
Aquila, OT text of, 8, 27n14, 161
Ararat, 179
Aristotle, 11, 91n34, 168
Athanasius, 3

Baal, 45, 118, 144
Babel, 199n51
Babylon, 74n146, 99, 199

Beatitudes, 37–38
Bered, 218, 220
Bienert, W., xi, 14
Book of the Testament (Jubilees), 5, 12, 115, 117, 118n10, 122, 133, 139
Butler, C., xi, 4n5

Cain, 12, 15, 16, 88, 110, 114–23, 125–30, 133–34, 137–38
Christ. *See* Jesus Christ
Chrysostom. *See* John Chrysostom
Church, the, 18, 48, 49, 69, 74, 92, 93, 97, 100–101, 103, 104, 146, 149, 178, 179, 180
Cicero, 91n34
Cleopas, 16, 180
Constantinople, Council of (381), 3
Corinth, 95
Cyril of Alexandria, 7

Daniel, 99, 199
David, 90, 95, 117, 118, 120, 129, 170, 203
Deconinck, J., xi, 12n27
DiBerardino, A., 3n1
Diocletian, 3
Diodore, 12, 15n42, 21, 122n25
Doutreleau, L., xi, xii, 4n7, 14, 17

Ebion, Ebionites, 17, 211
Egypt, Egyptian, Egyptians, 5n9, 6,

INDEX OF HOLY SCRIPTURE

Old Testament

229

New Testament